The Jungle Express

Books by Michael Bleriot

Memories of an Emerald World

The Jungle Express

Flying Naked

The Jungle Express

MICHAEL BLERIOT

MacGregor Books, Inc
Washington DC MMXII

The following is a work of fiction. Any resemblance to persons living or dead is coincidental.

Cover art by Allison Mattice

ISBN: 0983375135
ISBN-13: 978-0983375135
Library of Congress Control Number: 2012900124

Printed in the United States of America

To Steve Elling
who loved to fly and did it well

Contents

Prologue

THERE ARE TWO WAYS TO land a plane safely on a jungle airstrip and Rufus McGee didn't know either of them, which is why he crashed and strew airplane parts across half a mile of the only open patch of dirt within two hundred miles, leaving me to circle overhead wondering where else in Peru I could divert to land, if his passengers were alright, and whether the government was paying me enough to fly in the Amazon.

Rufus' excuse was that the approach at Site 17 (also known as Outpost Bita for the nearby river) was difficult, which was no excuse at all. He was flying a Beech King Air, a 10-passenger twin engine aircraft that was one-third the size of the C-27 Manny and I had just flown off the runway to make room for him. His true problem was that he was a lousy pilot. A fun guy, a great guy to drink beer with, and an old enough friend of General McKenzie at Southern Command that the latter was willing to hire him on as a contract flyer for one of his passenger shuttles, but a lousy pilot.

Rufus wasn't in our squadron, thank god, because he was a contractor and worked on the other side of the Panama Canal at the Quarry Heights headquarters. Still, because he flew planes for a living we all tried to like him. Pilots like to stick together. But in

Rufus' case it was hard. He'd wrecked more planes than some of us had flown. Just when we started to forget about the last tire he had blown or the last prop he had dragged through gravel, he would land another plane long and plop it into a swamp past the end of the runway. He just couldn't fly. And while good pilots can get away with anything among their peers, bad pilots can have a hot wife, a Nobel prize, and a million dollars in the bank and nobody will care. Rufus didn't have any of those things – and he still couldn't fly.

That's why he came in over the trees high and fast, bounced the plane way down the runway and off-centerline, and then swerved out of control far enough that his right wing caught on a tangle of ayahuasca vines – vines which are significantly more rigid and conservative than their hallucinatory properties might lead one to believe, in that they like to stay in one place and are willing to resist even sudden collisions with small American aircraft gone astray in remote sections of the Peruvian jungle. The ayahuasca sheared off the Beech's right wingtip like a paring knife dicing a carrot. That made Rufus panic and overcorrect by stomping on his left rudder. The Beech responded, veering to the other side of the runway (which was easy to do since the landing surface was only as wide as a suburban driveway) where it managed to find the only stake in the compound's perimeter fence high enough to hit his left wing – and hit it. That knocked another chunk off the plane, a jolt which threw Rufus against the throttles causing the engines to spool up instead of down and making them bounce back into the air. That was good because it let Rufus clear the second line of concertina wire that we always had trouble seeing anyway in the high grass. It was bad, though, because when he came down the left landing gear hit on an angle and ripped off, making the plane twist, tip, and dig in what remained of the wing. Beside me Manny braced for a fiery crash.

But Rufus got lucky: instead of cartwheeling down the remaining runway and crashing into the fuel tanks the Peruvians used to keep their radar going, his plane instead carved a series of lazy, counterclockwise pirouettes that stayed on the ground and allowed what was left of the right wheel to dig into the soft alluvial soil left from when the Bita overflowed its banks. One, two, three complete turns the King Air made, spinning and skidding its way down the remaining strip like a drunken figure skater as the twin propellers mowed the grass and threw hay into the air in a vortex of debris, before coming to rest by the sandbag wall that the soldiers erected to block snipers. It made me dizzy just watching.

Manny was dizzy, too, but with the instinct of most pilots he still jumped on the radio to join the action, not even waiting until the plane had stopped.

"Conch Two-Four, Conch Two-Four!" he called. *"Guys, are you okay?"*

George Eezie was Rufus' co-pilot. He had known Rufus when the two of them were in the Army but flew with him anyway, partly because he was drunk half the time and didn't notice McGee's screw-ups and partly because he was the only other contract King Air pilot the Army had bothered to hire. But even he agreed that Rufus sucked.

"*I...don't...know...,*" came George's centrifugal force-slurred reply. "*We're...not...done...crashing...yet.*"

After the dust settled, Manny and I looked down at the wreckage and wondered what to do. We had taken off not because we were done unloading our cargo but because the compound wasn't big enough for two planes. We still had a ton of rebar and a pallet of electrical cable clogging up our cabin. Rufus had promised that if we just got out of the way for a few minutes he would land, drop off his passengers, and leave again directly. He didn't have gas to delay, he said – but now neither did we.

"What do you want to do?" I asked Manny, holding the C-27 in a left bank. Quick math showed we had just enough fuel to make it back to Lima if we left immediately. The alternative was hoping we could squeeze back into Bita and borrow some gas from the troops. Manny was the aircraft commander so he had to decide.

He chewed his lip, studying the carnage below. Leaving a fellow pilot in a lurch was hard to do.

"Let's go get some Pisco sours," he sighed and pointed me toward the capital.

"You don't want to wait and see if they're alright?" Even if they were intact, Rufus and George were now stuck at the outpost for days, if not weeks. The least we could do, I thought, was give them moral support.

Manny looked down one more time. He was a really nice guy, the soul of human kindness, someone who would land a stolen Piper Cub in a prison yard to spring a buddy. On the other hand, Rufus was a lousy pilot.

"Nah," he said. "Screw 'em."

The Jungle Express

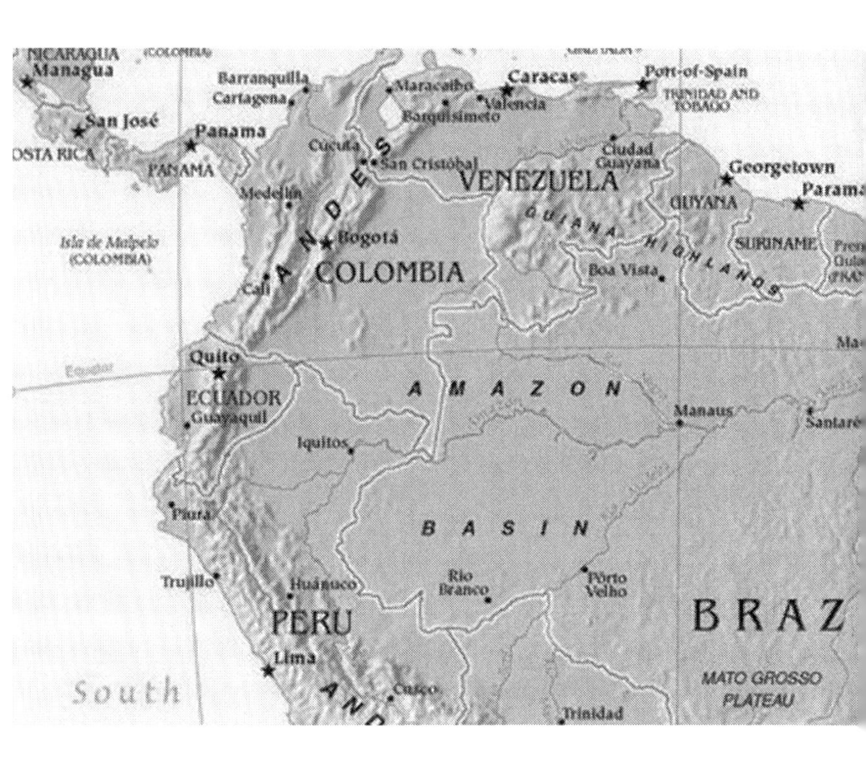
NICARAGUA
Managua
Barranquilla
Cartagena
Maracaibo
Caracas
Port-of-Spain
TRINIDAD AND TOBAGO
Valencia
Barquisimeto
San José
Panama
COSTA RICA
PANAMA
Cúcuta
San Cristóbal
Ciudad Guayana
Georgetown
VENEZUELA
Medellín
GUYANA
Paramaribo
ANDES
GUIANA HIGHLANDS
Bogotá
SURINAME
Isla de Malpelo (COLOMBIA)
COLOMBIA
Boa Vista
Cali
Quito
Equator
ECUADOR
AMAZON
Guayaquil
Manaus
Iquitos
Piura
BASIN
Trujillo
Huánuco
Rio Branco
Pôrto Velho
PERU
BRAZ
Lima
MATO GROSSO PLATEAU
South
Cuzco
Trinidad

1. Sloth

Speed is relative.

In the fall of 1990 I was flying. Two years earlier I had been in college. Now I was a pilot in the U.S. Air Force, being paid to fly people and things to remote places in Central and South America. In two years I had become an officer, learned to fly, and survived a short assignment in a huge cargo plane that sapped my pilot skills as much as my will to live. But in the last three months I had escaped to Panama and a smaller plane, one so new we didn't have manuals for it yet. I found a place to live, started a new job, and was learning a new language. The changes had come so fast it made my head spin.

For the next three years I lived and worked out of Panama, flying from an air base that sat near a Pacific beach on the edge of the jungle in what was left of the Canal Zone. Panama was hot, humid, beautiful from the air, alternately modern and backward depending on where you looked, and conveniently close to Colombia, Ecuador, and Peru where narco-traffickers used the vast expanses of the Amazon to ferry coca and cocaine from and to their labs and then to customers farther north. In our squat cargo planes we could fly from Panama to the vast *selvas* back of the Andes in just three hours to help the locals look for illegal flights. That rapid switch from a city to a jungle strip hundreds of miles from the nearest road was another change that never failed to disconcert.

Our squadron of C-27 airplanes was the only cargo operation the U.S. had south of the Rio Grande that could get into the jungle outposts local authorities used to monitor drug flights. So we flew a lot, moving from one location to another. We went to big cities but also to places that weren't on maps, and to some that were on maps but needn't have been as remote as they were. My companions were junior officers like me, with hundreds but not thousands of hours of experience. We learned most of what we knew by doing it. Most of the guys loved to fly, and most loved to jump from one sortie to another in a contest for bragging rights over hours in the air, experience, and miles logged. All ended up in Panama because someone else didn't want the job: more experienced pilots thought the assignment was dangerous, inconvenient, or bad for a career. In other words, we were the best of what was left. But because of the flying nobody minded.

In that first year in Panama we never stopped moving. Howard Air Base was the hub but we spent so much time out on the spokes and rim of the wheel that it was hard not to get dizzy. Launching before dawn to take advantage of cooler air, we would race south (or north) to get to our destinations, cruising high among the clouds or skimming low over the trees, looking for the right place to land or the wrong things to avoid. The latter included storms, dead-end canyons, and local militaries who may or may not have heard from their superiors that we had permission to be in their country.

Often we spent weeks away from home, ferrying troops and cargo from one remote site to another and congratulating ourselves at how industrious we were. It was hard not to feel that way in a land so sweltering and huge. Flying lightly over the infinite green forest, we seemed so productive compared to its inertia. The jungle didn't do anything, after all. It just sat there in its vastness, an immense, dark, choking expanse of life that spread up from Brazil to the furthest reaches of Guatemala like a living blanket. Flying over it was humbling – it could swallow us in an instant if our engines failed. Even if we survived a crash, everything from the soil to the treetops was designed to make us part of the food chain. But descending into the jungle as often as we did also encouraged a sense of superiority. Though we jumped from one site to another like anxious flies on a crowded table, at least we were doing something. We were in motion – frenetic motion, perhaps, since flying was always more important than the actual mission – but in motion nonetheless. The jungle just never seemed to appreciate our urgency.

One day not long after Rufus crashed his plane, I drove onto the base and immediately had to brake as the cars ahead of me slowed to a crawl. A sloth had come out of the jungle and crossed the twenty feet of grass to the one road that ran from the main gate to the base proper. God knows when it had done this as it was just now attacking the first of the two lanes. It moved with, well, sloth-like speed.

One of the cars ahead of me drove carefully around the animal as he flowed like cooling lava out of the grass. A second car started to do the same, then gave up and stopped. Another vehicle appeared from the opposite direction and stopped, too, blocking that lane as the driver peered out in curiosity. I shut off my engine and got out. It was obvious no one was going anywhere for a while. People rushed for their cameras.

The sloth was both revolting and cute, the impression depending on its pose at any given moment. It was also curiously underwhelming. I had never seen one before and examined it from different angles to see if there wasn't more to it. This one had thick grey fur that covered a gangly frame. Its skin sagged. Its head was tiny. Weighing maybe twenty pounds, the animal looked like an amiable koala bear on a crash diet.

When it moved it did so with ponderous deliberation, stretching out one long arm after another to pull its way across the ground. Each time it moved the floppy nature of its skin was apparent, as though this particular creature was wearing a hand-me-down hide from an older sibling. Bits of leaves and twigs clung to its coarse hair. Flies buzzed around.

"Ohhhh, he's gorgeous!" a female sergeant cooed as she moved up closer between the cars.

The sloth blinked as shutters clicked around him. Uncertain about pressing forward with so much attention directed his way, he sat back on his butt, short legs out in front and long arms to either side as braces. His face was serene – confused, maybe, but patient like a frail grandparent at a wedding when the photographer shouts, "Okay! Now just one more with the children..." It seemed as though emotion on the sloth's part was a cost-benefit calculation where the amount of energy required often didn't justify the effort.

A couple of guys tried to move the sloth out of the lane by stamping their feet and saying, "shoo!" but that was as effective as trying to scare molasses. We could have picked the animal up and tossed him into the grass but nobody wanted to do that, for two reasons. One was the fur, which looked mangier than a starving coyote's and a likely home to any number of diseases. The other was the scythe-like claws on the end of the sloth's arms. The animal never made threatening gestures but that didn't matter. They were sharp and clicked hard on the pavement.

About the time we were all settling down for a waiting contest that I didn't have good vibes about, the base security police showed up with a snare.

There were three cops. First they walked around the sloth the same way I had done, clearly wondering if there wasn't something missing. Then they discussed the use of the snare and who was going to do the honors. That fell to the lone female SP. She looked confident until actually trying to use the device at which point it became obvious none of them had paid attention in sloth-capture class. The sloth, though moving so slowly it was like watching rust form, somehow managed to avoid putting any limb in a position where a loop could be dropped over it, frustrating the SPs as they exerted more and more energy to accomplish nothing. It was a demonstration of animal tai chi.

Finally, after swapping the snare between them two or three times, the cops managed to drape the loop under one of the sloth's claws. The tallest SP took the pole and raised it carefully. The sloth allowed its arm to be drawn up as though grateful we were all finally getting somewhere. When its arm reached full extension he continued to hang on. The SP raised the animal carefully off the ground and – with direction from the crowd – carried it gently to the side of the road which the sloth seemed to have as its objective. The whole time the animal swung gently by one arm from the loop, round face showing a carefree willingness to be moved. His gaze was innocent and conveyed an inquiry that was infinitely Panamanian, one we could only interpret as, "What's your hurry?"

2. Pucallpa

Manny didn't intend to land at Pucallpa. He simply made a wrong turn crossing the Andes.

It wasn't easy to do but it wasn't hard, either. He and Jem were flying food out to Araracuara from Lima – a long haul from the coast out to the furthest reaches of the jungle – and they tried to stay below the weather by cutting up a canyon on the west side of the mountains. Except that there was more than one canyon and none of them went where the map said they did. Even better, no sooner had they committed to the mountains than the weather closed in behind them. Then their inertial navigation system died. The result was that after forty-five hair-raising minutes of squeezing between the cloud deck and the ground at 17,000 feet they popped out over the jungle without a clue where they were.

It had happened before. We were the United States Air Force and our squadron had the best tools available whenever we flew a mission – with the key word being "available." The only maps for most parts of the Amazon were TPCs, Tactical Planning Charts, with a scale of 1:500,000. We used them for the simple reason that they were what we had. Any pilot will tell you it's foolish to try to fly low-level off anything larger-scale than a 1:250,000, a Joint Operational Graphic or JOG. Above that scale roads and towns get omitted, rivers look larger than they are, and hills and peaks blend into the nearest range. Flying low with a 1:500,000 is like trying to find an address in Chicago using a map of the Midwest.

In fact, a smart pilot would fly using a 1:50,000 scale map. Unfortunately, there were no 1:50,000 scale maps of the jungle. There weren't even many JOGs. When there were, they were usually of small, isolated areas that some map-maker had once had an interest in or worse, were charts produced by the local authorities. Local maps couldn't be trusted. Peruvian maps were especially suspect as they often showed the world the way some politician wanted it to be rather than how it really was. I once saw a Peruvian JOG that had the border with Ecuador fifty miles north of where it was, showed a mountain where there was flat jungle, and that misplaced the Amazon river by twenty miles. The cartographers in Ecuador weren't any better. Their border, according to the map, was lined with towns that didn't exist. And their frontier encompassed a swath of jungle the size of Pennsylvania that had been seized by Peru in the 1940s – Ecuador just refused to recognize the transfer.

But then sometimes we gringos were in no position to complain. At least Peruvian and Ecuadorian pilots *had* maps.

When American pilots of the 155th Squadron out of Panama wanted to fly somewhere we searched our own inventory. If there was territory not covered by our collection we requested data from the National Imagery and Mapping Agency (NIMA) in Washington. NIMA and the Department of Defense would send us whatever they had, which often wasn't much. When Magellan went to the South Pacific 500 years ago he had better information than we sometimes got. Evan, our supply officer, once received a shipment of 60 charts, 48 of which contained nothing but huge white splotches where terrain relief should have been. In diffident small print a label explained: "Limits of Available Terrain Not Available." In other words, *Here Lie Dragons.*

It was into one of these white areas that Charlie Manson flew one black, rainy night, using his weather radar to avoid red areas on the screen which he assumed signaled the heaviest precipitation. He eventually flew between several of them and found his airfield. The next morning he stood blinking in the sunlight at the score of jagged peaks that surrounded the landing strip like watchtowers around a camp. Those peaks, not storms, had been on his radar. There were dragons, alright. Big dragons.

Even Erich Fetterman, our squadron check pilot who Rolo absolutely despised (he vowed that if ever he was about to crash the last thing anyone would hear on the cockpit voice recorder would be "Fetterman's a Nazi!"), had a record. He had picked up the occasional nickname of 'Rivers' in late August when he landed – not once, but twice – on the wrong airstrip north of Trinidad, Bolivia. He was using an ONC, of all things, a map with a scale of one-to-one million, which was even worse than a TPC. Using it to find a clearing in Bolivia was like looking for a grocery store in San Diego using a classroom globe. The ONC showed only one river where there were actually five. Fetterman's instructions were to land at the strip that ran parallel to the third river, which he did. Except that the third river was actually the second from where he was supposed to start counting. Later on he returned to the same strip in bad weather and did it again.

"It was a goddamned ONC!" he protested, to which Lt Col Rasmussen, our commander, dryly suggested that in the future we request the locals to erect large wooden numbers along the shorelines to help us out. Rasmussen could say that and get away with it. Anyone else would have sent Fetterman into a spiraling, nose-bleeding rage.

Sometimes the maps weren't to blame for us landing where we weren't supposed to. Like the time Mike Vaneya landed at Tingo Maria so his co-pilot could go to the bathroom. He and Kurt had eaten at a Chinese restaurant in Chiclayo the night before. Why, no one knows, since business acumen aside the distinguishing characteristic of Chinese restaurateurs anywhere south of the Rio Grande was indifference to hygiene. (Suspiciously, we never saw stray cats or dogs within blocks of the best restaurants.) Our best guess is that they were playing the odds: at Casa de Wang in Comayagua, for example, the chances you would get violently ill following dinner were about one in eight. Since the food was so good – and so cheap – many of us were occasionally willing to roll the dice. So of course Kurt was having intestinal disorders of the highest magnitude even before they got airborne the next day. The fumes he emitted were so foul and spelled such disaster for whatever might come next that Mike and the loadmaster decided an emergency divert was in order the instant they cleared the mountains. It just happened that the remote strip they chose was in dispute between two factions of the Shining Path. By relieving himself there Kurt single-handedly started a new front in the Peruvian rebel wars.

I had deviated as well, though less dramatically. On my first ride as a commander in Honduras I flew with Lowell Hendricks to a radar site on Isla del Cisne, far out in the Caribbean. Passing the exquisite tropical island of Roatan we were spotted by the controller of the only field there, who saw us while relaxing in a hammock by the runway. He called on the radio and invited us down to lunch. That day I politely declined, and the next also, but the third time he was so polite and convincing that I took the plane in. Lowell had a fit, nearly blowing capillaries in his temple as he protested that the shack man was probably setting us up for a hijacking. Or maybe that he was a drug lord trying to coax us in. But I couldn't see his reasoning. For one thing, if I was a drug lord looking to take down a plane I would say, "Land or I'll shoot you down with the Stinger missile I bought from Ollie North." I wouldn't say, "Come over for lunch." For another, what would a drug guy be doing on Roatan, a diver's paradise populated by Garafuna Indians and hardly the coke-pushing center of the Latin American universe? So we landed and had lunch, delicious fried fish with beans and rice. The islanders were enraptured by our visit and everyone including Lowell had a great time.

But he was still right and I was wrong.

Manny was wrong, too, in landing at Pucallpa, but it took three days and two more C-27s to find that out.

Like a lot of towns in the western Amazon basin, Pucallpa in 1990 was dirty, dusty, and ugly. Its buildings were cinderblock boxes topped with corrugated tin. Its streets were loose red clay. When it rained the din was deafening and the roads impassable. There were automobiles but most transport was by motorcycle or bus or the three-wheeled taxi that looked like a motorized rickshaw. On a hot day exhaust fumes lay stagnant in the humid air, mixing with the dust and making walking the streets a painful, choking experience.

The town stretched in unimaginative square plats along the Ucayali River, its port being the focal point of activity. The airport lay northwest of the town about a mile but Pucallpa was growing and it wasn't hard to see that in a few short years the houses and shops would reach out to its perimeter. Already two "restaurants" – shacks made of discarded plywood and sheets of plastic – had staked out claims among the weeds and garbage strewn by the road leading to the runway. Houses were popping up around them. Twice a week when the AeroPeru 727 from Lima (Monday morning) and the Faucett Antonov from Iquitos (Thursday afternoon) landed the owners of the shacks had an opportunity to sell their corn tamales wrapped in palm or banana leaves.

Pucallpa didn't look bad from a distance but down on the ground it had a foreboding appearance. Partly it was the uniform architecture – low, square, and dirty white. Partly it was the dust. Partly it was the knowledge that the town's isolation meant that law and order existed from inertia if it existed at all. And partly it was the birds. During the day, great flocks of vultures circled the squares and hovered over the port. At night they roosted in the eaves. Life in Pucallpa was hard and these aerial undertakers watched life transpire with only hunger to fuel their interest. Tourists were unheard of.

Economically, the people who lived there were like people anywhere on the back side of the Andes – mostly hardworking peasants and small business owners and mostly dirt poor. Little of their technology was advanced: there was no public phone system, for example. If you had anyone to call you found someone who had a working phone line and paid them for the privilege of using it. People worked to get by and to the extent they planned for the future it was a future much closer than citizens of more prosperous countries dream of.

As much as Iquitos, its larger, more prosperous neighbor to the north, Pucallpa was a frontier town. Both belonged in the region of Loreto but Iquitos, though it lacked access by roads, commanded more attention from the Lima government. There was talk of creating a new department to accommodate Pucallpa and reflect its separate identity but for now that was just talk. It remained on the back burner of official notice, a large town with lots of problems, some potential, and a key location for rebel movements, drug runners, and C-27 pilots who didn't know where they were.

When Manny and Jem landed at Pucallpa it was only weeks after the Peruvian government scored one of its first real successes against Sendero Luminoso. It wasn't much of an operation: government forces surrounded a house in the foothill town of Huanuco and in an hour-long gunfight killed five people inside. But the five were confirmed members of Guzmán's movement. More importantly, the house served as one of the rebels' regional hubs, filled with pistols, rifles, and propane tanks that Sendero used as bombs.

The rebels were suspicious: how did Fujimori's troops discover them? Rumor started it was with outside help. Further rumor said the American C-130s that flew over the country looking for drugs helped pinpoint the location. That was dangerous buzz because so far the rebels had refrained from targeting foreigners in their bombings or assaults. They did so under the unspoken, unwritten understanding that Sendero was looking to overthrow the government and the Americans were looking for drug runners and never the twain should meet. It helped that in general Sendero members were fanatical enough that they disdained the druggies almost as much as the government did.

In fact, all the rumors probably started somewhere in the Peruvian military among those who either sympathized with the rebels or who resented the U.S. "help" in their fight. But rumors were rumors. Not even Armando Guzmán could control what every member of his organization did. There were Sendero members who collaborated with coca growers and shippers – there were also radio operators and intel officers circling overhead who occasionally had the opportunity to listen in on rebel cell phone traffic or photograph coca fields in known rebel terrain. It was inconceivable that two such single-minded, mutually exclusive forces could avoid suspicions about the other. The potential for conflict was there and it increased with time.

Jem thought they had landed at Atalaya, a village some hundred miles to the south of Pucallpa. He was guessing, though, and it was a bad guess since Atalaya doesn't have a runway and is a much smaller town. Manny was sure they were further north but couldn't think of a respectable way to hop on one of the common traffic radio frequencies and ask something like, "Hey, does anyone see us flying around up here? Can you tell us where we are?" He and Jem both tried to use their navaids but the problem there was that three towns within 150 miles used the same frequency for their NDBs. Unless they already had an idea of their position it was impossible to verify which one of the beacons was directing them. And since an eighty-mile stretch of the foothills was swathed in white on their map, that helped them not at all.

So they landed. Manny circled Pucallpa's strip, saw no traffic, and made an approach.

The tower controller reacted the way everyone they encountered for the next three days would do so. Warily. He came out of the one-story tower with open squares where windows should have been and two antennae on the roof and stood anxiously in the doorway as the C-27 taxied up within thirty feet. Pilots in Third World countries hold an exalted status. Pilots of military planes with few identifiable markings are above that even. They don't make mistakes. They certainly don't land at fields just to find out where they are.

"Hey, son!" said Jem, jumping down the stairs as the propellers spun to a stop. "Where the hell are we?"

And if they do, you don't ask questions.

Jem didn't speak Spanish. He was from Georgia and spoke the South's version of English. He called everyone "son" regardless of their age and belonged to the school of foreign affairs that insisted anyone could understand you if you just spoke slow enough.

Matt Armand was the loadmaster. He didn't speak Spanish, either. It was up to Manny to communicate, therefore, and he did fairly well with the phrase book his wife gave him after a traffic incident where he accidentally called a local cop a "stunning bitch." The Peruvian controller listened nervously. Occasionally he raised an eyebrow. He didn't believe a word Manny said.

Manny was an Academy grad. Usually Zoomies can be identified by their carefully manicured appearance and incredible ignorance of anything outside of Colorado Springs, and while Manny was smart enough to fall outside the second stereotype he fit the first like a glove. He was polite, quiet, hardly swore, rarely drank, and squeaky clean. Literally squeaky clean. After hours in the tropical heat he still looked as though he had just scrubbed his face and combed his hair, so much so that senior loadmasters would often grab his cheeks to reassure themselves that their pilot was awake and ready to fly. He was a careful, conservative flyer and he didn't get excited when things went awry.

"Pucallpa," he said with a shrug after talking to the controller. "Okay, plot it and let's go."

But they couldn't go. When they started their generator the gyros wouldn't align. Then their emergency DC bus (which was really the primary DC bus but for some reason the Italian engineers designated it otherwise – perhaps because if you lost it you now had an emergency) wouldn't come on line. Finally, when they cranked the #2 engine all the fire lights in the cockpit illuminated at once even though there wasn't any fire. The plane they were flying was tail number 106. The fourth C-27 to be delivered to our squadron from the factory, after only three months it had a reputation for having gremlins, "queer-trons" that raced around in the electrical system and caused all kinds of unrelated malfunctions. Many of those queer-trons came from the supervisory panels. The "soup panels" were automatic junction boxes, the electronic equivalent of a committee of experts whose job was to make the electrical busses work without human intervention. Sometimes the committee got along, other times it functioned like Twelve Angry Men. Whether #106 had soup panel issues or was possessed by the devil no one knew. Manny's crew certainly didn't. They just knew the plane was broken.

While a crowd of curious onlookers formed along the road to watch them, Manny and his guys sat down on the red clay of the airfield and discussed their options. The one they decided on was to stay put.

Charlie Manson and Little Bud McIlhenny were in the jungle that same day. They were Shark 21, halfway through their two-week hub-and-spoke operation to various fields around northern Peru. They picked up Manny's call on the HF radio during take-off from Yurimaguas and called him back a few minutes later. They had Jerry Tunkelmann as their loadmaster ("the man from Tunkel") but more importantly they had Vince along as a crew chief. Vince could build a new plane out of shopping carts and Scotch tape so Manny's problems were solved if Shark 21 could just get to Pucallpa. Would they come?

"*Let me get this straight,*" Charlie said over the airwaves, his tone so dry it changed weather patterns as it bounced across the ionosphere. "*You landed in Pucallpa because you were lost? You were LOST, is that it? How do you know for sure you're in Pucallpa now? Maybe the guy on the ground is just lying to you. Over.*"

But they agreed to come. They would have to hit Iquitos for gas first but they would come.

It was a Tuesday afternoon. Shark 24 settled down to wait.

3. The Jungle Express

ABOUT THE SAME time Manny and Jem landed at Pucallpa I was shopping for a leather coat in Bogotá. Josh and I had flown in the night before so we could get up early in the morning and spend the day carrying Colombian troops around to outposts in the jungle. It was called the Local National Officer, or LNO, swap-out. But when our driver came to pick us up he had a message from Fast Eddie, the Bogotá station manager. Eddie said the troops weren't ready, that we would have to wait another day. So we were waiting.

Josh loved Bogotá. Before he got religion he could find his favorite things in life there: money, beautiful women, and nightclubs. That led me to believe that I would love it, too. But Bogotá is in the Andes at over 8,000 feet above sea level. Year round its climate is like a dusky fall day in upstate New York – which is great if you brought warm clothes. I didn't, so we were looking at leather coats.

Leather coats and blue jeans are the uniform *du jour* in Bogotá. Black leather is okay, brown leather is preferred. Brown leather that's a heavy suede means you've taken the time to get decked out. That's what I was looking at now, in the Anaconda Leather shop on Calle 63. Heavy suede, deep brown, with thickly-sewn pockets. If this didn't pull the local betties, nothing would.

"Josh, what do you think?"

"Not bad, not bad," he conceded. I waited. Josh never accepted anything the way it was. Already he had twice sent the shop owner searching the back room for jackets just slightly different from what was hanging on the racks. Josh was unfailingly self-centered. "You'll want to get rid of those little airplanes, though. Jeez, who thought *that* was a good idea?"

I hadn't noticed them until he said something. The zipper tabs were tiny metal models of old biplanes. Now that I did I was immediately decided. I would take it.

That night we were in the Zona Rosa when Jean-Paul found us. The Zona Rosa is the nightlife district in Bogotá, a happening neighborhood of narrow streets, nightclubs, and open-air cafes where everybody goes to see and be seen. We had snagged a table at Charlotte's, a open-air restaurant off Calle 82. It had a low rock wall around its perimeter and bonfires among the paving stones. It also served great *churrasco.* Crowds mingled in the restaurant and on the street. Music reached us from a club nearby.

Jean-Paul was our driver. He had another name but I never knew it. I always called him Jean-Paul because he looked like the French actor Jean-Paul Belmondo, right down to the easy fitting suits and the coolly indifferent way he flipped half-smoked cigarettes into the street. Fast Eddie assigned him to drive us to and from our hotel but Jean-Paul had the mysterious habit of showing up at other times as well, sometimes – like now – when we had no reason to expect him.

He sat down smoothly at our table and appraised the people near us. As usual he was impeccably dressed: a three-piece worsted wool suit, silk tie, and patent leather Armani loafers that gleamed in the firelight. He looked like he'd just stepped off a Milan runway.

Josh and I were amazed.

"Jean-Paul! What's up? What are you doing here – how did you know where we were?"

He shrugged like it was obvious. Even when he drove us around he didn't talk much but when he spoke it was in a suave, Spanish-accented Castilian, the *s* being pronounced like a *th* and the words running together. I wondered if he really was Jean-Paul Belmondo.

"Mr. Valladur would like you to come to the airport one hour later than planned. You may fly somewhere different tomorrow."

Josh said, "Oh? Where?"

Jean-Paul shook his head. His mission was simple and it was done. If he knew more he didn't let on.

The waiter, a middle-aged man formally dressed and with the confidence of one who knows he can juggle the demands of fifty people at the same time, breezed up to our table the instant he noticed the new arrival. We offered to buy Jean-Paul a beer. He waved us aside and ordered instead a mojito, specifying a Cuban rum and telling the waiter he would know if the bartender used anything else.

"You should not be here, you know," he said disapprovingly after the waiter walked away.

I raised an eyebrow. "In the Zona Rosa?"

"No, at this table. It is too near the sidewalk. You should choose a table closer to the inside, in the middle of the crowd."

Josh glanced that way. "But here we get to see the women go by. And there are a lot of them, by the way."

"There are also thieves and kidnappers and people who kill for a living," Jean-Paul noted blandly. "And you two don't blend in just because you're wearing leather coats."

I felt self-conscious. I had thought I was blending in.

"We might hook up," Josh pressed.

Jean-Paul nodded. "You might die, too."

"We've got the wall," I threw out weakly. In my Hollywood mind I saw us diving behind it in the event any shooting broke out.

"That wall? That wall is nothing." He looked at me. "That is a nice coat. Did you get it today?"

"Um, yeah, thanks."

"I like the airplanes."

I threw a told-you-so look at Josh.

He admired my coat then leaned back in his seat to see what else I was wearing.

"Why are you wearing Dockers?" he frowned.

"I didn't bring any blue jeans." I never packed blue jeans under the theory they made me look American. "And I like Dockers."

"They don't go with the coat."

"I like Dockers," I repeated.

"Then don't wear the coat."

The waiter reappeared with Jean-Paul's drink. Jean-Paul had a quick conversation with him, not all of which I understood it went so fast, but the gist of which was that we wanted to change tables. The waiter balked, looking at the crowded patio, but Jean-Paul's demeanor brooked no argument. The waiter moved off toward the bar. Moments later we saw him relocate a young couple from the back of the room. Reluctantly, Josh and I got up in turn and worked our way toward the table they had vacated.

That won't get us any unwanted attention, I thought, glancing around to see if anyone else noticed the game of musical chairs. No one had, or let on that they had. The twenty- to thirty-something crowd on the patio was too busy chatting, scoping out members of the opposite sex, or jabbering away on cell phones to pay attention to us. Jean-Paul was just paranoid and he passed the paranoia on to me.

"Oh, much better," Josh said sarcastically when we sat down again. A pillar for the bar blocked our view to the street. The parade of women was no more.

Jean-Paul cocked his head and gave a half-smile. Uncooperative clients didn't faze him.

He took two sips of his drink then stood up to go.

"One hour later," he said. "Be careful tonight."

"We've got no choice now," Josh muttered.

We bade him goodnight. He stood for a minute looking at the crowd and then walked casually out to the street, exuding cool. I wondered if I should start packing formalwear.

The next morning we ended up doing the LNO swap after all but now with an hour late start. Eddie heard about Shark 24 being stuck in Peru and anticipated that the Air Operations Center in Panama would redirect us to help Manny's crew. The AOC, however, for the moment left the task to Charlie Manson and his crew of Shark 21. That worked for Eddie, too. The Colombians were pressing him to have us haul twice as many troops to the interior as expected and Eddie agreed, thinking it would be no problem to get the AOC to agree to keep us in town a day or two longer. Eddie tried to appease the Colombian army whenever possible. For one they controlled the air traffic control system, such as it was, and could mess with Eddie's flights to no end. For another they ran the side of the airport on which he was located. If Shark 21 rescued Shark 24, then Eddie could offer our services to the Colombians for an extra day while at the same time appearing available to the AOC, thus looking good all around.

Eduardo Cortari de Valledur was a businessman, yet another one of the many people I encountered down south who was climbing the ladder of success by supplying rungs from whatever promising source happened along. He used his day job as Bogotá station manager to run several other businesses, including being a hub for Faucett air cargo and an exporter of Colombian emeralds. He financed at least one of the half-dozen 747s filled with roses that left for the States each day, was part-owner of a clothing store in the Adani Mall downtown, and had a stake in a cattle ranch near Medellín. He had so many irons in so many fires he needed a staff of six to keep track of them all.

But Eddie was on a more elegant level than Harry and Vince, our hyperactive mechanics who mixed adventure with dirty hands in their pursuit of the good life. Eddie didn't get his hands dirty. He dressed in European suits, smoked Cuban cigars, and decorated his office with photos of prominent people to show who he knew. His staff, other than Jean-Paul, consisted of six knockout women. Friendly, slim, and drop-dead gorgeous, "Eddie's girls" gave his business the aura of a shadowy high-class escort service. Yet if there was a driving goal that he was working toward beyond simply being rich it wasn't obvious. He was just always working and always working an angle.

Eddie liked organization. He liked it a lot. His own hangar, crowded with spare parts, cargo, and the occasional aircraft, was spotless and inventoried down to the smallest screw. Everyone who worked for him was neat and dressed like applicants to the Monaco jet set. The details. The details were what mattered most. And that was why Shark 24 could cause problems. If it kept us in limbo in Bogotá, it was a loose end Eddie couldn't tie up.

"Shark 21 had better get them out," he growled, stalking through his hangar with a pair of laborers in trail, using his Cojiba to point out to them what pallets needed to be moved where and when. Which crates were important could be ascertained by how much ash flew off the cigar when he pointed.

"Charlie will pick them up," Josh assured him. "He'll get down there as soon as he can."

"Charlie?" Eddie paused. "Charlie Manson? That man is crazy."

"That's why we call him Charlie Manson," Josh pointed out.

"Why?"

"Charles Manson? You know, the murderer?"

"I don't know that name."

Peru wasn't helping. Manson tried to get to Pucallpa on Tuesday but was held up in Iquitos by the controllers there. Since the flight was a last-minute deviation the controllers, suspicious, did what they normally did: refused to let anyone go anywhere while they waited for instructions from a superior. It was trickle-up bureaucracy at its worst. More than anyone else in the theater the Peruvians let anarchy reign in their government-military relations. The old president, Alan García, had been completely out of his depth in bringing order to chaos. The new guy, Fujimori, promised more control from above but no one saw it yet. We frequently received contradictory instructions as to what we were allowed to do in the country. Local power bases and overt nationalism made it impossible to stick to a plan.

Sometimes just switching from one controller to another would change our whole flight clearance. Different generals controlled different geographic regions and if they didn't want an aircraft there that was all there was to it. You didn't fly there. Appealing to Lima took days. Even then, if the embassy managed to get us clearance into an area controlled by one of the recalcitrant oligarchs, that same guy might just ignore the order from the coast and still say no. In that case our only recourse was to sneak into the field we wanted and hope nobody noticed – or at least didn't notice in time to keep us from leaving again. We did that often. It was a dangerous game but became such a regular occurrence over the vast jungle that after a while crews gave it little thought. We treated the whole country as a place where people were trying to shoot us down anyway, so whether it was by druggies, rebels, or the Peruvians didn't matter.

Even without the parochial generals, the *peruanos* were sensitive to suggestions they didn't control their airspace or their territory, which in many ways was true: Peru was simply too big and government resources too limited for anyone to know what was going on everywhere, let alone control it. But it was something the bureaucrats and especially the soldiers wouldn't admit. To cover for not knowing they overreacted. They used authority to show they had it, sometimes shutting down huge sections of airspace with no warning simply because they could. And as the months went on in my first year down south that attitude fed the trend among pilots to expedite flights by disregarding the local authorities altogether. Lima was useless. No one wanted to waste time arguing fruitlessly with some conscript behind a desk at a remote field or worse, a distance-emboldened voice at the other end of the HF radio. The Peruvians couldn't get their act together. It was much easier just to fly low and keep quiet.

As Josh and I winged our way around the back side of the Andes shuttling Colombian troops, I tried to picture Charlie Manson doing things the legal way, calmly discussing with the Iquitos tower employees how they could best expedite his take-off and why it was really in their interest to do so. I couldn't do it. Charlie was married to a Panamanian woman. He was used to pana-think, the term gringos slapped onto the Panamanian bent toward coming up with myriad reasons why something couldn't be done instead of one simple way to do it. He'd been south as much as anyone, spoke good Spanish, and had a bitingly sarcastic wit. He also had no patience for fools. No, things could not be going smoothly in Iquitos.

Somewhere over San Jose de Gortiari province Josh dialed up the HF radio to try to find out what was going on. Neither Shark 21 nor 24 was on the radio but the network monitor at Albrook Air Force Station was. She gave us a phone patch to the AOC, call sign Lobo, where the sergeant on duty had some information.

"*Yes, sir, they finally got airborne a few hours ago, over.*"

"*Confirm Shark 24 got airborne, over?*" Josh asked.

"*Negative, sir. That's a negative. Shark 21 got airborne. They were delayed departing from Sierra-Papa-Quebec-Tango but they did report a take-off time of, of,…oh, I have it here somewhere. It was a couple of hours ago. But their destination is a place called Poo-ca…Poo-ta…Pu-katka… something like that. Shark 24 is still on the ground. They have a maintenance problem. Over.*"

"No kidding," Josh muttered into the intercom. "AOC – masters of the obvious."

"Okay, Lobo, so Shark 21 is off the ground. Have they called in a land time yet? What I'm trying to do is find out if they're going to need us to head that way because if they do we're going to have to coordinate pretty soon. Otherwise they're spending another night down there."

There was a long pause on the radio.

"You didn't say 'Over,' sir," Ozzie Oswald, our loadmaster, said.

"Oh, crap," Josh replied, shaking his head, but quickly keyed the mike to say the magic word. If you didn't say "over" during a phone patch the net monitor didn't know when to throw the switch to allow the other party to talk, although that probably wasn't the case here since the guys in the AOC were no doubt just running around trying to find out what was going on in the theater. That was why Josh, and most of us, hated even talking to them. The more you kept home station informed, the more questions they asked and the more they wanted to be involved in everything you did. So many controllers think they can fly a plane from a desk.

Months later I found myself trapped on a small airfield in Bolivia feeling winds over 50 mph shake the plane. Winds like that were too strong to taxi (they could catch a wing and tip the plane over), much less take off, so we were stuck until they subsided. I asked a local when the winds usually died down. He thought about it a minute and then replied with confidence, "Christmas." So I called the AOC and told them I might be delayed a few days.

The AOC controller responded that according to his weather information there were no winds blowing in Bolivia.

"I beg your pardon?" I radioed in reply, my voice sailing three thousand miles and losing none of its edge.

"Our forecast shows no winds there, sir. There's no reason you shouldn't take off this afternoon."

My co-pilot at the time, Tommy Goode, burst into laughter. We were huddled in the cockpit, watching debris sail by in the gale outside and afraid even to open a window for fear of being sand-blasted by blowing dirt. The ropes that ran from our wings to stanchions in the concrete strained to hold the aircraft in place. I didn't find the situation funny.

"Then you come down here and pick up the plane, you jackass," I radioed back, *"because we'll be at the hotel."*

Now Josh waited, trying to keep his patience in check.

"I'll bet they don't know anything," he fumed. "But they'll want something from us."

"Uh, there's no land time yet, sir. But could you give us your position and status?"

"See?"

Outside, a high cirrus layer covered the normally bright sky. Random puffies wandered in the midlevels but between them the air was clear. Down below the ground was a hard grey, the deep green of the jungle reflecting the metal hue above.

"Also, please pass times for all take-offs and landings today. Over."

"Crap!" said Josh again but was spared the effort when all of a sudden Albrook started having trouble with the phone patch. In the middle of Lobo's request for us to repeat the times we lost the connection to Albrook altogether. Static hissed softly in the headsets where the voices from Panama had been. Occasionally a wavering tone like a riff from a Theremin sprinted across the ether but the monitor didn't come back. Josh didn't mind.

That night thunderstorms shot lightning across the Andes as we landed back at Bogotá. Fast Eddie was waiting for us in his office across the ramp from CATAM, the military parking area. He looked like he'd had a hard day. At least he had good company. Though it was past seven o'clock his bevy of Colombian betties was there in force. They smiled warmly at us when we walked in and I fell in love times six. Jean-Paul was there, too, lounging casually in a leather recliner, the trouser legs of his Italian suit riding high over silk socks and Gucci loafers as he crossed one leg over the other. Eddie's German shepherd, Little Eddie, was stretched out in front of his owner's desk. His name was a misnomer since although still a puppy he was now up to 95 pounds and almost five feet long. He merely raised his eyebrows and looked at us as we entered the office. He'd had a hard day, too.

Eddie tapped yet another Cojiba lightly over the ashtray, exhaling thick smoke at the ceiling.

"Gentlemen, gentlemen. We have a problem," he growled.

I took a seat by Marta, my favorite. Josh remained standing. He was tired, too.

"You know who the Lone Ranger is, Eddie?" he replied.

The non sequitur caught Eddie by surprise.

"Pardon?"

"The Lone Ranger? It's an American thing."

Eddie smiled, curious. He liked me and Josh but it wasn't good business to show it.

"Yes, yes, of course. The man on the big horse with the mask."

"Right," said Josh. "And his Indian friend Tonto? Well, there's this joke about how the Lone Ranger and Tonto are surrounded by hostile Indians and they're getting down to their last few bullets. The Lone Ranger turns to Tonto and says, 'Looks like we're in big trouble, my friend.' And Tonto says, 'What do you mean 'we,' white eyes?'"

Eddie nodded, waiting. The girls and Jean-Paul, who didn't speak English, waited, too, for all of us to call it a day so they could go home.

"Ah, I understand," Eddie finally laughed, puffing on his cigar again. "Well, okay then, maybe *I* have a problem. But my problem, in this case, is your problem, too, unless you can make yourself be in two places at once."

"How's that?"

"Your colleague, Mr. Manson, arrived in Pucallpa late this afternoon. Apparently he convinced our Peruvian neighbors that he was not going to commit some grand and terrible espionage by flying to an airfield not on his original itinerary so they let him go. Unfortunately,..." Eddie paused to stare at his cigar as though this was all part of a larger plan to cause him inconvenience, "...now he is broken as well."

"What? Noooo." I was incredulous. The C-27 didn't break. In three months of flying it I had yet to cancel or even delay a flight for maintenance issues. Now we had two that were stuck off-station? And Vince was aboard Shark 21, too. A wing would have to fall off before he conceded defeat.

"Yes, it seems he has difficulty with a fuel line."

"Hmm," said Josh. "That's not good."

"No," said Eddie instantly. "It's not. And here's why. Now the AOC wants you to go to Pucallpa – which, had they listened to me, you could have done today and then we wouldn't have this problem."

"What's the problem?" asked Josh. "No, wait a minute. What are we going to do? We don't have spare fuel lines to give them."

"He said you did."

"Eddie, you've seen our plane. We've got Jack and we've got squat, and Jack's on his way out of town."

"What?"

"We don't have anything. He's not taking our fuel lines to fix his problem. Then what'll we do? Sit in Pucallpa while he flies away? No way – not going to happen. I've been to Pucallpa. The women there are ugly." Too late, Josh paused and looked around the room. "Uh, no one here is from Pucallpa, are they?" he asked.

The girls just looked at him.

"Well," Eddie insisted. "If you don't have what you need tell me now. If I call tonight the parts you need will get here tomorrow morning on the C-21."

Josh and I looked at each other in surprise. Wow, the C-21, I thought. We must be moving up in the world if the AOC was willing to requisition a Learjet to bring us parts that fast.

Eddie read our thoughts.

"It was already scheduled. Some congressional aide is coming in to speak to the air attaché about drugs."

"Why?" said Josh. "Washington running short?"

Eddie shrugged. "Maybe. The plane is not for you."

So much for our high opinion of ourselves.

"So you can get parts if you need them."

Josh held up his hands. "Okay, hold on a minute. What parts does Manson need?"

"Fuel parts."

"But what, exactly?"

Eddie relayed the question to his staff. Marta jumped up and snatched a piece of paper that was sitting on the HF radio in the corner. She read from her notes in English, which was gutsy because she didn't speak the language.

"Capitan Manson say, tell Capitan Brite...Bri... Brit..."

"Breitling," Josh prompted.

"Breit-leen," Marta enunciated, pressing on. "Tell heem...we need special fuel, expenseev fuel. Tell heem...no Mexicans...*mejicanos. Sí, mejicanos.*" She was confused. "Tell heem...we need the eight-year-old. Eight-year-*olds.*" She said the *s* precisely.

"Eight-year-olds?" Josh repeated, incredulous.

"Sí, con ocho anos."

Uh-oh. I had a sneaking feeling I understood.

"Okay," said Eddie dismissively, waving his hands. "So it is not a fuel *line* he needs. He needs fuel, some kind of special gas."

Josh looked at me in disbelief. "You're not thinking what I'm thinking, are you?" he asked.

"That Charlie's a pedophile?"

"No, the other thing I'm thinking."

"I try never to think what you think."

"So what *are* you thinking?"

I was thinking of a margarita party at the Pinheads' house where a drunken Manson stumbled around with an empty glass demanding more of that 'special fuel.'

"I think either his plane has a new kind of carburetor or he's got an alcohol problem."

Marta stood watching us with wide eyes.

"He wants Scotch, Eddie."

"Excuse me?"

"He wants Scotch for some reason. He said he wants 'special fuel.' That's booze, usually tequila. But he said, 'no mexicans,' so it's not tequila. If he says eight-year-olds it's got to be scotch. Though why he wants eight-year-old is beyond me. That stuff is piss. I wouldn't touch anything younger than fifteen."

Eddie's face was blank.

"I do not know what you are talking about."

'That's got to be it, right?" Josh looked at me again.

I shrugged. "Makes sense to me – sort of. Maybe he needs it to buy somebody off."

Josh snapped his fingers.

"Bingo! That's got to be it. He wants scotch!"

Eddie was still two steps behind. His mind and linguistic abilities were just beginning to wrap themselves around the idea that he was being jerked around for liquor and he wasn't sure yet whether to be angry or amused.

"Manson wants whisky?" he asked. "That's what this is about?"

"Yes."

He threw up his arms, deciding to be angry. Ashes flew onto Jean-Paul's suit. Jean-Paul brushed them off and yawned.

"That Manson is crazy!" he shouted. "What does he think I am, a liquor store? The AOC is changing my whole schedule around so you can take alcohol down to that madman in the jungle!"

"Eddie," I tried to explain. "He probably needs it to *bribe* somebody so they can take off. *Una propina.* Manson's weird but he's not rude. He wouldn't drag another plane down there just so we could all get drunk."

Actually, Manson probably would do that but there was no sense in mentioning it. Josh looked up at the ceiling quietly mouthing what I had just said. He appeared to like the phrase, 'Manson's weird but he's not rude.'

"Then why didn't he just say, "Bring me scotch so I can take off?"

"Because he didn't want the AOC to listen in?" Josh suggested.

I nodded thoughtfully. Jasmina, Eddie's supply expert, saw me do it and nodded thoughtfully, too.

"Okay, okay..." Eddie had been ready to work himself into a lather but now had evidence pointing him the other way. Bribes he understood.

Still, for a moment he was unsure what to do. He jumped up and paced around the room, stepping over his dog each time he passed the desk. Little Eddie rolled onto his side and went to sleep. The girls and Jean-Paul watched their boss patiently, having witnessed his outbursts before. Marta came back and sat next to me again. I smelled lilacs.

"Okay," Eddie repeated. He stopped pacing and took a deep breath. "Let's say he wants...*scotch...*" – he bit off the word – "and I don't have to order parts. That still does not solve the problem we started with."

Which was?" Josh asked.

"The problem, *our* problem, is that I promised General Sosa you would go to Marandua tomorrow. They've been seeing more activity out there and think it will be attacked soon so he wants another forty troops. You were supposed to take them for him."

Marandua. I walked over to the map on the wall. Carmen, Eddie's smiling personal secretary, slid her typewriter out of the way so I could get closer. I liked Carmen. She was five-feet-nothing with jet-black hair in a long ponytail reaching down to the middle of her back. She was missing her left arm for reasons I didn't know but was still of supermodel beauty and the friendliest person I'd met in Colombia. She had such a pretty smile I'd taken to learning jokes in Spanish just so I could tell them to her. She pointed to a spot straight east of Bogotá about four hundred miles.

There it was. Out on the *Llanos*, the plains of eastern Colombia, vaguely between the Vichada and Ventuari rivers and a long way from anywhere you could call a taxi. There was no runway marked on the map. There was no town, for that matter. In blue pen someone had just drawn an X and written "SCXX – Mar." above it.

Josh looked over my shoulder. He took an expensive pen from his pocket and started taking notes. "Jeez," he finally muttered, "and I thought Minot was remote." Minot was an Air Force base in North Dakota. "What's out there, Eddie?"

"No scotch!" Eddie retorted. "Nothing. Yet another scenic location for our young soldiers to defend." He stifled a yawn and sat back down at his desk. "No, the FARC has been active out there for years. They have a 'working understanding' with groups over the border in Venezuela. They give each other drugs and guns, and the money the FARC makes from kidnapping and extortion they use to buy gold that Venezuelan smugglers pull from the rivers. Anyway, they are there. There is nothing there for them to make trouble with but they are still there so the Army has Marandua and Inirida Flats and other places to deal with them. Or at least keep track of them," he said dismissively, waving his cigar to suggest that it was all just a waste of time. "Lately there has been shooting around Marandua, snipers firing into the camp. You will see – it's so flat there is nothing to hide behind and bullets can go for miles."

"Oh, good."

"That is why Sosa wants the soldiers."

"Well, offhand it looks like a good two-hour flight," Josh said. "And with forty guys we can't take off out of here with a full load of gas. I don't suppose they have any out there to give us?"

Eddie's eyelids lifted just a fraction so he could stare at Josh across his cigar. *Are you kidding?* the look said.

"Then we can probably make it there and back but it'll be close. What happened to my pen?" It stopped writing all of a sudden and Josh spent several minutes getting increasingly frustrated trying to get it to work.

"Oh, I have no doubt you can make it there and back. If necessary we will get you clearance into Apiay to re-fuel." Apiay was a military base half an hour out of Bogotá on the back side of the Andes. "The problem is Shark 24."

"Oh, duh, of course," said Josh, remembering.

"Yes, 'of course.' *Claro.* The AOC wants you to go there tomorrow. You cannot do both."

No, we couldn't. Pucallpa and Marandua were in different directions, the one straight south and the other east.

"Can the general wait until Friday?" I asked.

Eddie hemmed and hawed.

"Let me re-phrase that, Eddie," Josh threw in. "*Tell* the General to wait until Friday." He tapped his pen again. "Hey, what happened to this thing? What the hell...? My father gave me this," he pointed out to me. "It cost forty dollars."

I ignored him, grateful that Eddie was the only other one in the room who understood English.

Eddie was confused by Josh's fixation but stuck with the original conversation.

"Nooo. I cannot do that. Or rather, I can, but it will not do us any good."

"What do you mean?"

"I mean, there's a good chance that if you don't go to Marandua you won't go anywhere."

"What does that mean?" Josh asked. "The AOC takes priority. None of us likes them but theoretically they do run this show."

Eddie studied his cigar. I got the impression he had already asked the questions we were now hitting him with and knew we wouldn't like the answers any more than he did.

"No, they don't. You need to go to Peru tomorrow. The general needs his troops to go to Marandua tomorrow. If you don't do one, you can't do the other."

"He's holding us hostage?" I was incredulous. "That's not likely to go over well back home. Didn't you say someone from Washington is coming in tomorrow?"

"No, no. You're not a hostage. You can always leave to go back to Panama if you want. But he won't let you change your itinerary to go to Peru unless you also change it to go to Marandua first."

Josh pursed his lips as he considered the situation. For someone who could throw a fit if his salad arrived at the same time as the entree, Josh was handling tonight very well. I got the impression he liked the various obstacles. He even seemed to appreciate the general's willingness to play hardball. I didn't.

"What an a...what a jerk," I caught myself.

Eddie nodded. "Yes, you are right," he said. "You were closer the first time. But that is how things work around here."

There were only two things I knew about General Sosa: one, he was a general, which you didn't become in Colombia without getting your hands dirty in one way or another; two, he ran or had run at some point the Colombian Army's 20th Intelligence Brigade, one of the units most implicated in human rights abuses over the years. The last I had heard from Josh who got it from Vince which made it gospel as far as we were concerned. How Vince knew was a mystery.

"Will we even have the crew duty day to do both tomorrow?" I asked. I walked over to look at the map and tried measuring distances with my open hand. "Or the gas, even if we stop at Apiay? That's a long way."

Josh shook his pen again to get the ink to flow. He did it so hard the pen flew out of his hand

and across the room. Pilar, Eddie's security chief, caught it as it sailed past. She was perched on a two-drawer filing cabinet and snared it with her left hand without even looking. The move was so fluid she could have been holding the pen the whole time. She handed it back to Josh, who eyed her with suspicion.

I took the pen and tied a piece of string to it, marking distances on the map and then measuring them against the scale at the bottom of the map.

"Why did you even promise him tomorrow?" I asked Eddie.

Eddie swung his feet back to the floor and got up again. "Because that is what the AOC wanted me to do," he said bitterly, walking around the front of the desk and nudging Little Eddie aside. "They said, 'Give the general what he wants' and then twenty-four hours later changed their minds. But you can't do that here. It's not good for business. They seem to think they can just switch schedules around at their convenience with no regard for the customer. In Colombia? No, no, no. Not a good idea. Sometimes the customer gets angry and refuses to let you change. And it's not good for me, either. What the AOC does not realize is that when I give people my word they assume I am going to keep it. I cannot just change things to deliver a bottle of *scotch.*"

He said '*scotch*' the way someone would curse after jamming their thumb in a door.

"Well, okay. Then why can't we just tell Shark 24 and Shark 21 to wait another day? They've got each other for company. They can all eat tamales and catch a tan for another twenty-four hours."

"Ah," sighed Eddie. "Yes. Yes, well. That is another piece of news for you. Apparently that is becoming a tricky situation."

The tricky situation was developing because no one at Pucallpa believed in coincidence. When the first C-27 landed at Pucallpa unannounced it caused a stir among the locals. Not the locals who repaired shoes and raised goats and wandered the streets in dirty cotton shirts and small-brimmed hats, but the locals who carried guns and kidnapped businessmen and believed the Marxist-cum-anarchy preachings of Armando Guzmán. Planes didn't land at Pucallpa. Well, sure, the civilian shuttles did, twice a week, but military planes didn't. Military planes with Americans on board most surely did not – and it took all of about an hour for word to get around town that the plane carried Americans.

When the second plane landed on Wednesday it raised even more questions. And when they both hunkered down for a second night on the cracked-earth runway with no apparent plans to leave, people began to talk. The rebels, suspicious, started moving people out of the foothills toward the town to learn more. The Peruvian military, a day and a half late but not asleep on the job, caught wind of the movements and sent a convoy of trucks rolling south from Tarapoto to meet whatever the Shining Path was up to. The situation was turning into Kurt's upset stomach times ten.

By Wednesday night the U.S. got into the act. American intelligence, through intercepts of the Colombian army's phone calls, found out that unmarked aircraft were on the ground in Pucallpa: they put two and two together and came up with thirty, concluding that the DEA must be running an operation all its own (though why the DEA would mess with a rebel movement wasn't clear) and fired off cables from the Lima embassy to SOUTHCOM headquarters demanding to know why the CIA wasn't involved. SOUTHCOM, not knowing why the CIA was asking the military anything but flattered nonetheless, volunteered to help in any way it could and asked the DEA for details. The DEA, out of Miami, denied all knowledge which only confirmed to everyone that they were running something. One of the funny things about the DEA was they had a rotten reputation with just about everybody they worked with. Not that they weren't effective, but they had a cowboy reputation which kept them from being even more effective and which, in this case, encouraged everyone to believe the worst about them.

Back at Howard, Lt Col Rasmussen was interrupted during dinner Wednesday night to field requests for air support from all three agencies and to answer questions like, Does Pucallpa have a runway? Has anyone been there? What kind of planes can land there? He activated the recall roster to bring in pilots to find out what was going on. That started a chain of events all its own. It was Wednesday, the best night to party in Panama with the exception of Tuesday, Thursday, Friday, and Saturday. Most of the guys in town were at the Pinheads' who were throwing another party, this one a belated celebration of Saint Crispin's Day because Evan had recently read Henry V. Every flyer in the unit was there drinking like a fish and cavorting in the pool with Chorillo prostitutes. After taking the call from the commander, the Pinheads kicked the whores out and found someone sober – Daisy, their real estate agent/communal girlfriend – to drive them to the base. Rolo went with them and so did J.C. Kurt Norris tried to follow them in his rumbling blue Blazer with its raised chassis and monster tires but got lost in his own neighborhood. He ended up parking across the only driveway to the El Dorado towers and refusing to budge until someone put the streets back where he remembered them. Mick Connor found him there an hour later, standing on his hood with a bottle of Jack Daniels shouting "we few, we happy few" while holding off a mob of Panamanians determined to push his truck into a ditch. They placated the Panas by inviting them back to the Pinheads' house for drinks, which the Panas then proceeded to strip bare when Mick and Kurt passed out by the pool.

And down in Pucallpa in the middle of it all sat seven Americans playing mumbly-peg and bitching about the mosquitoes.

"How about if we drop off the troops in Marandua and head straight south?" I suggested. "Is there anywhere we can pick up gas short of Iquitos?"

Eddie considered the idea and passed the question on to Sylvia, his logistician. She darted down the hall to another office and returned with a ledger and a black-and-white mimeograph of the map on the board with pencil markings all over it. She looked so much like she knew what she was doing I had to believe she would find something. After flipping pages for several minutes – and chewing on her pencil in an entirely distracting manner – she offered, "Leticia."

"Won't do," said Josh, studying the map. "It's just as far as Iquitos only further east. We need something within two hundred miles of Marandua."

That was like asking for a McDonald's in the Australian Outback. Sylvia chewed and flipped some more. Eddie suggested a few names but at each one she shook her head. "Calomar," she started to say but then immediately retracted it. When Eddie asked why she mumbled something about a fire.

Josh traced his finger along the places on the map and started calling off names. On Colombian maps airfields were indicated by a little silhouette of a bird. None showed anywhere near Marandua but he called off names anyway. "Riecito, Merida, Barinas, Mitu – "

"Mitu!" Sylva squealed. She held her pencil aloft and wagged it back and forth while flipping to the front of the book. "*Hee!*" she squealed again in triumph and carried the ledger over to Eddie to indicate an entry. He looked doubtful and said, "Not in two years." She replied something I didn't catch but looked quite sure of herself. Eddie shrugged and told her to make the calls. Sylvia brushed her hair over her shoulder and hurried out of the room, giving me a confident smile as she passed. Competence incarnate. We would be going to Mitu, I was sure.

And Mitu it was. Early Thursday morning we reported back to the airport where Sylvia gave us a sheaf of still-damp mimeographed diagrams of the Mitu area. Eddie wasn't in yet but Jasmina, his supply manager, took care of our flight clearance and weather reports. Jasmina was the only blond on the staff and always wore black. Black dresses, black skirts, black pant suits where the pant legs were a baggy silk that flowed around her legs like something an Arabian princess might wear. Like all the others except for Carmen she was tall and thin. Like all the others including Carmen she was beautiful.

She rarely spoke, though, and Josh tried to convince me she was deaf.

"She's not."

"She is."

"She's not!"

"Why, you think just because she's gorgeous she can't be deaf?"

"You think just because she doesn't yap the way you do she must be?"

"She is, I'm telling you."

"Five bucks says she's not."

"Oooh, big spender. Make it ten."

"You're on."

Before we walked over to the Catam ramp I slid over to the hangar doors where Jasmina was feeding Little Eddie.

"Excuse me, Jasmina," I said. She looked up and smiled warily. I always had the impression when talking to Eddie's girls that they were waiting for me to hit on them, which was doubtless what every crew that came through as well as any man who claimed to have testosterone in him did. Of course I wanted to but their beauty threw me off. Instead of chatting them up I always lost track of what I was saying.

"I had a question about these satellite pictures. Is there anyway we could get some with more detail?"

Jasmine took the pictures I showed her and studied them. It was a pointless question. She'd gotten the pictures over a fax machine from Howard.

Even the originals would have been useless since they showed the entire South American continent. The clouds were always in the same place – over the mountains – and there was never any way to tell how thick they were or what kind of weather they held. There were no reporting facilities where we flew.

She handed them back and smiled sweetly while shaking her head. "Mm-mmm," she replied.

Avoid yes-or-no questions, I thought.

"Well, what do you think of them?"

She smiled again and shrugged. Her pale skin and brown eyes were so perfect my resolve began to melt faster than ice cream in the jungle.

"Ah, err, well,..." I stammered, "will you be here when we get back? I'm sure we'll pass through on our way back to Panama and I could tell you whether these were accurate or not."

Oh, that was brilliant. Like she cared. My brain seemed to have stopped working. To keep from just staring at her I looked at anything else around her – pallets, the dog, the fans overhead. With my strained smile I looked like a white Ray Charles anxious for a bathroom.

Jasmina was patient. She had a lot of experience with men acting stupid.

"Mm-hmm," she nodded, giving me another delicate smile of such charm that Little Eddie could have bitten my leg just then and I wouldn't have noticed. Heck, Big Eddie could have bitten me.

Somehow I found my way back outside where Josh was waiting and watching. He carried a beat-up leather satchel that Sylvia gave him.

"You don't get laid a lot, do you?" he said scornfully.

"Shut up. Her smile threw me off-balance."

"Her smile knocked you down and kicked you around the hangar. You looked like my nephew asking for candy."

"Yeah, but what nice candy. Anyway, she talked. She's not deaf."

"She didn't talk. I watched the whole thing. She never opened her mouth except maybe to gag at whatever you were saying. Cough it up." He held out his hand.

"Doesn't prove anything," I muttered, but gave him the money.

We took off on the Romeo 1 SID and climbed to 14,000 feet before turning east toward Apiay. Romeo was an NDB located ten miles from the airport. It enjoyed its fifteen minutes of fame a few years later when the pilots of an American Airlines flight to Cali – which is down closer to the coast – entered its one-letter identifier into their autopilot's database by mistake: the plane's computer thought, "Romeo? Oh, that's up by Bogotá," and turned and flew straight into a mountain.

Josh and I decided that a stop at Apiay to pick up some gas before heading to Marandua was only smart. Apiay was forty minutes away on the east side of the mountains, right where the jungle began and a lot lower in altitude. We could take on fuel there that we hadn't been able to carry out of Bogotá because of all the soldiers Eddie had put in the back of our plane.

A fuel stop on the back side of the mountains was never a bad idea after leaving Bogotá. Still we had a dilemma. Not knowing anything about the landing surface at Mitu we didn't want to top off the tanks and end up being too heavy to land there; at the same time we wanted to make sure we got there with enough to divert to Leticia if the strip proved unsuitable. In the end we decided just to replace what we had burned coming out of the mountains. That would get us to Leticia – on fumes.

The turnaround at Apiay was quick. We were off again within an hour.

Staff Sgt Oswald sat in the loadmaster seat by the crew entry door, the better to keep an eye on the troops in the cabin. Throughout the flight he kept up a running commentary on their condition. Ozzie was one of the many Puerto Ricans in our squadron and spoke Spanish fluently. He had briefed the Colombians thoroughly on our 2 ½ hour trip out to Marandua but still they weren't doing well. Among other things, he reported, most had not used the earplugs he passed out to them. The C-27 was loud and if you didn't like being on airplanes to begin with or didn't wear earplugs, the noise made for a very rough ride.

"These guys here by the engines are hurtin' units," he informed us thirty minutes out of Apiay. "I'm guessing some of them have never been on an airplane before. They're probably not going to...oops, there goes one. He just puked in his hat. That's gonna start 'em off. They're all going to toss their cookies now. Ow, that's got to be messy."

"Load, didn't you give them airsick bags?" Josh snapped. Not only did guys puking stink up the plane, they also tended to miss whatever they were trying to puke into. This soldier made it into his hat but, guaranteed, not all of them would be so considerate. Sometimes we had to take a hose to the cabin after landing.

"Sure did, sir," Oswald replied with what-can-I-do resignation. "I also gave them earplugs but most guys aren't using either. They're all watching their sergeant. He's not using the earplugs and he's sitting on his airsick bag so that's what they're doing, too." He went off-comm for a minute and we could hear him in the back yelling above the noise of the engines. He was probably giving the sergeant hell. Ozzie, like most of our loads, was very proprietary over his part of the plane.

"Great," I said. "Once again we're going to deliver a bunch of deaf invalids to the fight."

Josh shrugged. "The life of a conscript," he observed.

Ozzie came back on intercom and poked his head up into the cockpit so nobody in back could see him chuckling.

"So much for leading the way," he said dryly. "I tried to get the sergeant to put his plugs in and while I was talking to him he threw a lung damn' near half-way across the cabin. Got it all over the guy who just yacked in his hat. This flight is gonna be UG-LY."

Sure enough, when we arrived at Marandua we had nothing but walking wounded on board. Despite the best efforts of the air conditioning system the plane smelled like a triage center at Gettysburg. I felt like puking myself.

Marandua was out on flat plains in eastern Colombia with nothing but grassland in all directions. The Colombians had built an outpost of sandbags and tin huts and surrounded it all with barbed wire. At each corner of the camp and halfway down each side was a sandbag bunker but that was it for vertical relief.

The runway was outside the perimeter on the south side of the camp, its bright orange dirt standing out like a wound on the pale green and yellow landscape. It was clear and wide and flat. Had it not been a different color from the grass we would have had a hard time making it out. Even now if we ran off the side or either end of it all we would do was mow the outpost's lawn.

We landed and taxied to the far end of the strip. Josh, sitting in the left seat, turned the plane around there and lowered the ramp.

"Alright, Ozzie. They can get out here. Thank them for riding the Jungle Express – and tell 'em to take their bags with them."

I twisted in my seat to get a look in the cabin. Many of the soldiers were disregarding Ozzie's admonitions, so anxious were they to get off the plane, so he was picking up and hurling the white plastic bags after them. But the soldiers were bunching up on the ramp. From what I could see their sergeant was holding them back.

"Hey, Ozzie, what's up? Why aren't they getting off?"

Sgt Oswald walked to the ramp and had a shouted conversation with the Colombian NCO.

"Sir, he says they don't want to get off here. It's too far from the camp. They want you to taxi closer to the gate."

Josh looked at me in disbelief.

"You've gotta be kidding me," he said. "Ozzie, tell 'em to get the hell off my plane."

"I'm not kidding, sir. They don't want to go."

"Hey, look," I pointed. Out the front windscreen we saw a jeep pull out of the camp at the front gate, which was nothing more than a loose roll of concertina wire that a gloved soldier carried out of the vehicle's way. In the jeep were two armed soldiers and a third who stood in back, manning what looked like an M-60 machine gun. They drove the twenty yards to the runway and sat there, waiting.

Josh threw his hands in the air.

"Let me get this straight," he said to no one in particular. "The fricking runway is three seconds from the camp and safe enough to land an unarmed airplane on, but it's too dangerous for the guys who are on the plane to get out and walk?"

Ozzie had nothing in the way of a response. "They're not getting off, sir," he said simply.

At that moment the soldier with the M-60 spun ninety degrees to his right and loosed off two long bursts. Smoke rose from the barrel of his gun as we heard the dull *thud-thud-thud* above the sound of our own engines.

"What the...?"

We looked left out into the grassland but saw nothing where the gunner was firing, nothing but endless waste-high acres of thin waving stalks. It was like shooting Nebraska.

The jeep rolled forward then turned into the grass. The gunner kept firing. That is, until he fell backwards clutching his chest, sprawling across the spare tire and almost falling out of the vehicle. Then the jeep turned and raced back to the gate where dozens of soldiers collected. Some of them had

M-16s. They spread out along the fence and began shooting where the M-60 guy had. From the cockpit we still couldn't see anything that resembled a target.

Ozzie walked back to converse with the sergeant.

"Sir," he called. "The sergeant says there's a sniper out there."

Josh shook his head in bewilderment. "No kidding!" he yelled back. "But how the hell does he know? He's on my damn aircraft!"

"He says they do it all the time. That's what they fear most out here."

"Who does what all the time?"

"The FARC. They shoot into the camp."

I looked to the left again. They could have been shooting from Brazil as flat as the ground was. There was nothing but grass in sight.

"Is there anybody out there?" Josh asked me.

"I don't see anybody. But I don't think that gunner had a heart attack."

Josh released the brakes.

"Unbelievable," he muttered. "We're sitting here like a fat cow."

He taxied us forward to mid-field. The soldiers outside had to stop shooting as we moved up to the gate and blocked their view of the prairie. They jumped up and ran down the concertina wire to get to a new position. Except for the M-60 gunner we saw no other casualties from return fire. In fact, the gunner himself was now sitting up in the back of the jeep which had parked inside the gate. He looked dazed but healthy and with the help of the driver was probing his chest for a bullet wound. Nobody was actually behind any shelter. The troops knelt only behind concertina wire. Even the third soldier in the jeep simply sat in the passenger seat as though waiting for us to move so he could drive around some more. To my untrained eyes it was a strange battle indeed.

We stopped so close to the gate our right wing hung over the gloved doorkeeper. When Ozzie lowered the ramp our troops piled out. In a cloud of orange dust blown up by the props they jogged to the safety of the camp as the jeep backed up and the M-60 gunner groggily resumed his position. This time he pointed the gun in a new direction...right at us. Sitting in the right seat and therefore able to see him up close and personal, I felt threatened until I realized he didn't even know he was doing it. Then I felt worse. He was another conscript, a poor teenager in an ill-fitting uniform with a long neckerchief and a cap that blew off the instant we taxied away. His wound magically healed, he now watched the plane in open-mouthed fascination as though noticing it for the first time, not even looking out on the plains where everyone else was still shooting. I hoped his finger wasn't sitting on the trigger.

When we were airborne again Josh pulled the propellers back to a cruising angle to save gas. There was a loud *wha-wha-wha* as the blades did their lopsided-washing-machine thing before finding the beat and spinning together. That minimized vibrations throughout the plane, and the din inside settled down.

I noted our fuel and pulled out my whiz wheel to compute whether we would have enough. Josh did the same but he bent the slide rule portion of his own slide rule and then had trouble getting the two pieces to move together.

"Hey, what happened to my whiz wheel?"

"Looks like the fuel's going to be closer than we thought."

"What the hell happened to this thing?"

"I have us getting there pretty close to bingo," I concluded.

"I've had this ever since pilot training," he said, holding it up. "How could this have gotten bent? You'd think they would have thought of that when they designed it."

"It's a piece of metal," Sgt Oswald observed. "Metal bends."

"You want to hear my fuel calculations?" I asked.

"Why does my stuff always break?" he groused in response.

I laughed, which only made him angry, so I tossed him my calculator to use. We both figured we would have five minutes to land the plane after getting to Mitu. Any more delay and we wouldn't be able to divert to Leticia.

"This sucks!" Josh decided after running the numbers again.

"What does?"

"What do you mean, what? *This.* We're out here in BFE, Bumfuck Egypt, heading for a field we don't even know if we can land at, and we may not have enough gas to go anywhere else. This sucks!"

"I don't know what you're getting all worked up about. We knew we would be close on gas before we took off."

He tossed his broken whiz wheel onto the dash and turned to look at me like I had two heads.

"Does anything tick you off, Bleriot? Anything?"

"Lots of things tick me off."

"Like what? What ticks you off? Please, please share with us."

"Dude, what's up with you? Where did the mood come from all of a sudden?"

"Nowhere, nowhere. I just want to know what ticks you off. Come on, Ozzie wants to know, too. Don't you, Ozzie?"

Sgt Oswald had turned his seat toward the writing table and was reading a book.

"Yeah," he said unenthusiastically. "I'm on the edge of my seat."

"See, he wants to know."

"Well," I agreed. "You and your PMS moods tick me off, for one."

"Okay, see, now there's a start. My PMS ticks you off. What else?"

"The ugly Panamanian women that you date – they tick me off."

"Oh," he held up his hands. The plane drifted into a left bank so he put them back on the controls. "Now you're getting personal. And how could the women I date – who aren't ugly, by the way – how could they upset you in any way?"

"They *are* ugly. I've seen them. And they tick me off because they lower the standard for the rest of us. Ugly women go out with you, their ugly friends see that and figure, 'Hey, I can get an American, too,' so then they're all pushing to go out with an American. We don't need that. We need the good-looking Panamanian women lining up to go out with us."

"There are no good-looking Panamanian women," Josh corrected me, obviously having considered my theory.

"Ah-ha! Then how are you going out with one?"

He thought for a minute.

"Okay, my point was," he started over, conceding nothing, "My point was that apparently there are things that tick you off but one of them is NOT that we're out here over God's green acres looking for a place to get fuel and not sure we're going to find one. That doesn't seem to bother you."

"No, not at all."

"Why not?"

I whipped out the papers Sylvia had given me.

"Because I have faith in the black-haired beauty. Beautiful women never let you down."

"Ha!" Ozzie grunted into the intercom. "Never trust anything that bleeds for five days and doesn't die."

"Sgt Oswald doesn't appear to agree with you," Josh said, looking at the loadmaster. "He's crude but sincere and in this case he's right on the money."

"That's right," Ozzie agreed. "And I know. Beautiful women *always* let you down."

He sounded like he knew whereof he spoke which made me wonder since Ozzie – though a great loadmaster and probably a wonderful human being – was one of the ugliest men I had ever met. If he had regular opportunities for beautiful women to let him down then I was going to shoot myself.

"Anything you want to tell us, load?" Josh asked.

"No, sir." Ozzie went back to reading his book.

"Alright, then. Let me see those surveys."

Sylvia's surveys weren't real surveys. Real surveys had geographic coordinates, runway dimensions, approach path guidance, obstacle clearance, and hazard information, not to mention a precise sketch of the entire area. Sylvia's survey looked like drunken scribbling on a cocktail napkin. There was a sketch of a river and of a runway alongside it, the outline of a house or hut on the opposite shore, and then a trapezoidal shape in the middle of the river marked *La barca.* The second page had names and dates from previous refuelings, none of which had involved a C-27, and the third was an unevenly-inked mimeograph of an unidentified map showing Mitu as a small town in the middle of somewhere. It was impossible even to tell the scale of the drawing.

"Mmm," mused Josh in mock appreciation. "Oh, yes. Very helpful, very helpful. I like the colors, and these lines...I like what she's done with them. These will be very big in Paris next spring." He tossed the pages back to my side. "Not!"

"You know, with all these negative waves floating around the cockpit it'll be a wonder if there's any gas for us there at all. You should be optimistic if only to inspire your crew."

"Uh-huh. Easy for you to say, you don't have the A-code. And as for my crew, if they were worth anything they would have talked me out of this half-assed operation while we were still in Bogotá. To hell with Sosa."

He was right about one thing. It was a lot easier to be the co-pilot on ever-changing flights like this. Everyone had inputs to the decision but only one guy carried the responsibility and that was the pilot-in-command, the guy with the A by his name on the orders. Then again, when we ran out of fuel and crashed the ground wasn't going to care who was in charge.

We found the Vaupes River just after eleven o'clock. I say we "found" it like that was an accomplishment: since it ran east-west across our flight path missing it would have been difficult – the important thing was we recognized it for what it was.

Our map showed a sharp turn in the river twenty miles upstream of Mitu. We used that as a waypoint thinking it would be easier to see than a small village hidden in the trees. But when we arrived overhead the spot we found the entire river to be just like every other river in the Amazon Basin – a lazy, winding, oxbow-laden ribbon of brown silt cutting its way through the jungle. There were lots of turns and almost-complete loops. The waypoint was nowhere to be seen.

We turned east to follow the water, staying high and watching the INS tick down the distance to the coordinates we had pulled off Fast Eddie's wall map. Fifteen miles, fourteen, thirteen... There wasn't a town in sight. There weren't even any villages along the river. Our fuel gauges hovered above bingo. Josh grew anxious. I knew it because his ears and neck always turned red when he was about to have a fit. Right now his ears were hidden by his headset but his neck flushed pink. As the gauges moved closer to zero with no runway in sight, the pink sank into an angry, frustrated crimson.

But then ten miles out we spotted a clearing in the trees, a long patch of light green that looked suspiciously man-made, and for a minute we deluded ourselves into thinking it was Mitu. Josh's flushing subsided. Then common sense prevailed. This clearing wasn't a strip. As geometric as it was the ground was too swampy and the scattered trees in the middle of it were too big for the area to host aircraft. It was just a clearing. We continued downriver. Josh's neck grew scarlet again.

Then at three miles we struck gold. He called it out.

"I've got something. Well, I *think* I've got something." Then, "Jeez, this is going to be good."

The river ran straight for a mile then banked to the north. Where it curved there was a white beach on the south side that followed the flow of the water. A pier jutted into the river at the near end of the beach. There was a hut at the base of the pier and across the water from it stood a two-story house jammed tight against the tree line. A charred hole high on the west wall of the house gaped at us, the yellow plywood boards that patched it from the inside staring like a jaundiced eye out over the river. Josh pulled the throttles back and went into a leisurely descending turn so we could get a closer look.

"Hey, there's the boat," I pointed.

Chugging up from the direction of the border was a rusty shallow-draft riverboat. It was steel with a cylindrical black tank balanced amidships like a cast iron Buddha. The hull was painted white as was the tiny wheelhouse, but the dirty brown of oxidation had attacked both schemes and was the dominant color everywhere. Clouds of black smoke popped rhythmically from the stack as the boat made slow progress against the current.

"There's somebody in the house," Ozzie called from the back.

A child – a girl – appeared on the landing in front of the house. An adult woman joined her. Both looked up as we circled overhead. I waved through the window. Neither waved back.

"How're we going to land on that?" I asked my usual question as we spiraled through two thousand feet.

"I don't know," Josh answered, looking out the window. "I'm looking for guns right now. When I don't see any I'll look at the runway."

The boat reached the last curve upstream from the house and rounded it at a leisurely pace. A man appeared at the stern beneath the cover of the wheelhouse. He wore a blue shirt and pants that were in shreds from the knees down. As we passed overhead we saw another man half-submerged in a hatchway on the starboard side. He bailed water with a canvas bag, leaning down to fill it through a hole in the deck then rising to throw it over the side before it all leaked through the bag. He stopped bailing and waved when we flew over. At last, a friendly gesture.

"Jeez, buddy, keep bailing," Josh muttered. "We don't want you to sink until we get our gas."

Josh passed me the controls for the overfly of the runway so he could concentrate on studying its surface. I descended to five hundred feet and slowed to 170 knots. In the back Ozzie was banging around.

"Hey, Ozzie," Josh ordered. "Open up the hell-hole. We want to be armed on this one."

"Already there, sir," came the reply.

The hell-hole was a hatch in the floor right behind the cockpit where we stored the chocks and intake covers and occasionally beer since the hole stayed cold at altitude. The door was almost invisible and had a lock on it. For that reason we also kept our guns there.

I went back up the river two miles and turned around to make a run-in the way we were most likely to land. At five hundred feet we could see the bend well enough, the water bulging like the fat part of a worm before making its patient turn to the left. The pier came into sight before the landing area did. Then the "beach" showed up. It turned out not to be a beach at all but simply a chopped-scraped-burned-cleared area on the south bank. It paralleled the water like a crescent moon peeled from the sky and pasted onto the edge of the trees.

"It's curved," Josh pointed out in frustration, the way he would reprimand a waiter who twice brought him the wrong wine.

"It sure is," I agreed. Where we needed to land definitely wasn't straight. The initial heading looked to be 120 degrees but the far end pointed east. And that in less than a mile. After two hundred yards of landing roll if we didn't jink left we would barrel off into the jungle.

"Can you believe this? They can't even build a straight strip out here!"

"Eddie said it wasn't much."

"He was right."

"Who do you suppose built it?"

"From the looks of it, volunteers from the Chicago Lighthouse for the Blind."

"Funny, the survey showed a straight strip," I mused.

"Ha!" was all Josh could say to that.

We cruised by. Looking out his window Josh conceded the surface of the strip looked solid. It was October, after all, the rainy season, so a hard surface was a big plus. Though high in its banks, the river hadn't started flooding yet.

I started a left turn to a downwind. As we cruised over the boat both men smiled and waved, the one in the wheelhouse stripping off his shirt and swinging it around over his head.

"Well, Mr. Aircraft Commander?" I asked. "You want to land or divert?"

"Well, Mr. Co-pilot," he replied. "Do you think we have the gas to divert?"

"No, our five minutes is up."

"Neither do I. What do you say we land?"

"Cool. Shall I do the honors?"

"Negative. If we're going to die I'll be the one who kills us. Ozzie?"

"Sir?"

"You ready to crash in the jungle?"

"Oh, yes, sir. All ready." Sgt Oswald climbed back up into the third seat and put his seatbelt on. He wore his boonie hat and a 9mm pistol in a holster strapped to his leg. He had another pistol, his own .45 Colt, tucked into his belt, and slung the strap of an AR-15 around the arm of his chair. Our loadmasters always got into the mercenary role with enthusiasm. Maybe it was all the time they had to think about it during flights. All Ozzie needed was a bandolier of cartridges to look like a Mexican revolutionary. Pancho Villa, the later years.

"Alright, this is what we'll do," Josh briefed. "I want to give them enough time to pull up to the pier so they're out of the middle of the river. If we have to go around it's going to be a quick left turn over the water and I don't want to pull a kamikaze if they're still in the way. We'll get the props into reverse fast but lay off the brakes so the nose doesn't dig in.

Mike, be ready to come on the controls quick. We're going to have to be turning all the way through the landing and when I go for nose wheel steering you'll get the yoke."

"Roger."

And that's exactly what we did. When the riverboat dropped anchor abeam the pier Josh turned final, aiming at the part of the runway still hidden by the trees. With barely two thousand pounds of fuel on board we weighed just less than forty thousand pounds, light by our standards and a weight that allowed us to slow to a veritable crawl of 94 knots. When the edge of the sand came in sight Josh cracked the throttles back and dropped onto a perfect glide slope for a steep approach. I split my attention between the approaching ground and the right wingtip, the latter of which was brushing the tree line.

"*Fwoom!*"

The ground was soft. The gear didn't make the satisfying *whump!* it normally did when pounding down on concrete or gravel. The loamy soil sucked up the rear wheels and gave a quick jerk to our forward motion that threatened to slam the nose gear down early. But Josh saved the nose and delayed reversing the props. Then the forward wheels on the main gear met the ground and increased our footprint over the surface.

"Left...left..."

"I got it."

"More left!"

The nose came down.

"Your controls!"

"My controls."

We stopped with a thousand feet to spare. The crescent of the runway was so pronounced Josh could look over his shoulder out the left window and see where we'd touched down.

"Uh, well, that worked out," he commented.

"Yeah, sort of, I guess. Nice landing."

"Thanks."

Sweat poured down his face. We opened our windows to get airflow through the cockpit.

The air outside was heavy and wet. From the sky the river and jungle looked like a clear, clean, dry tableau. Down on the ground they were anything but. The air was pungent with heat and the smell of damp greenery. A carpet of some kind of tropical clover covered the east half of the strip, interwoven with vines. The sun dappled leaves on the edge of the tree line and boiled off dew that clung to the lower branches, leaving wisps of steam to float above the weeds. As always, light was frustrated penetrating the canopy. Instead it danced on the trees and created a sparkling vision of glistening plants fronting a black interior. It was as though the jungle wore a diamond choker. I had the feeling that if we broke where we were, the vines crushed beneath our tires would rise up and cover us within days.

"Ramp's clear," Ozzie called. He hopped out of his seat rifle in hand and ran to the back of the cargo compartment.

"Roger." Josh reached up and flipped the switch over his head that opened the cargo door and ramp. There was a *clunk* as the bolts unlocked, then the upper door rose inward. When it reached the ceiling it locked in place and the ramp took its turn to lower. It locked out at ninety degrees, level with the cabin.

"You're clear," Ozzie called, squatting on the ramp with the rifle in his lap. "How are you going to turn this thing around, sir?"

"Good question," was Josh's answer.

"Don't turn right," I advised. "You've got a tree off the right wing."

"Well, I can't turn left until I turn right. The strip's not wide enough."

"Use differential power."

"It's still not wide enough."

"It looked wider from the air," I commented unhelpfully.

"Yeah, it did."

"Keep going forward. I think the trees break out up ahead."

They did. There was a divot in the tree line a hundred yards up which allowed Josh to angle the plane right and then spin it back to the left a hundred and eighty degrees. With the left prop in reverse and the right one forward and some careful nose wheel steering Josh turned the plane with a dozen feet to spare on the water side.

"Okay," he breathed. "Now if we can do that again at the far end we just might get out of here."

At the beginning of the strip the two boatmen were already running out a two-inch hose. They worked quickly. I wondered, and then stopped wondering, what operations they normally supported out here.

Facing the approach end, we shut down the right engine. Ozzie was outside before the prop stopped spinning. He jumped off the ramp and ran to the water's edge to intercept the boatman dragging the hose. Seeing him dressed like a stressed postal worker didn't faze the locals at all.

"*Hola!*" the one with the hose called. He was short and lightly-built. If he weighed over a hundred pounds it was only because he hadn't cut his hair for years. It grew thick and greasy in all directions, stopped only by a canvas cap with a five-pointed star sewn into the top. His face was small and square and cracked from a deep tan. He could have been a hard twenty-five years old or an easy fifty – it was impossible to tell. He smiled upon greeting Ozzie and then was all business, as though he and his partner, too, were at some risk with an idling boat full of fuel out here in nowheresville.

Very quickly they got the motor on the Buddha going. It *chug-chug-chugged* in concert with our idling prop.

The driver of the boat waved but stayed on board. His square-faced partner did all the work, moving nimbly across the crumbling pier and hopping from plank to plank with the assurance of one who knows which ones will hold and which will not.

I hopped out of the right seat and went to the back of the plane. As per Josh's instructions, for the whole refueling operation I stood by the ramp with an M-16 while Ozzie and the boatman worked the hose.

The nozzle on the hose was the kind used on automobile gas station pumps so the process didn't go quickly. Ozzie had to climb up on the wing and point the hose right into the tank – the old-fashioned way. If the hose didn't clog we would be lucky to be done in twenty minutes. The speed of the gassing wasn't the only thing that worried me, though. Was the fuel any good? There was a filter built into the tank port but I shuddered to think what we were going to be running our engines on.

Josh worried about that, too, but mostly he was nervous about sitting in the middle of the jungle. Neither of the boatmen was armed that we could see and they always stayed in sight except for the few times the one on the boat dropped below the gunwale to hammer on the Buddha's pump. But the fact was we were a sitting duck and were going on nothing more than Eddie's word for our safety out here.

"How's it going?" he said into the intercom.

"Fine," I replied. I'd taken my headset out back and run a comm line from the troop door. "Ozzie's up top and the two guys haven't moved."

"Keep an eye on them."

"What do you think I'm doing?"

"Knowing you, day-dreaming. For all we know these guys are Tupac Amaru just waiting to kill us and take the plane."

"I doubt it," I said, watching the intensity with which the boat driver monitored the pump. "'Always trust your car to the man who wears a star.'"

"What's that supposed to mean?"

"It means they're working pretty hard for guys who want to kill us."

"It could be a cover."

"For?"

"For other rebels to sneak up on us."

"They don't need any help. We're aircrew who barely know which end of the gun goes where."

"Well, when in doubt empty your clip."

"I wouldn't hit anything."

"They don't know that."

"Come on, these guys are legit. Well, maybe not legit but I think they intend to sell us gas. If they were going to kill us they would have done it before they started pumping. Otherwise, they're wasting they're own product. Capitalism, my friend. Besides, what are they going to do, steal our plane?"

"Maybe."

"Give me a break. You and I were barely able to land it here. You think the average recruit to T-A would be able to take off? Stealing this plane would be a lousy idea."

"They could brag about it to the world press."

"After they crashed?"

"Maybe."

"What reporter in his right mind would come out here to see it?"

Josh was unconvinced. He kept stretching from his seat to look out the right window and back through the cargo compartment.

"It could be a trap."

"If it is, when the attack comes I'm going to hide out back here on this grassy knoll."

"Whatever. Keep an eye on them."

Josh being Josh, what he was really worried about was the money. Also in the hell-hole was Sylvia's satchel containing ten thousand dollars to pay for the gas. In one sense, paying ten thousand dollars for any amount of fuel in South America was highway robbery but in another – well, all we had to do was look around. There weren't many Texaco stations in Mitu. Forking over ten thousand dollars to keep a twenty million dollar plane in the air wasn't a bad deal.

All we wanted was four thousand pounds. Eddie had instructed that we pay the men the whole ten thousand dollars regardless of how much gas we took on. He'd muttered something about good business, the concept – though dear to him – obviously at conflict with his sense of cutting a deal. Josh shared his feeling. Anywhere else all of us would have wanted to take on as much fuel as we could simply to bring down the price-per-pound. Here, however, the more gas we took the harder it would be to take off. Josh and I figured the minimum we needed to get to Leticia was four thousand pounds. The minimum was all we wanted.

Josh was reading my thoughts.

"Hey," he called from up front. "At ten thousand dollars for four thousand pounds, we're paying them about seventeen dollars a gallon."

"So?"

"What do you mean, 'So?' That's a hell of a lot of money for gas that you can get for a buck and a half."

"Where?"

"Anywhere."

"Not here."

"That's two thousand."

"That's two!" I called up to Sgt Oswald.

Ozzie finished with the right tank, snapping the cover on the tank port back into position. He crawled across the top of the plane to the left side, dragging the nozzle. Square-Face heaved on the hose to give him slack.

"Yeah, but even out here that's a rip-off," Josh continued. He spoke as though he had done a marketing survey of the relative costs of supplying stolen aviation fuel in the Amazon Basin.

"Uh-huh," I agreed absent-mindedly, looking past the boat to the woman and girl on the porch of the river house. The girl wore a pink dress and stood with her arms leaned on the railing of the porch. The woman stood behind her with her hands on the girl's shoulders. They looked mestizo, not pure native. "Why don't you tell these guys that and see if you can talk them down?"

"I'm thinking about it," Josh said stubbornly.

"You do and I'll shoot you myself."

"Huh?"

"Just give them the whole bag and let's get out of here."

"You're pretty free with other people's money."

"You're pretty tight with it. You're so tight-fisted if I gave you some coal to hold two weeks later I'd have a diamond."

"What? What...where do you...what are you talking about?"

The girl on the porch turned to look upstream. She said something and the woman turned, too. I couldn't see what they were looking at and the cord wasn't long enough for me to move far from the plane.

"Hey, I think someone's coming down the river," I said into the mike.

Josh leaned over the center console to my side of the plane but the trees blocked his view.

"Who?"

"I don't know."

"*Ey, Choco!*" the man on the boat suddenly called to his companion. Square-Face kept hold of the hose but stepped to the other side of it to look back. His partner on the boat reached below the gunwale but hesitated, decided to wait, and stood straight again. Now neither of them was looking at our plane.

"Hey, more slack!" Sgt Oswald called from up top. He jerked on the hose, getting Square-Face's attention. The little man hoisted up more hose then went back to looking at the river. He didn't look nervous; he didn't look angry. His face was a mask.

"How much more do we need?" I asked Josh, who was monitoring the gauges. We would probably have to put a little more on the left side since the number 1 engine was still running.

"Eighteen hundred pounds."

Now the women alternated their glances between us and whatever was coming downriver. The way they did it prompted me to flip the safety off the M-16.

A canoe hove into view. It was a dugout, a *cayuca.* Long, with tapered bow and stern and covered planking at both ends. There was one man in it. Like our refuelers he was small and dark. Instead of a shirt he wore a vest with various flashing pieces of metal hooked to it. He had a hat with a flat brim that reached so far to left and right it shielded his shoulders from the sun. The way he moved as well as the few features of his face I could see suggested he was older than our gas suppliers. Yet he was alert. With an eye on us and the refueling boat, and with one long paddle trailing in the water, he casually steered his craft through the current up to the base of the house on the far bank. Our refuelers watched him as he drifted in.

"Huh," said Josh, settling back in his seat. "Dad's home from the office."

No one else came down the river. The face of the little girl on the porch followed the old man in the dugout as he floated closer, eventually nudging the prow against the shore near the house. The woman on the porch went into the house, returned with a burlap bag, and walked down to meet him. The man with the hat kept looking our way. Our boys from the boat stared back. Nobody waved or called hello or made any signal they knew each other.

"Gas?"

"Fifteen hundred."

"We'll be here forever."

"What's your hurry?"

"I'll feel more comfortable in the air, that's all," I replied, then called above the idling left prop, "Ozzie, how you doing?"

Ozzie kept his eyes on the nozzle but raised a hand to give me a thumbs up. He was in an awkward position, half-sitting and half-crouching on the wing to avoid the hot surface of the roof.

Across the water the woman leaned out and held open the bag. The old man took his eyes off the boat and the plane long enough to reach between his feet and pull up a three-foot-long fish from the bottom of the dugout. It was a *paiche,* a delicious fish found in all the waters of the basin. *Paiche* could grow to six feet long and weigh over a hundred pounds. This man had gotten lucky and found a good-sized one. But then he showed it wasn't only luck by pulling up a second fish, this one even larger than the first.

"Hey, dinner," Josh commented from the cockpit. "You think they're going to invite us over?"

The man in the hat reached down into his canoe again.

"Jeez, how many fish does he have in there?"

This time he pulled out a gun. It was a rifle. I couldn't tell what kind. It had a short stock, a bolt, and a long barrel, so long that he seemed to take forever pulling it up from the bottom of the boat.

"What is *that*?" came the question from up front. I didn't answer. Now that somebody else in the neighborhood had a gun, my hands, already sweaty on the M-16, gripped it tighter.

The woman paid no attention to the gun. She closed the bag with the fish and with effort swung it over her shoulder. Without a look back she carried it up the porch steps, past the girl by the railing, and into the house. But even before she sank into the darkness of the doorway her man had his unwieldy firearm out. He pointed it right at my head. At least that's where I thought he was pointing as all I could see was the dark hole of an open barrel. In reality he was probably aiming at the boat. Probably.

"Hey...hey...what's he doing?" Josh said. "Hey,... Mike?...Mike?"

"Uh, um.."

"Do something, Mike."

I am doing something, I thought. I'm panicking. In fact the only clear thought to go through my head was that I should try to look unimportant. Maybe he was low on ammo.

Boat Man and Square-Face had remained unmoving and poker-faced since the canoeist's arrival. Now, seeing him point a rifle their way, they seemed unsure what to do. Boat Man crouched. Then he hesitated as though that wouldn't be fair and stood up straight again. Square-Face never let go of the hose that Ozzie still had pointed into the tank. He half-ducked when he saw his partner do the same, then stood straight again on the other's lead. When Boat Man changed his mind again and ducked, Square-Face did the same. It was like watching two kids practicing to be a jack-in-the-box.

The old man pulled the trigger.

"*BOOM!*"

Every bird for miles flew into the air in fright. Ozzie, who hadn't been paying attention to anything but the hose and the tank, was so startled he almost fell off the wing. There was a tumbling *whoonh-whoonh-whoonh* sound overhead as the bullet went high and crashed into the trees behind me, knocking down a good-sized branch. Though it sounded like a record winding down, the shell must have been massive: it traveled with the speed and momentum of a cannon ball.

I stood there like a mannequin while the old man pointed and fired his ancient musket. Now I, too, half-ducked – and remained there like a half-ducking mannequin. The situation was surreal. One minute we were in a tropical paradise calmly doing business with black market fuel smugglers, the next a backwoods poacher was taking shots at my head. My mind struggled to catch up.

Josh shouted something into his headset. Up top Ozzie looked sideways at the man on the opposite shore. Judging that for the moment he was in no danger, he repositioned himself lower on the wing and kept refueling. Square-Face, too, made no move to reel in the hose. He crouched lower, however, which enabled him to escape from line-of-sight with the canoeist by hiding behind the hull of the boat. His partner on board also made minimal efforts to conceal himself. He spent several seconds ducking, scampering, and making other slow-motion unproductive movement but then eventually reappeared above the gunwale with a rusty .30-caliber carbine in hand.

Great, I thought. Now there are two of them.

Oddly, we all failed to do what every nerve in my body was telling me to do: run like hell. I wanted to but reason prevailed long enough to ask me where I would go and what I would accomplish once there. And to be honest, I wasn't sure how bad the situation really was.

Our erstwhile comrades from the boat, for example, looked concerned, but their concern had a resigned nature to it. Boat Man, in particular, leaned on the Buddha like he had just acquired today's newspaper and would read it while waiting for the refueling to end. He levered the breech of the well-worn weapon trying to work a round into the chamber, looking for all the world like a man who knew he had something to do today but couldn't quite remember what it was.

Separated by fifty yards of open water, the old man in the canoe struggled through mechanical difficulties of his own as he reloaded his weapon. He worked carefully and made no attempt to take cover or get out of his craft. It finally crossed my mind that I should shoot him.

From the cockpit, Josh could only see the canoeist and a small section of the hose running overhead.

"Mike! Mike! What the hell's going on? Is anybody hit?"

"No," I said as though watching the whole scene from afar.

"He shot at us! What'd he hit? Are we hit?"

"Nothing. He missed."

My brain started working again. Shoot him, a voice said. Then I saw the hose at my feet and my priorities jumbled themselves like clothes in a dryer. We needed gas, not a fight.

The pump on the Buddha chugged away.

"How much gas do we still have to go?"

"Screw the gas! Are you crazy? We need to get out of here!"

The canoeist fixed his gun at the same time that Boat Man cleared his. The long barrel came pointing our way again; this time its large black hole gaped menacingly at the peeling blue paint just above the waterline amidships. Boat Man leaned around the Buddha and shoved the carbine toward the opposite shore. I half raised the M-16.

"BOOM!"

"Pop!"

Again there was a *whoonh-whoonh-whoonh* as the gyrating mass of the mysterious giant round sailed clear overhead. This shot was further to the left than before and plowed into the forest sixty yards behind the tail of the C-27. Now even Josh could see the man's aim was way off.

"Man, he must hate those trees," he commented.

Indeed, for such a long barrel the old man had miserable aim. He was shooting point-blank at a boat the size of a garage and so far hadn't hit a thing. The charge behind each bullet was to blame. It was so powerful that when it went off the recoil almost knocked the old man into the water. Each time he fired, the cayuca canted wildly. It came close to capsizing and the old man ended up with the barrel pointing at the sky.

"Pop! Pop!"

But Boat Man didn't do any better. He had repeating-action technology on his side but all his rounds – approximately four for every one from the old man – went so wide we couldn't tell where they hit. He fired fast, carelessly, as though the goal were to expel the bullets rather than actually strike anything with them. His expression was anxious innocence, someone trying hard and seeking affirmation that he was doing the right thing. When he reloaded he didn't hurry. He leaned on the Buddha out in the open, balanced the carbine stock against his hip, and every few seconds looked over his shoulder to see how the old man was doing.

The old man was doing fine but was slow. He sat in his canoe and painstakingly pushed giant cartridges one by one into his own rifle. His position on the water and in the canoe was awkward. Shooting at us was difficult because he wasn't pointing directly our way. The bow was parallel to the shore so he had to twist halfway around each time he fired, a position that looked uncomfortable even before the recoil. Like his opponent, he also made no effort to correct it or to get out of the other's sights.

"BOOM!"

"Pop!"

"BOOM!"

"Pop! Pop!"

Josh's voice turned from panic to disdain.

"Jeez, these guys are bad shots."

No kidding. I lowered my own gun. Shooting in self-defense didn't seem quite so critical now. Ionescu could have staged this battle.

Even the girl on the porch thought so. Bored, she turned and went inside.

"You know," I said to Josh, "I get the feeling they've done this before."

The firing slowed down, the initial "fury" – if I can use that word – subsiding into a rhythmic schedule of shoot, counter-shoot, rest, reload. Josh watched through the windshield like it was widescreen TV. I kept an eye on the old man to make sure he didn't suddenly correct his aim but more and more began to look around – to see if Josh's conspiracy theory might be valid. Someone creeping up from another direction, perhaps, or worse, filming for Candid Camera.

"Got the gas?" Ozzie called. He at least was still prone up top.

"Got the gas?" I relayed.

Josh checked the gauges.

"Got it."

"Got it!"

"*Oye, amigo! Basta!*"

Square-Face yanked on the hose and scooped up the slack. Boat Man lay down his carbine to help. The old man in the canoe, seeing them prepare to leave, hesitated before his next shot and watched, waiting. Ozzie dropped back into the cabin through the cockpit hatch.

I jumped into the plane and tucked the M-16 behind the seats.

"Close the ramp!"

The ramp came up and the door swung down to meet it. By the time they latched I was in the seat. Ozzie opened the hatch in the latrine and positioned himself there now with his own rifle, resting it on the case of scotch we were taking to Manson. The position let him cover both Boat Man and Square Face as well as the old fisherman across the way. I didn't blame him given the unpredictable nature of our temporary companions but so far they were all too absorbed in their own work to pay any attention to us. The refuelers readied their boat for departure. For his part, the old man finally moved – he climbed carefully out of his canoe, lay his rifle down long enough to pull the dugout onto the shore and into the grass, then went back to the shore and stood there. Retrieving his rifle he held it at his waist, watching the activity a hundred feet away. The gun was longer than he was tall.

Josh punched the starter switch on #2. The right prop started to turn. When it did it caught Boat Man's attention and he looked up in alarm. He yelled something. When none of us reacted he yelled again and waved, then jumped down to the pier and started hopping from plank to plank to make the shore.

"Hey, one of 'em's coming back!" Ozzie said anxiously.

Boat Man jumped off the pier into the grass and waved his arms some more, shouting and running toward us.

"What's he want?"

"I don't know. He looks mad."

"Don't let him come to the plane!" Josh shouted.

"He's not stopping!"

"Wait," I started to say, "He..."

There was a burst of automatic fire and rounds plowed into the grass at Boat Man's feet. He stopped like a giant bungie was tied to his back, feet going in reverse while his arms and head still wanted to go forward. Square Face looked up in alarm from where he was loosening the mooring rope. Across the river the old man laughed.

"Holy shit! Ozzie, don't shoot!" I yelled into the mike.

"You said to stop him!"

"I didn't!"

"I did," Josh admitted.

"Yeah, someone did."

"Okay, okay! But he didn't say shoot. Stop shooting!"

"I stopped! I'm not shooting!"

"What are you doing?" Josh asked.

"I just realized – he wants his money!"

Josh stopped and smacked his forehead.

"Oh, god. Sorry. Oh, hey, yeah, I forgot. Jeez, that's embarrassing. Ozzie, get that bag out."

"You going to cover him?"

"We don't need to cover him!"

I gripped the console with white knuckles. The #2 engine fired up and went to ground idle, making the panel shake as we rumbled in place. "Jesus Christ, we almost shot him when all he wanted was the money."

"He should have said something," Josh said.

"He's outside!"

"Well, okay."

"I can't believe we almost shot somebody."

"Yeah," he agreed. "We would never be able to get gas here again."

"Is this the bag?" Ozzie held up a tool bag from the hell hole.

"No, the leather one! It's under the chocks. Come on, Ozzie, how many bags of money do we have in there?"

"You know," Josh continued. He twisted in his seat as Ozzie found the right pouch. The wheels of larceny started to turn. "Wait a minute. Wait a minute. Hold on to that money, Ozzie. Let's think about this one."

"Think about what?" I asked.

"Hold on, hold on. I've got an idea here." He held up his finger to make the point.

"Think about what? Give him the money and let's go!"

"Well, that's what I'm saying. Just how much do we want to give them?" He reached for his kneeboard with its pad of paper. "I suggest we revise the contract..."

I threw my shoulder harness off and leaped out of my seat. Grabbing the bag from Sgt Oswald I leaned into the latrine and flung the whole bag out into the grass. The satchel landed at Boat Man's feet.

"What are you doing?" I heard Josh scream above the engines. He half-climbed out of his seat but then remembered the engines were running and reluctantly sat back down.

Boat Man picked up the bag and ducked away from the spinning prop. He crouched down and opened the straps to look inside. When he looked up it was with a delirious face. I threw him a thumbs up with a shrug – enough? He nodded and beamed from ear to ear, giving me a thumbs up in return. More than enough.

Ozzie nodded. "Good call," he said

I climbed back into the right seat. Josh's face was ashen. He tried to talk, half to chew me out and half to complain about the money, but he couldn't complete his sentences.

"Shut up!" I barked. "Let's get out of here."

On cue the old man decided he was tired of waiting for his game to begin again. The funny stuff was over and his opponent was still alive. There was another *BOOM!* loud enough that we heard it in the cockpit. God knows where the bullet went.

"Oh, jeez. Grandpa's at it again," Ozzie muttered. The old man was on the wooden platform, fiddling with the bolt to chamber another round. "How about him? Can I shoot him?"

"No! Yes! No! Oh, hell, I don't know," I admitted in frustration.

"I can just wound him," he offered. Now that he'd fired once he was spring-loaded to do it again.

"Hang on. He's not doing any damage yet."

"Well, if his bullets are big enough for that barrel they could put a hell of a hole in one of our engines."

"I can't believe you just did that," Josh broke in, working to control his temper.

"Dude, somebody's shooting at us. Would you stop worrying about your checkbook?"

"If we still had that money we could offer him some to stop shooting at us," he countered.

"They could puncture a tire, too," Ozzie continued from the back.

"It's not even our money."

"That's the beauty of it. Ten grand tax-free."

"Maybe a few warning shots would get him to put his head down..."

"You would sell your soul for a few thousand dollars? Not to mention give a raw deal to armed guys who just saved our butts?"

"Saved our butts, my butt. They're businessmen. Crooks, yeah, but this is a business. All they want is a few pesos to feed their families but nooooo, you go ahead and pay tourist rates to top off the tanks."

"He could hit a fuel tank, too," Ozzie droned on.

"...not to mention that the next time someone comes out here the fuel's going to cost even more. That's the way a market works: if they know you're willing to pay ten grand then they'll start asking for fifteen."

"Yeah, that's where I would be aiming if I were him. One round would ruin our day."

"Could we just get out of here?" I pleaded.

"Alright, alright," Josh threw up his hands. "If you're finished playing the Good Samaritan, that is. You're sure there's nothing else in the back you want to toss out to them? Some tools, maybe, or perhaps extra ammo for their guns? The way that guy's shooting he's going to need it."

"You know, a hole that big – our tanks just might blow," Ozzie persisted from the latrine.

No kidding. I had been waiting for the old guy to hit us there ever since he pulled out his gun. So far, however, he was more a danger to the forest. I knew we would be justified in shooting him but it was a hell of a thing to kill someone on principle.

"Ozzie, just hold your fire."

"Can't I even lay down a few shots that way? Just to get him to back off."

"No!"

"Jeez," he sulked. "You guys never let me shoot anyone."

Josh finally threw his notepad onto the dash and turned back to the business of flying. He pushed the power levers up.

"Alright, let's get out of here before Mike starts going through my wallet and I have a total breakdown. Ozzie, ease off your trigger figure and see if we can get out of here," he directed. "I promise, if we crash you can shoot anyone you want starting with the copilot. For now we need to turn around. Can you cover us out the left side?"

"Yeah, out the troop door I can."

"Then do it."

Boat Man ran back across the pier as Josh pushed up the power lever on #1. The little man moved fast now, a handful of bullets at his feet apparently warming up the blood. In one deft movement he scooped up the mooring rope and leaped to the bow of the boat to join his friend. Immediately they drifted away from the pier.

The C-27 was moving, too.

This was going to be the trickiest part of the whole operation. I looked out the right window to where our wing was already over water. The boat would have to move farther before our left wing would clear the Buddha as we came around.

"Watch that side," Josh instructed needlessly. "This is going to suck if we sink in."

That was the understatement of the year.

"Right's going into reverse."

As we budged from our parking position he lifted the right lever over the detent and pulled it down. The right prop dropped into a comforting roar as the pitch in the blades retreated. Josh pushed #1 up more. The Mighty Chuck started to do its thing.

"Not too much," I warned. "You don't want to dig the nose wheel in."

"Well, I have to clear the weeds, too. It's not exactly a wide turn."

"No, it's tight."

"Tell me how tight. I can't see."

"You're good, you're good. Just don't push it any more or the nose wheel won't make it."

To tell the truth I wasn't sure it would make it anyway but there was nothing Josh could do: he was already spinning the aircraft on a dime. The nose wheel sat below us and about two feet aft so a visual wag from our seats was that if we just barely passed over something the nose wheel should miss it. *Should* miss it.

"Hey, the tail's hittin' trees," Ozzie said from the back. "Not bad, but don't push it back any further 'cause there's some big ones coming up."

Josh shouted in frustration. There was nothing he could do. We were moving and there was no backing up.

"Keep it coming, keep it coming..." I coaxed. We were halfway around the turn.

"How's that side?"

"Good," I lied. "Dry enough to hold us."

One good thing as we passed the ninety-degree point was that the boat had moved. It drifted from the pier and now backed with the current, so our wing didn't clip its stack. Boat Man was in the wheelhouse, looking over his right shoulder as he reversed engines.

"BOOM!"

I'd forgotten about the old man. He had issues, apparently, and still felt the need to express them with his blunderbuss. By the time I turned to look, the recoil had swung his rifle so high that I had no idea where the bullet went. It didn't come through our windscreen, however, so we had that going for us.

"Bring it around, Josh. Almost there. Power up! POWER UP!"

The plane started to sink in on the left side. We could feel it up front, a lurch to the left and sudden deceleration. Josh yanked on the #2 power lever and pushed the other throttle full forward – just in time. The C-27 broke free and bounced to the right. We were lined up.

"I'm not stopping! You guys ready?"

We hadn't computed TOLD but it was way too late for that now.

"Ready."

"He's going to shoot again," was Ozzie's response. The boat was drifting into our eight o'clock, behind the wing and between us and the old man.

"If he hits us, kill him," Josh snapped.

He matched the power levers and pushed them up. The needles swung to our emergency limit.

I held the yoke. As the grudging turn of the tires in the clover became a takeoff roll I pulled the controls into my lap. We hadn't talked about it but the smart thing here was to do a soft-field take-off: get airborne as soon as we could regardless of whether the plane was at climbout speed. That would allow us to break free of surface friction and accelerate in ground effect – long enough, we hoped, to point the nose up without stalling and clear the trees at the strip's end.

We hadn't covered a hundred yards before it was clear we weren't going to make it.

"Power..." I coaxed.

"I don't have any!" Josh yelled back as though I were accusing him of hoarding.

"Go left, then."

Josh's hand was still on the steering toggle by his left leg. I couldn't see but assumed he had a death grip on the trigger – I would have. The trigger closed an electrical circuit, which opened a valve that ported hydraulic fluid to the actuator on the twin-wheeled nose gear. The whole device worked wonders while taxiing but became extremely sensitive at high speeds.

A branch smacked the right wing.

"Left..."

We jerked left on Josh's steering but now the plane's speed was in a touchy region where it was too slow to fly and yet too fast to move the nose gear safely. The nose bounced left, hit uneven soil, and corrected even further to the right.

"The other left!" I shouted.

"You've got it!" he yelled back. "Steering's not working. Bring it left!"

The strip was curving and we weren't keeping up. Another tree slapped at the right wing. As light as we were the tires beneath our seats bumped and slipped in the soft dirt. I stepped on the left rudder pedal and held the ailerons far over in the same direction. Two-thirds of the strip was gone. The end was coming up fast. It wasn't a dramatic drop-off or concrete wall but it was still the end. Beyond the clover the grass grew thick. Cattails as high as our cockpit told us the ground gave way to water. When we hit it the gear would sink in and we would splash to a sinking, muddy, belly-flopping halt that the Chuck would never recover from.

But that was at the end. If we didn't keep up with the turn we would never make it that far. Before then the right wingtip would finally meet a branch or tree trunk that didn't budge.

"Left!" Josh cried again, and put his hands on the yoke as though the controls could go any further over than they were. Five hundred feet remaining. A young greenheart tree, long limbs and spare trunk boasting some of the hardest wood in the world, grew taller and fatter in the corner of my eye as it raced toward us from the one o'clock position abeam our old tire tracks. It was going to shear our wing right off.

The right wing lifted.

We weren't fast enough to fly or even rotate yet but air still poured over the wings. With the right aileron pointing straight down the camber on that side did what it could to produce lift. And what it could do was tilt us left.

Had I been outside watching our takeoff I would have thought we were drunk. The right wing lifted and the left one dropped, far enough that the position light on that side traced a furrow in the surface of the river. The left prop mowed the cattails growing up at the water's edge.

"Back right."

"No!"

"I've got water over here."

"I've got TREES over here!"

The greenheart flashed by underneath the raised right wing. With full rudder we careened to the left following the track of the airstrip. We had a hundred feet to go.

"Rotate!"

The airspeed indicator hit 87 knots. It was time to fly. The right gear was off the ground and we were bouncing along like a water skier in choppy waves but the controls were already in my lap. There wasn't any more I could do. From here it was up to physics.

"Rotate!" Josh pleaded. His hands were on the yoke now, too, and I could feel him trying to muscle the plane into the air.

In the back Ozzie struggled to keep his rifle pointed out the troop door.

"Are we going to crash?" he asked innocently. "Should I put a seat belt on?"

Just before the water I wrenched the yoke right and shoved forward to lower the wing's angle of attack, then yanked the controls back again into my lap. The nose came up as the cattails tried to slap us in the face. The main gear gave one final bounce on the weedy bank and then followed us into the air as though flying had been their intention all along. The C-27 finally did what it did better than almost any other plane: launched itself off the ground and started climbing like a wayward rocket.

"Left – no, level!"

I shoved the controls forward again to level us off a mere twenty feet up. We had accelerated so slowly on the ground that we still needed another dozen knots to fly higher than one wingspan from the surface.

A triumphant yell came from the cabin. We banked left to get away from the trees and then back right to follow the water's flow. From his perch in the open troop door Ozzie was getting the VIP tour.

Neither Josh nor I spoke right away. At the eastern bend to the river, with the airspeed shooting through 160 knots, I pulled back on the controls and shot us up and over the tree line in a rapid climb to five hundred feet. Altitude had never looked so good.

"Gear up."

Josh didn't reply but raised the handle.

"Flaps up."

My hands trembled and my throat was dry. I concentrated on looking out the window and flying the plane, taking great care each time I glanced at a gauge to confirm what it was saying. For some reason being very specific was suddenly important. One hundred eighty-*seven* knots, not one-eighty-five. Thirty-*one* hundred psi in the hydraulic system, not three thousand. Dead people didn't sweat details.

Josh's face was set in stone, an anguished mask of death-narrowly-averted. But then he surprised me by taking a deep breath and hooting with laughter.

"What's so funny?" I asked.

He didn't answer right away. He just cackled away, leaning on the dash in a contagious, gut-busting guffaw. Josh wasn't a big laugh kind of guy – he was more the sarcastic hit-and-run type – so seeing him doubled-over got to me. I began to chuckle.

"Don't...do...that...at home, boys and girls," he managed to say. "We're...experts." At the word 'experts' he collapsed in fit of giggles. I caught the bug and joined him.

"What are you guys doing up there?"

"Flying," I gasped out, which made us laugh harder.

Eventually Josh took a breath and held his hands out in front of him.

"My controls," he said, choking back snorts.

"Your controls."

He banked us right and pulled the power back to mid-range. Six hundred foot-pounds of torque per engine could move us along quite comfortably at 200 knots. When he let the nose fall through the horizon we picked up even more speed than that.

"We going back?" Ozzie called from the cabin. I looked over my shoulder. He was standing by the troop door and had been about to close it.

"Are you kidding?" Josh exulted, his laughing fit having completely changed his attitude. "That little feat we just pulled *demands* a fly-by! Am I right?"

To tell the truth, I would have been happy to continue on our way in a straight-and-level cruise. But the sudden exhaustion that came as the adrenalin drained away brought me into Josh's loopy mood.

"You are right," I agreed. "I hate to admit it and hope it doesn't become a trend, but you are right!"

"I mean, hell. We've shown enough poor judgment today – one more little stunt can't hurt."

"I've got my seat!" Ozzie yelled, and sat back in the doorway with one foot dangling into the slipstream.

Josh brought us around to the west and dropped to tree-top level. With the sun overhead our shadow raced along the canopy just ahead of the nose, a black probe that pushed through the trees to smooth our way. The airstrip at Mitu was a mile-and-a-half distant. By the time we reached it we were doing 240 knots.

The blue-and-white riverboat came around the bend from the house, chugging downstream. As we flew past, Boat Man and Square Face looked up and waved their shirts over their heads, their big smiles evident even from two hundred feet. Ten thousand dollars went a long way toward making friends out here.

The old man from the canoe was walking through the grass to his house when we buzzed the river. He looked our way and showed no emotion whatsoever. Which was good, since the only emotion he'd shown thus far had been expressed through his rifle. The woman from the house and her little girl came back to the front porch. I waved through the window as I had before, not expecting any response. The woman gave none but the little girl, surprisingly, finally smiled and waved back.

When we passed over the far end of the strip, Josh hauled back on the controls and launched us into a seventy-degree climb with a steep turn to the left to bring us around to the east. From the ground the C-27 must have looked beautiful, its squat body thrown flat against the sky like the high silhouette of a man-made star. The gunmen stopped shooting to watch. In the cabin, Ozzie jumped to his feet to enjoy the view. Restrained by his harness, he stood spread-eagled in the open doorway looking straight down at the airstrip that had almost claimed us for a trophy.

"Hey-heyyyyyy!" he yelled into the brilliant sunlight. "Woo-hooooooo! Welcome to the jungle express, baby!!! Welcome to the jungle express!"

4. The Jungle Express 2

"You guys going *to land tonight?"* came the call over UHF.

"I don't know," Josh replied carefully. *"Should we? You tell us."*

We were in a holding pattern at five hundred feet over the trees twenty miles north of Pucallpa. We'd filled our tanks at Iquitos and pressed on to the south but now were leery of joining Shark 21 and 24 on the ground.

"Well, where do I start?"

It was Charlie Manson's voice. I knew that because his sarcasm sliced the frequency spectrum in half as it sailed through the ether.

"All I want to know," Josh broke in, *"is if we land, can we take off again? What's holding you up? Is it mechanical or the locals?"*

"Both. Manny's bird had bus issues but Vince fixed those. Now we're, uh, guests of the locals. Did you bring the scotch?"

"A-firm. A whole case."

"Good. The local knee-breaker won't let us leave until he gets some. And I hope it's good stuff 'cause this guy seems to know his kilt-juice. He might back-track if it's junk."

I went into a shallow turn around a tree-fall while Josh grew frustrated.

"What guarantee do you have he'll let you leave even when he does get it?" he demanded. "*Come on, Charlie. The way you're talking I'm thinking of air-dropping this stuff to you.*"

There was a sardonic laugh over the radio.

"That's probably not a bad idea. No, we think he will. Vince has been doing the negotiating and we think he's afraid of Vince."

"Hell, I'm afraid of Vince," I said.

"The problem is, the situation's changing on the ground here so if you're going to come in you probably want to do it sooner rather than later."

"Why's that?"

"Well, I don't know what they're doing here but a whoooollle bunch of guys with guns have shown up since yesterday afternoon. Some are in uniform but most aren't. They're popping up all over the place looking mean at each other – I think there's a good chance we're about to get caught in the middle of a turf war."

Josh looked at me in disbelief as he keyed the mike.

"Charlie, why are you telling me that? Are you trying to convince me to go away? I'm not landing in the middle of somebody's war."

"Well, that's just it. If you come in tonight you might miss it. Oh, hang on..." There was the sound of yelling and the radio clicked on and off. Josh, Ozzie, and

I waited, watching the minutes tick by. I made lazy turns around the jungle.

"*Okay, disregard,*" Manson's voice finally came back. "*You won't miss it. I just heard some shooting over in the city. Looks like things have kicked off. It's not close, though. Let us know what you guys are going to do, okay?*"

Things were just never easy. It was now past five o'clock which meant it would be getting dark in an hour. The sun crept toward the horizon beyond the mountains, sending our shadow far to the east even as we tooled around over the trees.

The problem – one of the problems – was that the Peruvians didn't allow anyone to fly at night in their airspace. You could occasionally get a waiver to fly under instrument conditions if you were going in or out of Lima but getting a waiver to fly VFR over the jungle was out of the question. It was a simple matter of control related partly to safety and partly to illegal drug flights. Of course, on practical grounds it was a pointless rule. Drug runners were running drugs, after all, so they didn't worry about violating a law banning night flights. Even if they did there was no way to enforce it. It wasn't like the Peruvian Air Force flew at night or could find anyone if they did. On the other hand, drug runners didn't fly at night over the jungle anyway. It was too dangerous. If you lost an engine you had to land in a river and if you couldn't see the river you were doomed.

Josh and I discussed our options. *If* we landed, and *if* we didn't get shot in somebody's firefight, and *if* the local extortionist didn't confiscate our plane, then what? Even if he wasn't in on the liquor scam the guy in the tower might just follow his rules and forbid us from taking off again since there was no way we could get out of the country – or even to another airfield – by nightfall. Then what? Did we take off anyway and incur the wrath of official Peru? And where would we go? We hadn't filed a return leg to Colombia yet – another country, by the way, which prohibited night VFR flights. Our options weren't good.

"Um, Charlie. We've come to the conclusion that you suck."

"That's helpful. Hey, the food's good down here if that's any consolation for you. We've got this little girl who brings us corn tamales. If nobody shoots her she should be by again in an hour."

"Are you guys staying on the airfield?"

"Hell, yeah, we are. You think we're going to leave these planes on public display? Besides, it's not like there's a Marriott down the street."

His transmission was punctuated by several staccato bursts of what sounded like static. Then, thinking it might not be static, we looked out the window toward the town. A thin trail of black smoke rose from the far side of the city. Somebody's vehicle had just met an untimely end.

"Charlie. Charlie, is that gunfire behind you?"

There was no immediate answer but eventually Manson came back.

"Shark 18, say again?"

"Is that gunfire?"

"Uh, yeah. Hey, I don't want to sound nervous or anything but that last bit of shooting was a lot closer. We've taken a vote and decided we all want you to get your butts down here so we can leave. This place has stopped being a pilot town and is now officially soldier-ville."

A second voice broke in at that moment. It was Jem on the radio in #106.

"Hey, hey, Shark 18. This is Jem. Hey, son, y'all gonna land or what?"

Josh waffled, wondering if Jem was a more objective source of information.

"I don't know, Jem. You really think we should? I mean, if that fight moves on we could come in later."

"Well, hell, son. Never ask a barber if he thinks you need a haircut. Get on down here! My southern ass is about to get shot off."

"Okay, okay. What are conditions at the field?"

"Conditions?" Jem's voice was incredulous. *"You mean the weather, the wind, the strip, or the war?"*

"Jeez," said Josh. "You know, I'm getting too old for this kind of stuff."

"You're twenty-eight."

"Well, I feel like I'm forty." He pointed toward Pucallpa and sighed. "Go on, land. God forbid this day should end on a quiet note."

I pointed the plane toward the buildings in the distance.

"Never mind, Jem, we're coming in. Should we talk to the tower or just land?"

"Well, there're trucks on the runway right now. They put them there to keep us from leaving."

Josh threw his hands up in frustration. I went back into a turn.

"That's good information, Jem! Thanks for mentioning it. How're we supposed to land if there are trucks there?"

"Well, just hang on, son. We'll see if we can get them to move."

"If they'll move the trucks for us to land," I asked no one in particular, "why don't those guys just take off while the runway's clear?"

Josh passed the question on to Jem.

"*Now*," he drawled, "*they're not stoopid. If they see us start up our engines, they'll be all over us like fleas on a dog.*"

We held for another ten minutes while the crews on the ground did their coordinating. Fortunately, gas was no longer a problem for us. We could hold for an hour and still be able to get across the border.

While we waited I got on the Satcom radio and tried to pass back to the AOC what was happening. The AOC hated it when C-27 crews used the Satcom. Technically we were allowed to as it was more secure than HF transmissions but since there were few nets available on the satellite the AOC gave priority to the photo-surveillance C-130s. Unfortunately, 'giving priority' was understood by many AOC operators to mean 'ignore other calls.' I got hold of nobody.

"You want me to try the HF?" I asked Josh. My tone indicated I wasn't thrilled with the prospect.

Josh wasn't, either. "I don't want every ham radio operator in the Western Hemisphere to know about this," he said.

Another voice popped up on the radio.

"Shark 18, Shark 18. This is Shark 24. Switch frequencies to Cheap Suit and go secure."

We dialed up 299.5 – twenty-nine ninety-five – and hit the cipher button to encrypt transmissions.

"You up?"

"We're up."

"Hey guys, this is Matt. How you doin'?"

"Better than you. We're airborne," Josh replied. *"What's up, Clunk?"*

Matt Armand was the loadmaster on Manny and Jem's plane. He was called 'Clunk' because he was a big guy with a big head that was constantly knocking into things like doorjambs, car roofs, and low-flying birds. He was twenty-two, low-key, and competent.

"Vince wants to know if you brought any guns."

"Yeah, some. Three M-16s and our nine-mils. Why?"

"He just wants to know. I think it's in case they give us a hard time about leaving."

"Do you guys have any?"

"Just our pistols."

"I thought Charlie said they were afraid of Vince," I commented.

Josh frowned. "I guess he figures they'll be more afraid of him if we show up looking bad-ass. Oh, *Ozzie!*....You get to play commando again."

Sgt Oswald grinned like a maniac. "Heh-heh! Ozzie get guns now." He hopped down to the hell-hole.

"Shark 18, Shark 21."

Manson again.

"Go ahead."

"Okay, here's what we're thinking." Manson's voice had an edge to it now. *"They're moving the trucks. I think they'll stay out of the way. Get in here as fast as you can and land but keep your engines running."*

"That's a no-brainer," Josh muttered.

"What we want you to do is pull in as close as you can to our two birds. You'll see there's not much of a ramp to park on but do it anyway. Get close and make as much noise as you can. If they see us start up they'll freak out so we need your engines to cover the noise of our APUs when we crank. You copy?"

"We copy."

"Land, somebody get out, make a big show of not being concerned about leaving again. If the tower guy gives you a problem just blow him off."

"No problem there," I agreed. I turned the plane back toward the north edge of the city again where Pucallpa airfield lay. While Josh talked on the radio

I aimed to set us up on a ten-mile final so that when he was ready we could just blitz straight in.

"What are you going to do?" Josh asked. *"Do you guys have gas? Are you ready to go?"*

"We…we're…hang on, hang on."

The radio went silent, then it was keyed again and we heard shouted conversations with irregular popping in the background. Out the window more columns of smoke – some black, some white –appeared between the buildings. Somebody was having a major firefight. Josh gripped the dash in frustration.

"*Okay,*" Charlie's voice came back up. *"Things are changing fast down here. I'm not sure Cifuentes is the guy in charge here anymore."*

Josh and I looked at each other in confusion. 'Who's Cifuentes?' he mouthed. I shook my head.

"Charlie, who's Cifuentes?"

"He's the guy who wants the Scotch, the guy who controls the airfield and the trucks blocking your way. And a guy who likes carrying lots of guns. But some other guys have shown up. I'm not sure who they are. Recommend you get here ASAP before they turn out in force."

"Great," Josh said bitterly. "Goddammit, goddammit, goddammit! Let's get in there. Random shallow – no gear or flaps until we're close."

The adrenalin came back. This was twice in one day that I was getting a rush strong enough to make my feet tremble on the rudder pedals. I turned from where I'd been heading for a straight-in approach to the runway and now made a beeline for where I figured the threshold must be. We had about a forty-degree offset – which was good. It would let us get that much closer and then kill our speed in the turn to final.

We practiced random shallow approaches all the time at Howard. Walt was a master at bringing the plane from any direction at treetop level and dropping it onto the runway. I wasn't a master. Timing was everything.

The critical decision was where to start the slowdown. If we decelerated too early we would be exposing ourselves to all the smoke-makers in the city who might decide to start taking potshots at an airplane. If we slowed too late we could overshoot the runway and have to go around and try again – embarrassing under any circumstances but hazardous here because it would ruin our element of surprise. I kept expecting Josh to take the controls for the approach but so far he made no sign of doing so. I decided to err on the conservative side. When the airport finally came in sight I picked a clearing in the trees one mile from the approach end to start my slowdown.

"Okay, where's the runway? Where's the runway? Shit, where's the goddamned runway?" Josh slapped the dash in impatience. Our altitude was so low it was hard to tell which buildings flanked the field and which were in the city itself.

"There!" Ozzie pointed from the third seat.

I'd pointed too far to the left but that was okay since I was also too fast. I banked hard to the right and chopped the throttles to idle, then brought the nose back to the left. The maneuver worked wonderfully for bringing us from 260 knots to just under 200 in less than a mile. In spite of myself I'd set us up perfectly.

"Flaps ten."

"Flaps ten!"

"Flaps mid."

"Flaps mid!"

"Gear down."

A road ran along the edge of town parallel to the runway. I noticed as we made our second turn that a long line of military trucks was backed up on its narrow surface, fighting with normal traffic on the narrow street to move the same direction we were heading. Close off the right side as we flew down final a building was on fire. Smoke poured out from under the eaves while flames licked the exterior wall.

"Flaps full."

"Flaps full!"

The end of the runway flashed by as we dropped out of the sky. I didn't worry about locking the brakes since Pucallpa's strip was six thousand feet long. The surface was pale asphalt and loose gravel. Dirty rubber streaks stretched along the surface from planes that had landed before. In the seconds where I should have been thinking about almost anything else, I wondered who the pilots were whose planes had made those streaks. Did they ever worry about being shot?

Whoomph!

We hit in a gentle descent. The shocks sucked up the impact to make it seem a feather-like landing.

"Ozzie, ramp's coming down!"

Josh hit the switch as soon as the nose wheel touched. With his help I put the props into reverse but almost immediately brought them back forward to keep our speed up.

"There they are," Josh pointed. "Take it all the way down."

"I'll swing the right wing over their nose and pivot left."

"Okay, but don't tap the breaks too hard."

"I won't."

"You always do. Just use the left brake."

"I will."

"The left brake only. Got it?"

"Yes!"

Shark 21 and Shark 24, tail numbers 104 and 106, were parked next to each other in a dirt pull-out at the far end of the field. Both pointed toward the runway with their tails hanging over the chain-link fence that separated the airfield from the street. A dozen bystanders stood at the fence looking in. At least two of them had automatic weapons in their hands.

"There's Charlie. Get up there! Get up there! Make the turn!"

Under Josh's hyperactive tutelage I stomped on the left brake abeam the planes, skidding to a halt and pivoting the nose of our plane, left to set the ramp pointing toward Shark 21. Josh climbed out of the seat before we stopped. Looking up out my right window I could see the two tower controllers. They leaned on their open window sill talking into a microphone. Probably talking to us, I thought. We hadn't called them and in fact had turned the radio down on final approach, not wanting to be distracted.

"Stay inside!" Josh told Ozzie. The loadmaster crouched at the ramp hinge out of sight of those outside, his pistols and M-16 at the ready.

Josh ran to the back of the plane.

"Get a gun!" Ozzie yelled at him.

Josh spun around and ran back to his helmet bag for his holster and pistol. He didn't like to wear them while flying. After he strapped them on he headed back toward the ramp.

"Don't forget the scotch!" I called.

Josh shouted something unintelligible above the noise of the engines and returned once again to the front of the cabin for the liquor.

"*Shark 18, we're starting up.*" That was Jem's voice.

"*Roger,*" I answered. "*What are your intentions?*"

"*I'm thinking of finishing this tour then getting out and going to the airlines.*"

"*What are your intentions RIGHT NOW, Jem?*"

"*Oh. We'll get the APUs up. When Charlie's ready we're both going to do simul-starts and hope to get out of here before they can react.*"

A simul-start was when we started both engines at the same time. Our flight manual for the C-27 said the pressure from the aux power unit wasn't strong enough for that but we had learned that it was.

"*Why don't you just start right now?*"

"*We're waiting on Charlie.*"

A new voice broke in.

"*Manson wants to give the guy his scotch.*" It was Little Bud Blair, Manson's co-pilot in Shark 21, and judging from his tone he had his own opinion of Manson's sense of priorities.

"*Chickenhawk!*" I called over. "*Glad to have you along.*"

"*Screw you. This place is too hot.*"

No sooner had he spoken than there was a crack like someone breaking a stick over his knee. A bullet had struck Josh's sliding side window. It hit on an angle, ricocheted off the steel frame, and left a vertical crack eight inches long in the plexiglass. A second *crack!* followed right after it in the same place. That round penetrated the glass, caromed off the frame, and dug itself into the sheepskin headrest of Josh's seat. I felt the blood drain from my face.

"Ozzie, we were just hit! Somebody's shooting at us." I toggled the radio. "*21 and 24, this is 18. We were just hit. Let's get moving!*"

Bud, in his excitement, flipped his radio switch instead of the intercom so for the next ten seconds we heard him shouting instructions to his loadmaster. When he finally stopped transmitting, Jem's voice, much calmer, came over.

"Hey, son. Try not to die all tensed up. 1-8, roger. We'll keep an eye out. Ah think it was probably a stray, though. I can see the street and nobody's shooting there. Lots of folks runnin' around, but nobody shooting. Ah don't think we're even in range."

"Trust me, we're in range."

"Well, Ah don't see 'em."

Sgt Oswald couldn't, either. "I'm looking, sir. Ain't nobody back here pointing a gun at us. If they were, I'd have shot them by now. There's a hell of a lot of action back at our eight o'clock, though, about two streets down."

"Copy," was all I could say.

The two men in the tower disappeared and then came back into sight on their deck. This time there was a guy in a uniform with them. They all grabbed the radio microphone at once and struggled to be the one to yell into it. In their haste they ripped the wires from the wall.

"Capt Breitling's coming back."

Josh jumped back up on the ramp and yelled something in Ozzie's ear. Fearful of getting my head shot off, I nevertheless opened my side window and leaned out as far as I could to see behind us. To our right I saw Manny running for Shark 24.

"21's turning," Ozzie advised from the back.

Seconds later Jem hit his starter switches and both props started to turn.

The tower controllers and their soldier companion stopped shouting and stared at our three planes in amazement. Then they went into another flurry of waving arms and shouted orders. All three started yelling at the half-dozen civilians standing around at the base of the tower. The men on the ground they were shouting to ran to the vehicles they had only recently pulled off the runway and that were now parked on the far side of the tower. I slid my window closed.

In two perfectly-timed jumps Josh vaulted from the cabin into his seat.

"They're ready! Let's get out of here. My controls!"

"Your controls. They're going to block the runway again." I pointed to the running men.

Charlie Manson saw the same thing and called over the radio, "*Hurry up, guys! They're going to block the runway again.*"

"No kidding!" Josh shouted. He took his feet off the brakes and we began to roll.

Just then there two thumps from the back of the plane.

"Those weren't strays," Ozzie called up. "Do I have permission to fire at these clowns?"

"If they're pointing at our plane, you do," I answered. I was through with moral dilemmas. The bullet in the window ended my patience.

"I'll see if I can just scare them." Ozzie raised the ramp and lowered the cargo door halfway. He lay on the upraised floor and aimed at the edge of the fence line behind Shark 24. There two raggedly-attired rebels with AK-47s were positioning for another shot. Why they were shooting at us when Shark 24 was so much closer was beyond me. Maybe it was because we were moving.

"Where are you going?" I asked Josh. Behind us Sgt Oswald let loose a volley of shots.

Josh winced hearing the gunfire. "I'm going to do what you did," he explained. "We have to delay those guys getting out on the runway."

I wasn't sure what I'd done that he wanted to emulate so I just watched. Josh used the nose wheel steering to take us around Shark 21 and then point the nose right at the trucks starting up by the tower. Our right wing went directly under where the controllers stood.

"You going to hit them?" I inquired as we bore down on the small fleet of vehicles.

"Not if I can help it."

He didn't. Everywhere except on the runway itself the surface was dirt, including at the base of the tower. What Josh did was drive at the trucks until the last second, then pivot around the left main gear the same way I had done to park us five minutes earlier. Except that when I'd parked I'd had the power in idle. Josh kept the power up to full throttle and came so close that when we turned our right wing passed over the nearest vehicles. In the front seat of one Toyota Hilux there were looks of terror on two men who thought they were about to be ground up by a propeller.

But that was nothing compared to what came next.

The prop wash from our plane generated twin tornados of dust as Josh spun the plane one hundred and eighty degrees. The controllers and all the truck drivers were enveloped in a blinding maelstrom of sand, rocks, and dirt. One truck that had started to move turned right when the driver could no longer see and slowly collided with that part of the fence that stretched past the runway centerline. The driver opened the door and fell out into the dust.

Over the radio we heard a cheer and Charlie Manson saying, "*Beautiful! Beautiful!*"

Josh wasn't ready to celebrate.

"*Go when you're ready,*" he snapped. "*We can't sit here all day.*"

No, we couldn't. Our engine intakes had to be sucking in some of all that dust.

The other two planes needed no prompting. Already they could see a jeep pushing through a broken part of the fence further downfield. In unison they both started to move. Shark 21 made a beeline for the runway. Their cabin door was open and I saw Vince lean out to strafe the fence line with his pistol. Shark 24 stayed on the infield.

"*24, you're clear to go ahead of us,*" Manson called.

"*We're gone. You can have the runway,*" Manny radioed back. He and Jem pushed their power up and bounced down the dirt track that paralleled the asphalt. One of the trucks had been parked their earlier and now the jeep from downfield came at them from that direction. It was a short game of chicken, however. The C-27 lifted off five hundred feet short of a collision. By the time they rotated Manson and crew were rolling. Josh released our brakes again.

"Ozzie, you ready for take-off?"

Sgt Oswald climbed coughing into his seat. He'd meant to cover us again as we passed the tower but gave up when the same dust storm that blinded the drivers poured in under the cabin door. He thrust out two thumbs up.

"Flaps ten," Josh ordered as the front wheel bounced up onto the runway asphalt. The first two Chucks were going for maximum speed and had stayed low after lift-off. Josh was going to get a best climb instead.

"Flaps ten."

We lifted off in twelve hundred feet but not before hearing one more worrisome thump in the body of the plane. Josh pulled the nose up just as we had out of Marandua. We didn't cover much ground but we climbed like a bat out of hell, maybe leaving a few shooters on the ground looking up in amazement rather than along the sights of their guns. We kept the climb going until we hit five thousand feet. There we pushed the nose over, raised the flaps, and put Pucallpa off our tail.

"Shark 18, Shark 21. You guys okay?"

Nobody in our plane answered right away. Josh looked at Sgt Oswald but he was already climbing out of his seat to find out where the damage was.

"We'll let you know in a minute," I called back. *"We took a few hits and we're trying to find out where they are. How are you?"*

"We're good. A sprained ankle and busted up shoulder. Shark 24?"

There was silence on the radio. If I leaned forward and looked down among the treetops I could still see Manny and Jem's plane, skimming the jungle about two miles off Shark 21's left wing.

"Shark 24?"

More silence.

"Can you guys reach them?"

I tried. Finally, a reply.

"This is Shark 24 on Victor guard. Come up Fingers secure."

Manny's call came over the secondary receiver. I dialed up 123.45 and pushed its cipher button.

"Hey, we've lost our UHF," Manny told us. *"I think one of the antennae was hit. We can hear you but can't transmit on that radio."*

"*Okay,*" Charlie Manson radioed back. *"Let's use VHF primary for ATC and secondary for interplane. You guys have any other damage?"*

"*Just to me,*" said Manny. "*I banged my knee.*"

"If it makes you feel any better we had a casualty of our own," Manson called. "*I saved a bottle from the case I gave that lying bastard Cifuentes and then dropped it climbing into the seat. Now the cockpit smells like a Highland distillery. Dalwhinnie Limited Edition, too.*"

"That's your excuse?" I pimped.

"That's my story and I'm sticking to it," he insisted. "*Have you figured out your status?*"

Sgt Oswald leaned into the cockpit and pointed toward the left side of the cabin. "Two above the gear. One through the left troop door. We won't pressurize but otherwise I don't see damage."

"We've got three holes in us so we can't pressurize," Josh answered. *"Otherwise we're fine."*

"Okay. Then you guys follow us. We'll stay clear of weather and work along this side of the Andes until we

find someplace to cross. I don't think I need to mention we're going to have to cross the border ASAP."

"*Yeah, that would be fahn,*" Jem called from Shark 24.

Now that we were airborne again, Josh calmed down. His voice shook but the loopy relief tried to break through, replacing the stress that had been taking years off our lives for the past eight hours. He even indulged in some spontaneous generosity.

"We did it," he said, trying to smile. "You guys did great back there. I can't believe we pulled that off."

"Yeah, that was okay," Ozzie agreed. He was the calmest of all of us. Putting a plug of tobacco behind his lower lip he got a dreamy expression in his eyes, reflecting with satisfaction on the two times today he got to shoot at somebody.

"Something? That was incredible!" Josh insisted. "We pulled off a miracle back there! We're a damned good crew!"

Yeah. He was right but we had also been lucky. My feet still trembled.

"Don't get all warm and fuzzy," I said. "We could have died."

"I know it. And I'm not warm and fuzzy. I'm just trying to recognize good work. And trust me, this has been the worst goddamned day of my life. Land on a fucked-up runway, get shot at by Daniel Boone, risk my life for a few bottles of whiskey...I'm too old for this. One more shock to my system, just one more, Bleriot, and you'll have to carry me out of my seat."

He settled onto the sheepskin and took a deep breath. After a moment, though, the whistling at his ear became impossible to ignore. He opened his eyes and glanced left. When he did, I saw his neck flush through three shades of red in an instant.

"Aw, come on," he growled, "what the hell happened to my window?"

5. Tailpipe Kilo

"How did you get a Humvee?" Rolo shouted above the roar of the engine and the whine of the tires grinding into the gravel road. He was in the right seat which in a Humvee looked like he was sitting on the far side of a room.

"I asked for it!" I shouted back.

"Asked who? The SP's?"

"No, are you kidding? Air Force cops wouldn't hand out a vehicle to a pilot."

"Then who'd you get it from?"

"The motor pool on Fort Kobbe."

"Why would they give one to a pilot?"

"They didn't. They gave it to an officer. You show up with rank and they just assume you have a right to whatever you want. Go Army!"

The Humvee hit a pothole and bounced hard, throwing us against our seat belts. Its suspension was designed for survivability, not comfort, so every time we jolted over anything larger than a soda can it felt like a cannon ball was shot into the undercarriage. But it kept moving.

"Did you have to take a test?"

"A written one."

"A written one?" Rolo couldn't believe it. "A written test qualifies you to drive a three-ton armored vehicle?"

I smiled. "It does for the Army."

We practiced airdrops at a number of clearings in and around the old Canal Zone, some of which were located on Empire Range. Empire Range was a swath of jungle twenty miles long and ten miles deep on the west side of the canal, an ancient forest of dark hills and triple-canopy jungle. It belonged to the Army.

Throughout the American presence in Panama the U.S. military used the range for everything from survival training to infantry movements, from airborne assaults to munitions storage. It was also used as a live range. Tons and tons and tons of ordnance fell on Empire over the years, both in well-marked clearings and in impenetrable jungle. Everything from rifle-launched grenades to napalm, not to mention uncountable rounds fired from hand-held weapons, had exploded in, around, and over the forest, pockmarking the ground, downing trees, and killing or scaring whatever local species happened to be in the way.

In time, often a short time, the jungle always recovered. Viewed from the air there were few areas that looked to be associated with military training. But hidden in the trees and high grass was a legacy of destructive potential. For all the hundreds of munitions that detonated a certain number didn't – and nobody had a clue where those were. As a result the entire range was a live wire. The potential for an accidental explosion existed everywhere within its borders since no one could tell for certain where every round was loosed over the decades. Even Panamanian squatters avoided the area.

The exquisite irony of paradise-as-bomb made Empire Range a charming land of contradiction. It was one of the most naturally beautiful and artificially savage locations on earth.

That's why we were in a Humvee.

We were heading for Kinzer DZ. Kinzer was a drop zone we hadn't used before but our normal zones were busy: the Army was practicing air assaults on the field at Gatún, and Dublois-Coats DZ – next to Veracruz Beach – had construction equipment on it where the Civil Engineers were trying to drain the swampier sections. Major Byron dug the Kinzer survey out of long-forgotten files and sent Rolo and me to check it out.

Walt wanted to upgrade Evan and Jem in airdrops; Rolo and I were to retrieve the bundles. I volunteered because I heard the word airdrops and thought it meant we would get to jump. Rolo was picked because he was standing in front of the scheduling desk when Major Harmon needed a body.

"Alright, well, there's nothing I can tell you from the map except to keep going," Rolo announced. He had a 1:50,000 map of the south end of the range. On it he had highlighted the road we needed to follow.

There were roads in Empire Range, lots of them. None were paved. Only one was even graded, the one that ran next to the canal. On Rolo's map Kinzer DZ was a clearing right next to the road we were on. All we had to do was get to it.

"What time is it?" he asked.

"Ten-thirty."

"What time is Walt going to call?"

"Ten forty-five."

We missed the clearing. Our road wound through the jungle like it wasn't sure where to go, turning so often I was always wrenching the steering wheel one way or the other. Usually the trees pressed so close their branches met overhead. Sometimes they backed off in favor of high grass that towered straight up for eight feet before curving over to brush the roof of the Humvee. In areas where rain had washed the road lower than the forest our view of the grass was surreal, as though a mutant lawn was trying to curl over us from both sides.

On one such stretch the ground was so sunken that we never realized the tree line behind the grass had stopped, paused, and then started again a hundred yards on. We only saw our mistake when we noticed our timing from the highway had gone too long. At ten-forty I began the painstaking process of turning the Humvee around on the narrow road. Rolo monitored the radio.

"Tailpipe Kilo, Tailpipe Kilo, this is Shark 18. Radio check."

Walt's voice crackled faintly through the mike. Rolo propped the receiver on the open window and extended the antenna. He spoke into the telephone handset.

"Shark 18, this is Tailpipe Kilo. Got you weak but readable."

"Yeah, you're weak yourself. Very weak, but I don't think it's the radio. What's your location, Rolo?"

Walt had lousy radio procedures.

"We're not sure. We think we overshot the DZ and we're on our way back."

"Do you need us to guide you in?"

"Where are you?"

"We're about ten miles out to the northeast. We'll call overhead the DZ."

"Copy."

"Guide us in, no way," I said to Rolo. "Keep your eyes open. Let's find this thing."

I floored it down the road back the way we had come. We didn't need to go far. As it turned out we were only a quarter mile past the clearing. The area's slope as well as the high grass was deceiving – we had driven right past Kinzer thinking it looked like every other bit of jungle. Coming from the opposite direction the drop zone was more obvious.

I stopped the Humvee and climbed out. Rolo clambered onto the hood to see over the grass.

"Not so bad," he said. "If you're a landscaper in need of work."

"The grass is shorter away from the road. Grab the chairs."

Just then Walt and company roared overhead at three hundred feet. I looked up and could see Jerry Miner, the skinny old chain-smoking loadmaster who had joined the Air Force when God was a second lieutenant, waving from the right troop door.

"That's it. That's it. You've got the right clearing," Walt announced to us. *"Just keep going in and you'll get to the center."*

"No kidding," I said.

"He's priceless. Never met a microphone he didn't like."

We walked to the center of the clearing where the grass not only shortened to knee-level but changed from yellow to green. That suggested somebody had done a controlled burn during the last dry season. The new stuff hadn't had time yet to catch up with the old. Mosquitoes took notice of our presence and rose from the grass to investigate. Rolo pulled the radio from his rucksack and tossed me a Mark XIII flare.

"That might help with the bugs," he said. *"Shark 18, this is Tailpipe Kilo. We've set an Impact Point and are popping smoke."*

The C-27 disappeared below the tree line to the south. Even with the road the clearing was no more than a hundred yards in diameter and the trees around it rose a third that distance into the sky. It was impossible to see anything within thirty degrees of the horizon.

"Copy, you're popping smoke. We're going to set up for a run-in – give us a wind check at :03 for a drop of :06. Time now 10:55."

"Tailpipe Kilo, roger."

I removed the cap from the smoke end of the signaling device. The Mark XIII had an orange cap for its smoke side, a black one with bumps on it for its flare side. The smoke was for signaling during the day, the flare, obviously, for signaling at night. If it was too dark to see you just felt for the bumps to know which end was which. "Things go bump in the night" the instructors had said.

I pulled the tab clear. A burst of flame shot out of the tube followed by orange smoke. I set it on the ground and watched the smoke billow into the air, staining the ground and grass around it.

We retrieved a cooler and our lunches from the Humvee and set up camp. The smoke chased away the mosquitoes but we slathered on sunscreen and repellant anyway and swapped our ball caps for boonie hats. Depending on how long Walt's training went, we could be out there for hours.

The training was in airdrop, which in simple terms meant throwing something out of a plane and having it land where you wanted it. It was harder than it looked. Evan and Jem were with Walt as students: they had to learn to figure a run-in course, factor in winds, altitude, temperature, and airspeed, and compute a CARP, a Computed Air Release Point, all while flying the plane and navigating themselves over the jungle at only a few hundred feet. The CARP would be that point on the ground where they called "green light" to the loadmaster, who then tossed a sandbag tied to a parachute out one of the troop doors. The sandbags weighed only twenty pounds but with a smaller chute they represented fairly accurately the "throw" and trajectory of a soldier with his gear. Calling "green light" too early meant the bag landed in the trees; calling it late meant the same, as did being too far left or right of course. Landing in the trees, in addition to being an inconvenience, was dangerous. A soldier loaded down with gear could break his leg or his neck plowing through branches eighty feet up. Airdrop was one of those many things about flying that looked easy when viewed from the ground. In reality it was a fine balance of skill, coordination, planning, and luck.

"One minute to wind check."

Rolo had a portable anemometer that he held over his head. It looked like an alarm clock with a fan through which the wind could flow. Right now the fan was still. The air around us wasn't going anywhere. It wavered like a crowd on a subway platform, not doing enough even to register on the gauge. That lack of motion made the day hot. Despite a high layer of clouds that blocked the sun, heat built up over the range like steam in a kettle.

"Wind check. Winds light and variable at four," Rolo said into the mike.

"Copy. Light and variable at four. Do you guys still have the smoke going? We can't make it out from here. But we're flying pretty low, not that you guys would know about that."

That was vintage Walt. Talk, talk, talk. Most guys wouldn't even have acknowledged Rolo's call. Walt had to, though, because he was always in motion. Since either Jem or Evan was in the other seat and doing all the flying, Walt had nothing to do but correct their mistakes and key the mike.

"Negative."

The smoke from the Mark XIII dissipated. We had only two. The next one being our last, I offered it to Rolo.

"Your turn."

He popped the smoke and held it aloft, walking back and forth across the LZ for the twenty seconds it took the device to burn out. Another cloud of orange drifted over the grass.

"LZ in sight, twenty seconds."

The sound of the C-27's engines rolled in over the trees behind us. They were making an approach from the north again. Even as we turned we saw the bundle clear the right troop door.

"Um, that would be short," Rolo commented matter-of-factly as the sandbag disappeared into the trees.

The plane cruised overhead.

We stared at the jungle where the bundle went in, each waiting for the other guy to volunteer.

"Flip you for it," I offered.

"You've had jungle survival," he countered, referring to a two-week course I'd done on the north coast shortly after my initial check ride.

"Yes," I agreed. "And that means I know how much it sucks in there. That's why I'll flip you for it."

We flipped. I lost.

"Don't worry," Rolo said. "If that's any indication of how they're going to do I'll see you in there. Or rather, I'll be in there and probably not see you."

I picked up one of the walkie-talkies we had brought along and headed for the tree line. As I walked away I heard Walt call asking for a drop report. Rolo responded with a location in distance and bearing. I didn't hear him use the word 'boondocks,' though he could have.

It took me some minutes to get inside the jungle. Before I tried, I rolled down my sleeves, put on my gloves, and jammed my hat down tight.

Finding the bundle would be next to impossible. I knew that before I left the clearing but it struck home once I was inside the trees far enough to get a good look around. The sandbag was green. The parachute was green. The parachute lines were green. I stared at the trees around me and felt like I'd crawled inside a bell pepper. We were wasting our time. Most of the other drop zones, such as Dublois-Coats, were big enough that we laid out an Impact Point, an IP, using orange panels and then just walked across the grass to pick up anything that landed far from the "X." If Walt and his students kept missing the zone here we would soon be out of bundles.

"Hey, Mike," Rolo's voice came in a burst of static from the walkie-talkie. He was only two hundred feet behind me but completely out of sight. *"You find anything yet?"*

"Some primitive tribes and the lost treasure of the Maya," I replied, *"but nothing in the way of bundles. It's dense in here."*

"Copy. They're setting up for another run, this one from the west. If they miss I'll go get it."

"Roger."

I walked around, stepping only where I could see and looking for anything out of the ordinary. I looked at the tree trunks for parachute cords and at the ground plants to see if any had been crushed by the bundle. Nothing.

Fifteen minutes later I still hadn't found anything. Mosquitoes attacked my neck and I rolled up the collar on my BDU blouse to keep them away. The C-27 approached again, this time off to my left. I heard it pass over the clearing; seconds later came the call from Rolo.

"I'm mobile."

They missed again, this time long.

I was just about to give up when I happened to look up. What caught my eye was the smooth bark of an espave, one of the monster trees of the jungle. The story went that when conquistadors arrived in the New World they asked natives to point out a tall tree from which they could view their surroundings. The Spanish called the one provided the *es para ver* (it's for seeing), since shortened to espave. This one ran straight up for fifty feet and then curved an 'S' in a successful attempt to find sun and shoot through the canopy. My eyes were following its winding path when I saw what looked like a heavy vine hanging above the 'S'. It was the bundle. The high-speed parachute hadn't been fast enough to break through the upper branches of the canopy. Instead the fabric shredded and caught and the sandbag now swung slowly sixty feet off the ground. And it would for a long time to come.

"Bagcatcher 2, this is Bagcatcher 1."

"Go ahead."

"Yeah, Rolo. I found the first bundle but there's no way to get to it. We would have to put Tarzan on a contract for this one. I'm on my way back out."

Way off through the trees I heard him make a decent attempt at a Tarzan yell.

"Copy. I'm still looking over here."

It took a while to get back to the clearing. As I broke into the open Walt flew overhead on their third pass. Nothing came out the door, however, which was just as well since they were offset to the east.

"I called a no-drop since we weren't ready," Rolo reported. *"But they're going to do one more pass and then depart on a low-level."*

"Okay," I called back. *"You can wave them in now. I'm back in the clearing."*

"They're requesting smoke. They're not seeing the clearing until the last second."

I looked around. We had used both smoke devices. I could light the flares but that wouldn't do them any good.

"We're out of Mark XIIIs," I radioed. *"Tell them I'll see what I can do."*

The grass around the lawn chairs was too short to be of much use so I moved to the south edge of the clearing and hacked at the high grass with a small machete we had brought along. I had a knee-high mound by the time Rolo called back.

"He's three minutes out."

"Roger. Popping smoke. Tell him it's white this time."

I twisted off the bumpy end of the Mark XIII. Flipping up the tab, I held it at arm's length and yanked the string. There was a pop, a fizzle, and then a four-inch burst of flame shot out. Holding it at the base of the grass I tried to set the pile aflame. At first the intense blaze of the flare sucked away the oxygen needed to start another fire so I had the absurd situation where I held a torch to dry grass with no effect. However, the sparks flying out the side of the device started a fire of their own which quickly climbed the side of the haystack. I tossed the flare onto the pile. White smoke climbed into the air.

The C-27 came in over the trees from the east this time. They were still offset to the left. That was probably due to the fact that whoever was being trained was in the right seat and unconsciously drifting to the left to make it easier to see out his leg window. But the drop when it came was good. It hit on the road just twenty feet from the Humvee, the parachute collapsing onto the sandbag.

"Good drop! Good drop!" I called to Rolo. *"Tell him eight o'clock for forty feet."*

Rolo passed on the call and then said he was on his way in. He said he hadn't found anything but a few minutes later when he appeared at the edge of the clearing he had the bundle slung over his shoulder.

"I thought you didn't find anything," I said.

"I didn't. I looked all over and decided to hell with it, then practically stepped on it while on my way out." He coiled the parachute lines around the sandbag and tossed it by the cooler, then started to pick burrs off his flight suit. When one of the burrs jumped up and took off running down his sleeve his face twisted in disgust.

"Good god, you spent two weeks in that stuff? I could barely move and couldn't see anything even when I did. How did you stay in there without going crazy?"

"Who says I didn't?" I countered.

"That bad?"

"Almost."

"Is Rasmussen going to make all of us go?" He didn't sound enthusiastic about the idea.

"Depends on the flying, probably. Carl Diehrmann and I were doing nothing in August so we volunteered. If there's down time and you're just sitting around, the commander might send you, too."

"Great. Another reason to pray for missions."

He unzipped his flight suit and wriggled out of the sleeves, tying them around his waist. Then he took off his t-shirt and rubbed suntan lotion on his arms and chest.

"We're in PCH," I said. "Aren't you worried about getting too much sun?"

Rolo scoffed. "Peak Cancer Hours don't apply to people from the Mediterranean. We live on sun."

I sipped Gatorade and adjusted my boonie hat to make sure it kept my nose in the shade.

"You're from Cincinnati," I corrected him. "And you're mother's maiden name is McKinney. You're as Irish as a pint of Guinness. You have as much in common with the Med as I do with Fiji."

"You are wrong, my friend. I'm Greek at heart. You're just jealous."

"Your heart may be Greek but your skin is from County Clare. Don't whine to me when you burn."

"*Efharisto*, for your concern."

"You're welcome."

Rolo Metzger and I were roommates not because we were great friends, although we got along fine, but because we both needed a place to live and knew we could get more for our money if there were two of us to split the rent.

Rolo was an easy-going city kid from Ohio, the youngest of eight children in a Catholic family that single-handedly kept the immigrant stereotype alive and well. In high school he played football and dreamed of going to Notre Dame. Told he was too small to make it on a college team he briefly tried to be a real-life "Rudy" and moved to Indiana to lobby his case. Reality being different from the movies he soon returned to Cincinnati and plotted his next course. Somehow – even he didn't remember the details – he decided on the military.

He applied to Annapolis, was rejected, then applied to West Point, convincing his congressman to sponsor him by bringing his parents, seven brothers and sisters, and twenty-two assorted cousins, nieces, and nephews (all of voting age) into the district office to vouch for him. The academy accepted him but on a conditional basis: his grades from high school not being the best but his football record speaking for itself, the faculty wanted him to improve his GPA first by attending a military prep school for a year. Rolo did, going to St. Michael's Military Academy in west Texas where he learned to wrestle, drink a lot of beer, and sneak into Mexico on Friday nights to pick up hookers and dog tacos. And he studied, at least enough to up his GPA.

West Point turned out to be more a notional experience for Rolo than a lead-in to a professional military career. There was the academy and there was Rolo, and never the twain did meet.

It wasn't that he didn't try and it wasn't that he couldn't meet standards. It was more that early on in the Long Gray Line he decided that while military life was interesting and challenging and occasionally even exciting, it wasn't what he thought it would be. It just didn't light his fire. There was nothing wrong with the regimen, the discipline, the uniforms, and all that – it just wasn't something worth getting too worked up about. Being part of the academy, a group, a team – whatever team it might be – mattered. Rolo was a great team player. The other stuff – the straight creases, the precision marching, the spotless rooms: all the attention-to-detail nonsense that makes the military academies what they are – he blew off. But he was such a popular guy he could get away with it. No one got too angry if he sometimes showed up late for a work detail or if his boots lacked the proper shine. He was punished, sure, and yelled at by red-faced seniors, but when an upperclassmen chewed him out during an inspection for missing a belt loop, Rolo could maintain a composure that was nine-tenths professional and one-tenth "Dude, get a life," and nobody minded. Granted, he spent a *lot* of time 'walking the line' – pulling all-night guard duty after a full day of classes, but none of that was tasked out of spite. It was what his superiors had to do and it was what Rolo had to do, and everybody accepted it at that.

What did light his fire still was football. And wrestling. And coaching. Though he didn't make the academy gridiron team he got to wrestle and helped to bring in all kinds of awards from the eastern conference. He spent so much time on athletics that his grades suffered. By his junior year he was in serious competition for the 'Goat' award. The goat was the person who ranked last in his class at graduation time. Everyone else in the class gave the goat a silver dollar. It wasn't much of a goal but if you already knew you were near the bottom it was one worthy of consideration. And Rolo worked hard to achieve it.

He lost. In the end he ranked third from last, which in a way was worse than being last because he had lost at trying to lose. But again, being who he was Rolo shrugged and moved on.

The Army initially blew a gasket when he announced he wanted to cross-commission to the Air Force to become a pilot. Then someone at the Point reconsidered, realized it was Rolo they were talking about, and signed the papers.

He returned to Texas for pilot training at Laughlin Air Force Base. Happily, it too was on the Mexico border. But at some point he hooked up with the wing commander's daughter who had just returned from a year abroad as an exchange student in Athens. From then on Mexico was out and he developed a fanatical attachment to all things Greek. That included Greek food and now one of his catch-as-catch-can goals in life was to become a chef and open his own restaurant. He worked at it by cooking whenever he had the chance, claiming that everything came from one of "Grandma Metzger's famous traditional secret recipes." Rolo's self-applied nickname was Kristo, though nobody in Panama ever called him that except to cheer him up when he was upset about something. It simply made no sense. And as a name, 'Rolo' was goofy enough.

The liaison with the wing commander's daughter benefited him in more ways than one. At graduation Rolo did well enough to get a plane – which was something because the Air Force was starting to assign some pilots to desk jobs – but it was a slick C-130 to Dyess AFB, Texas. It was a nothing assignment to nowhere. His girlfriend encouraged him to try to change it but Rolo, even though he didn't want to go to Dyess, thought he should go with the flow. If the team wanted him to go to Dyess, he would go to Dyess. She thought otherwise and worked on her father. It took a while. Rolo went through Herc training at Little Rock, Arkansas, and then moved to Texas, where he languished patiently for two months as she and her father sought to save him from the "four fans of freedom." The sympathetic O-6 made some calls. At some point he talked to an old friend from his own pilot training class. That friend was our squadron commander.

"Hey, there's a Greek restaurant that opened up by the Marriott," Rolo said, stretched out in his chair. "I was thinking about asking around for Friday night, seeing if anybody wanted to go."

"Near the Marriott?" I tried to picture the area. "What's it called?"

"The Greek Restaurant."

"Catchy." Panamanian entrepreneurs were remarkably un-imaginative. There was a German restaurant on Federico Boyd Avenue called 'The German Restaurant,' and an Italian place in El Dorado called 'The Italian Restaurant.' "I'm sure we could get a crowd. What time did Walt say they would be back?"

"About forty-five minutes. You know, this would be a lot easier if we were using Dublois-Coats."

"It would. Dublois-Coats is bigger. The engineers are working there, though."

"What did you say they were doing?"

"Draining it."

Dublois-Coats was wide and flat, so big that nobody ever dropped bundles into trees there. But there was another hazard. Parts of it were dry but parts were wet and because of the high grass you never knew which was which until you drove or walked into the wrong place. Sometimes bundles drifting down from the sky *splooched* into the mud and disappeared just as thoroughly as if they were caught in the high canopy. Most of us put up with the conditions but the previous month Garb Taylor had driven out to the zone with Colonel Hunley in Hunley's personal SUV. It was meant to be a tour of Wing facilities but Hunley's Montero got stuck in the mud and sat there for three days. Lo and behold, this month the zone was being drained.

"Who dropped the first time?"

"I think it was Evan."

"So Jem should be next. They'll probably do a few patterns just to use up the rest of the bundles. They have ten total, right?"

"Eleven."

"Well, they've got ten now. Let's hope they put the rest in the DZ."

No such luck. A short time later Jem made a five-minutes-out call. Rolo gave him the wind report while I trotted to the high grass again to build another fire. Even with the smoke they missed the clearing, coming in from the north and dropping the bundle over the road so it drifted way into the trees on the far side of the Humvee. It was so far off-target that Rolo and I just looked at each other and shook our heads.

"Tailpipe Kilo, Shark 18. Drop report?"

"Give me the radio," I said. Rolo handed it over.

"Shark 18, this is Tailpipe Kilo. Twelve o'clock for two hundred yards. We're not going to be able to get that one back."

Walt replied, trying to sound reasonable.

"Um, Mike? We really need the bundles back if we can get them. It didn't go that far long, did it?"

Rolo sat up in his chair and shaded his eyes to look where the bundle had dropped into the trees. "Tell him not yeah, but hell yeah. That baby's gone."

"Shark 18, we would need a National Geographic expedition to go after that one. No kidding."

"Ha-ha! See if you can find Diegel Doone!" Walt cackled. When I didn't answer there was a long pause, then he added, *"Okay, we'll try to drop the next one shorter."*

The trick to airdrops in the C-27 was to be on course, get the winds right, and use the same picture out the window every time. Walt's technique was, when the winds were light watch the target disappear beneath the nose and count one-potato, two-potato, three-potato, four – then call "green light." It wasn't scientific but it usually worked. Of course, we usually dropped to zones bigger than Kinzer.

Another problem was that everyone's picture out the front window was different. If a pilot sat higher or leaned forward or slid his seat back just an inch, the target disappeared beneath the nose a few seconds later or earlier than it did for the other pilot across the cockpit. A few seconds was long enough to send someone into the trees. At Kinzer it was long enough to launch a bundle into the next county.

On the next run-in the C-27 cruised low over the trees on the same heading as before. This time the bundle left the plane directly over our chairs but that was still too late. The parachute opened, pulling the sandbag up short in its plummet to the ground and causing it to swing like a pendulum. It dropped into the trees just the other side of the Humvee, on the same magnetic line as the previous one but much closer.

"My turn," I said, getting to my feet as Rolo called in the report. I could imagine the frustration in the cockpit.

The far side of the road was bordered by kuna grass ten feet high. I paced back and forth before it like a sapper examining a castle wall and eventually gave up finding an easy way in. Instead I crunched through it with short steps, pressing down the stalks with my boots so they didn't spring back up and slice open my hands and face.

This bundle I found in a hurry. Retrieving it was another matter. Like the first one the parachute and lines were hung up in a tree. Unlike the first one they were closer to the ground, the sandbag twisting slowly only seven feet from the dirt. I could jump up and grab it except for one thing: directly underneath was an ant hill four feet high. It pointed like a cannon at the sandbag that threatened to crush it only a few feet above. Red ants swarmed over the mound.

"Hey, Mike! What were you using to build a fire?" Rolo's voice followed a static *beep* from the radio on my belt. Even though I couldn't see him we were still close enough that I could also hear his voice in the clearing as he made his call.

"The grass by the Humvee. Use the machete."

"Copy. They're setting up for another run-in. You find anything?"

"I found it. It's on top of an ant hill."

"Whoa-ho! Leave it, it's not worth it!"

"I'll see what I can do. You have the next one."

"Roger."

There were two possibilities the way I saw it. I could knock down the ant hill and then jump for the bag, or I could snare the bag and pull it toward me. Attacking the ants was extremely unattractive, as was climbing onto the hill. 'If it doesn't stick you, sting you, or bite you, it'll give you diarrhea,' my jungle survival instructor had said. The ants definitely fell into the stick-sting-bite category. I looked around for a vine.

From behind me I caught a whiff of smoke. Rolo was building a fire.

I found a vine that was supple and strong enough to fill my need. I tied a loop at one end and stood back from the base of the ant hill, stretching forward to raise the loop under the bag. It was harder than it looked. When I found what I thought was a perfect angle I realized I was standing in the trail the ants used to get to their mound. A dozen had already swarmed over my boots before I stamped them off. I moved around to the other side.

The smell of smoke grew stronger.

Finally I snared the bag enough to pull on it. Luckily, only the parachute itself was snagged, not the lines. I pulled until the branch it was caught on broke. The branch fell into the mound, creating a furious commotion among the ants, but the sandbag and chute landed at my feet. I picked them up and beat a hasty retreat through the kuna grass.

The air around me turned a chalky white.

Even before I got to the road I felt the heat. The tall grass above the Humvee was a wall of flame. As I got to the vehicle the crackle of burning stalks turned to a roar. Smoke poured up into the sky from a line of fire twenty feet long.

"Rolo?"

I ran around the fire to the clearing. Rolo stood there with his hands on his hips studying the inferno like it was a math problem rather than a blaze that might engulf our vehicle at any minute. The last Mark XIII flare smoldered at the fire's edge. As I ran up Walt's voice came out of the radio at Rolo's feet.

"Hey, we can see the smoke now. What are you guys burning?"

Rolo picked up the mike. Great clouds of gray smoke billowed above the flames as the fire marched in both directions along the road.

"Just some stuff. As you can see, the wind is calm."

"Copy, stuff. Shark 18 is three minutes out."

"Tailpipe Kilo copies, three minutes."

The fire moved parallel to the road, burning all the yellow grass but only smoldering at the newer, green shoots. Rolo held up his hands to preempt me from making any snide remarks. We watched the blaze peak and then falter as it struggled to find fresh fuel. Together we stamped out flames that tried to make an end run around us to hit the lawn chairs. Since the road was several feet lower than the clearing, the grass there burned itself out before it could singe the Humvee's roof. The Army's vehicle was safe.

"I've been thinking," I said eventually. "Perhaps when you open your restaurant barbecuing shouldn't be on the menu."

He turned up his nose, refusing to be baited. He did stomp harder at the flames, though.

The fire burned quickly, so quickly that by the time Walt flew over it had almost exhausted itself. Even so the rising smoke was so thick that Jem in the right seat offset even more to the left to avoid it. His drop was right-on fore-and-aft but the bundle drifted over the tree line to the east. Rolo dropped the mike and sprinted to catch it.

"I've got this one!" he yelled over his shoulder.

"By all means," I said. "You've accomplished enough here."

The bundle stayed in plain view but clipped the top of an umbrella tree at the edge of the clearing. The sandbag crunched through the upper layer of the tree's cap, eighty feet up where its wide leaves fanned out over smaller trees below. The lines passed through but then the canopy snagged, stopping its descent. The whole package dangled high above the ground.

Rolo stopped running and slapped his thighs in disgust.

"Un-fricking-believable!" he exclaimed. "I can't do anything right today!"

Suddenly the lines to the canopy snapped. The bag plummeted like an oversized coconut to the base of the tree. When it hit, it blew up.

The explosion lifted Rolo off his feet. Dirt flew up in a geyser, showering everything within a hundred feet and masking the white plume that continued straight up through the branches. The remaining flames in the grass blew out. Even the Humvee rocked on its axles. The tree itself trembled and began a slow lean into the forest, ripping through foliage until it came to rest in the crotch of a neighbor's trunk. Every branch from twenty feet down tore free and blew up into the canopy above.

The shock wave from the explosion carried all kinds of debris. When a twig nicked my neck I jerked my head in response and thereby missed some of the larger items. One sounded like a zipper on fire until the 8-inch stick that produced it flew past and buried itself in the molding of the Humvee's door.

The bundle disintegrated.

The airplane was a quarter of a mile away in a right bank, turning around to a downwind heading. The radio lay face first in the grass but from it we still heard Walt's muffled voice.

"Oh, good, you've elected a pope. What are you guys doing now?"

I hid under a lawn chair waiting for more explosions. I'm a pilot, I kept repeating, much as I had when I'd endured the jungle course. What am I doing with my nose in the dirt?

After Walt's call it was quiet. The birds that earlier chirped their presence around our every move now held back, waiting to see if we had other surprises in store. On the far side of the clearing embers smoldered where Rolo lay in the grass. For all I knew he was dead.

But then he moved. He looked around – left, right, at the tree, then across the clearing to me. Bits of grass stuck in his black hair and dirt dusted his face. His mouth made a firm, disbelieving O.

I got to my feet. The chunk of wood in the Humvee wouldn't budge but the door still opened. I swung it back and forth on its hinges, watching the stick curve through the air like a weapon, and tried not to think what it would have done to my head.

Rolo got up slower, first to his hands and knees, then to a crouch. He stayed in a half-crouch and walked away from the blast gingerly, the whole clearing now a mine field as far as he was concerned. When he got close he watched me play with the door.

"Aren't you going to ask me if I'm okay?"

"No. I'm trying to imagine my head on a pike."

He pointed his finger at me.

"We're done. Day's over."

He collapsed into a lawn chair and sat looking at the sky. Hundreds of feet up, great curls of dirty smoke hung listless, letting thermal currents from below push them into various shapes that he found worthy of intense study. Since he looked like he had just been burrowing in a compost pile I let him alone. For a while we sat in silence. Then to calm his nerves he closed his eyes and began talking. To himself. About food.

"Tzatziki," he murmured. "In a nice pita with lamb. Browned in oil...no, in water...just the water... salt, cucumber, a little onion...that'll do...alright, okay…, alright, okay… some garlic...some pepper..."

He would be alright. We would get back to the squadron and have a beer, and he would be alright.

As usual it was Walt who had the last word.

"Hey, guys, the smoke's starting to clear. Can you make more? We want another pass."

6. Apiay

Apiay was an interesting place to spend happy hour so long as you wore body armor.

It was a small Colombian Air Force base at the bottom of the Andes, forty miles to the east of Bogotá and eight thousand feet lower. A nearby town shared its name. Both were tucked close to the mountains but so far beneath them that flying there from the capital was like sliding down a ladder. To avoid a long descending loop out over the jungle and back into the airfield, whenever we signed off from Bogotá Radio we instead chopped the throttles and coasted down the backside of the cordillera in a valsalva-clearing descent that probably looked to anyone outside like we were a Stuka bomber going for a kill.

Apiay was out of the mountains but it wasn't in the jungle. Jungle was near, spread out in menacing darkness on the horizon, but it wasn't on the base. The base instead had trees that were tall and spare and thinned to an ornamental presence. Undergrowth was cleared away. In its place grew stands of bamboo that didn't cause the same claustrophobia as a tropical wood. The bamboo clumped like mutant weeds and prevented anything bigger from taking hold of the grounds.

While jungle didn't dominate the landscape the way it did, say, around Mitu or Araracuara, farmers around the town and troops within the base still had their work cut out for them to hack and burn places they wanted to keep clear. It helped that a narrow corridor stretching north of Apiay along the mountains stayed fairly dry. In some meteorological aberration this section of the foothills enjoyed a temperate microclimate where rains came and went but nature didn't suffocate everything under a humid carpet of green. True jungle only started some miles to the east and south. The closest representation Apiay had was a twenty-acre hardwood forest near the north end of the runway, across an open field that a local farmer plowed.

I liked Apiay for the tamales. An old local woman had an arrangement with the base commander: she brought a pushcart onto the base each day and sold the soldiers chicken and beef tamales wrapped in palm leaves. I liked them because they were good, they were cheap, and because she parked her cart only a hundred yards from the best viewing area for the afternoon strafing.

Mike Vaneya told me about the strafing. I flew to Apiay with him on my first LNO swap-out, a monthly flight where the 155th helped the Colombian army move soldiers around its far-flung jungle outposts.

Normally the way it worked was that we flew into Bogotá and spent the night. Then on Day 2 we flew empty out of the capital and down the mountains to Apiay. In Apiay where we had better power due to the altitude, we loaded troops and fuel and then started a three- or four-leg trip around the eastern basin to places like Las Delicias, Orocué, San Jose del Guaviare, Leticia, and Marandua. And of course to Araracuara. We didn't go to the same places every time and our loads varied but the days were always long and the flying good. Nights we would land back at Bogotá. That would go on for two or three days until the Colombians had everybody re-distributed. Then we would fly home.

Occasionally the number of car bombs and kidnappings in the capital increased to a level that made the embassy uncomfortable. When that happened we couldn't spend the night in Bogotá. Instead we stayed at Apiay.

"Safety meeting," Mike announced.

"A what?"

We had been on the ground for an hour. I had already eaten four tamales. There was no beer allowed in camp so Luz and I were sitting on cots drinking warm Cokes. Luz would finish a bottle and then try to entice a column of ants running along the floorboards to crawl in, reasoning that if he could get enough of them inside and then take the bottle elsewhere he would solve our ant problem. It was an exercise in futility but it gave us a metaphor for our caffeine-induced discussions of the entire counter-drug effort. Besides, there was little else to do at Apiay. The camp was run by the Colombian army, a no-frills organization if ever there was one. It was small – existing only to support the runway – and there were no luxuries. No one was allowed to go downtown due to warring drug cartels and no one from downtown – read, women – was allowed to come into the camp. On top of that, the three of us were the only Americans.

"A safety meeting," Mike repeated. "The commander is a major who spent a lot of time working with our MilGroup up in Bogotá. He likes how they do regular safety meetings to remind people of local hazards so he called for one this afternoon. He wants us to show up."

Local hazards?

Luz and I looked at each other. We were on a military outpost in a Third World country. Colombia was in the middle of an insurgency and the region around Apiay was infested with gangs of drug smugglers who staged tit-for-tat killings on the streets of nearby towns. In addition to the bullets and bombs, there were hazardous roads, dark foot paths, poisonous bugs, deadly snakes, malaria, dengue fever, and the thick mold on the walls of our bedroom that even bleach and Lysol couldn't kill. What hazards could the major possibly want to brief us on?

"HIV," the major announced a half-hour later. "Today we will discuss HIV and how to prevent contracting it."

He held his meeting outside because other than thc aircraft hangar the camp didn't have a building large enough to hold forty soldiers and three visiting airmen. We sat on chairs and plank benches.

"How long will this go?" I whispered to Mike.

"Maybe an hour. Why?"

"I just had four tamales. An hour may be too long."

We sat in a clearing yards from the runway. As locations for meetings went, this one wasn't bad. All the buildings of the compound sat off to our right, clustered at the end of the strip and visible through the trees. To our left were more trees that backed up to the perimeter fence. On the other side of the fence was the main road between Apiay and Villavicencio. Across the runway was the open field and on the far side of that the twenty-acre forest. Strong rays from the late afternoon sun kept the whole scene bright despite the foliage. They made it through the leaves overhead to dapple us with shards of light so the whole clearing looked like the rustic floor beneath a stained-glass window.

"Todo el mundo conoce el sida," the major began his lecture. He stood next to an easel with the runway and forest as his backdrop. On the easel was a flipchart

that he had gone to great lengths to prepare. One page after another showed numbers reflecting the spread of the disease, graphs of affected countries, and mortality rates. There were also a fair number of pictures of prostitutes which elicited much attention from the audience and at least one comment of, "Hey, I know her."

It was during one of these sessions of catcalls and whistles that a splinter of wood from the top of the easel suddenly flew into the air, accompanied a second later by a distant *pop*.

The whistling stopped. The major steadied the easel which had tipped forward. He checked his watch and looked behind him.

"*Es temprano*," he remarked. He motioned to a private at the front of the crowd. The private leaped to his feet, saluted, and ran off through the trees to the hangar.

"AIDS is everywhere," the major continued. "Even in our beautiful country..."

I looked at Mike.

"What was that?"

"Easel malfunction," he answered, chewing a Slim Jim. We were at the back of the gathering but both he and Luz moved off their chairs and sat on the ground. From there they could barely see the major because of all the soldiers blocking the way.

"What are you doing?" I whispered.

Mike shrugged.

"More comfortable," he replied and motioned that I join them.

I was going to argue but just then there was the sound of another gunshot. It was far-off and the report echoed from somewhere across the empty runway. A small branch in the tree above our group fell onto soldiers in the third row.

"Is somebody shooting?" I whispered.

Mike held a finger to his lips and pointed up front, indicating he wanted to hear the lecture.

When the branch fell some of the soldiers stirred. A few made comments. The major called for attention and quelled the murmuring. He looked at his watch again and then toward the hangar.

"It is important to wear protection when engaging with your loved one," he continued in a loud voice.

At the hangar the wide doors slid open. A handful of soldiers who had somehow managed to skip the AIDS briefing pushed the detachment's OV-10 Bronco out into the sunlight. A dandy in a dark blue flight suit followed them. He was one of two pilots assigned to Apiay and it was clear from his walk that he relished his privileged status. He stepped carefully, arms swinging wide, looking for all the world like he had just stepped away from a cold beer at the officers club. He paused only when he got too close to the sweaties moving his aircraft. Then he stopped and waited, one hand fingering the scarf while the other tapped a note pad strapped to his thigh. Actually there was no note pad there – it was just a black velcro strap for *holding* a note pad. I guessed the note pad didn't exist and the strap was there because it looked cool.

The pilot's flight suit was immaculate, his sunglasses stylish. He wore a thin white scarf tucked in at the collar. He didn't touch the plane until the mechanics positioned it abeam the runway. Then he did a perfunctory walk-around, tapping a few panels and kicking the tires. It was a show inspection, not a real one, the kind pilots do to demonstrate that they *could* delve into the plane's airworthiness if they wanted to but this time, on this one occasion, they wouldn't.

Watching the guy climb into the cockpit I remembered a cartoon I'd seen once. It showed a woman in an office building in front of a plate glass window. Outside on the street three men in uniform looked in her direction, primping and posing. The woman was embarrassed until a co-worker told her, "Don't worry, Marlene. They're not trying to get your attention. They're pilots and they're looking at their reflection."

"Condónes, gomas, preservativos, profilácticas, profilácticos," the major rambled on, looking off into the distance as he espoused the utility of condoms. *"No importa la palabra, pero es muy importante la cosa."*

A third gunshot made it to our ears just before the engines of the Bronco would have drowned it out. The bullet blasted a hole through the center of the flip chart, neatly removing the main attraction of a photograph that showed two detached hands demonstrating how to put a condom on a cucumber. The soldiers burst into laughter as the major, exasperated, put his hands on his hips and threw an angry glance toward the tree line behind him. As he did so, the Bronco started up. Minutes later it roared past us on its takeoff roll.

Mike was on the ground, taking cover behind the Colombian soldiers who remained seated in neat rows ahead of us. He rolled to one side and propped himself on an elbow to see the flip chart, clucking in satisfaction.

"That was a hell of a shot!" he exclaimed. "Took the rubber right out of her hands!"

I got down on the ground beside him.

"Somebody *is* shooting at us," I insisted.

"Yeah," said Mike as though it was obvious, which it was.

"Who?"

"Some guy over there in the forest."

"But why?"

"Don't know. They say it's a FARC sympathizer but for all I know it could be a disgruntled farmer or one of the druggies."

"They say...? You mean this has happened before?"

"Yeah," Luz said, sipping a Coke and scanning the ground at the base of the easel for the remains of the picture, thinking it might be worth saving. "Every day. Once in the morning and once in the afternoon. Usually doesn't hit anything, though. That was a good shot."

"Once in the morning and once in the afternoon, somebody shoots into the base?" I repeated. "Then why the hell are we having a safety briefing *outside*?!"

Mike checked his watch. "Because normally he doesn't start until dusk. He's early."

The Bronco climbed out and made a sharp turn to the right, not even reaching pattern altitude before the pilot descended again on an angle for the forest directly across from us. The whine of the engines reached us across the open fields as he began his dive.

The OV-10 is a cool-looking plane. It's not pretty but in terms of utility and a design that did exactly what its customers wanted it was hard to beat. It was built as a lightly-armed observer/forward air control platform for the Marines in Vietnam. Nobody could argue the Marines didn't get what they were looking for. Twin tail booms met to support a high-mounted horizontal stabilizer. A long flat wing supported two Garret turboprop engines. The fuselage pushed itself forward from the wing, the cockpit mostly plexiglass for maximum visibility. This one still had machine gun turrets on twin attachment points. As the pilot made his dive we saw white smoke billow from the guns even before we heard the rattle of automatic fire.

Our briefing was put on hold. Nobody can pay attention to a lecture on STDs while an air strike is in progress. Even the major stood aside to watch the show.

"Oooo, that must have hurt," Mike said as bullets ripped the base of the tree line a hundred yards away. He clapped appreciatively. By the forest clods of dirt leapt into the air. Leaves flew off the trees.

"Buen tirar! Buen tirar!" the soldiers shouted as the Bronco peeled away at only a hundred feet. The pilot climbed out over the forest to set up for his next pass. He had obviously done this before. At maybe a thousand feet and at the top of his climb he stomped on the right rudder. The plane, already slowing down, whifferdill'd to the right to point itself parallel to the edge of the forest as it started back down.

Smoke poured out again from the Bronco's guns. The *pfttttttt-pftttttt-pftttttt* of the bullets reached our ears as the tree line took another pounding. Good shooting, indeed.

"How long does this go on?" I demanded.

Luz shrugged, not looking away from the attack.

"He'll probably make one more pass and call it a night," he said.

"And they do this every day?"

"Every day, twice a day," Luz affirmed. He watched the show transfixed.

Every day, twice a day. Watching the damage done to the forest at each pass I wondered how close the trees had been when all of this started.

The Bronco pulled up one last time, the pilot performing another beautiful turn in the sky, sliding the plane around the apogee of its climb so it looked for a moment like the craft stopped in place and pivoted on an invisible support. The nose swiveled and dropped. Together, man and machine dove again to shoot up the same piece of real estate. At the bottom of that run the pilot banked hard right at a hundred feet and curved around the western corner of the base to line up perfectly on final to the runway. He touched down maybe six minutes after take-off. The sortie was a model of efficiency that would have made Frederick Winslow Taylor proud. If the Bronco had burned more than a hundred pounds of fuel I would have been amazed.

All through the aerial assault there was no sign of the sniper. No bullets went up toward the Bronco (judging from the lack of evasive action on the part of the pilot) and none came toward our briefing area. For all we knew, the sniper had packed up and run away when he saw the Bronco taxi.

In our clearing, the soldiers resumed their seats. The major turned away from the runway as the

OV-10 landed. He paid no more attention to the field behind him.

The plane taxied to the hangar where the mechanics waited. The pilot shut down the engines and hopped out. He exchanged only two or three words with the ground crew and then walked away. Back to the club, probably. The mechanics pushed the plane inside.

"Pues," the major before us said, wrapping up his lesson. *"Preguntas?"*

No one had any questions. I looked at Mike but he scrunched up his nose to indicate he would decline the opportunity.

"Bueno," the major concluded. "Just remember: It is important always to have protection."

7. Guatemala

EVERYTHING IS RELATIVE, and relative to Bob Harcourt and Jerry Miner I'm an excitable person. That became clear when I flew with them to Guatemala in January to ferry road equipment to the locals.

Bob didn't breathe, ever. His chest never rose and fell to satisfy demand from his lungs, so I had to conclude he didn't have lungs and somehow had mastered the ability to soak up oxygen through his pores. With respiration thus a luxury rather than a necessity his nervous system operated just above flat-line level: he never got excited, never raised his voice, and moved like an octogenarian grateful for not needing a walker. Lt Col Rasmussen liked Bob because he was "calm." Calm? I thought he was a walking coma victim. The Four Horsemen of the Apocalypse could have ridden up to his house and Bob would have offered them a smoke.

Jerry Miner would have offered them a whole pack of cigarettes. He would have done that because he always had several packs on him, as well as a stainless steel cigarette case with the words SMOKING KILLS in bold letters across the front. In three years of flying with him I never saw Jerry without a lighted cigarette in his hand. That included the time he and

I broke a plane in eastern Colombia and had to camp out for a week, using plastic bags hung from trees as camp showers. Jerry smoked even while showering, carefully balancing his Marlboro on a branch while soaping up, then taking a deep drag before getting back under the water to rinse off. Life for him was lived through a blue haze of floating ash. He greeted crises and boredom alike with half-lidded eyes and an unhurried puff on a glowing butt. No doubt he would have been a jittery, nervous individual had he ever been deprived of his nicotine but in all the time I knew him he never was.

Bob had been to Guatemala before but only as a tourist. I was making my first trip and flying as his co-pilot. We had a small but heavy load in the back: hand tools, bags of concrete mix, some truck parts including four tires, and a portable asphalt cooker that looked like a Ben Franklin stove on wheels. Jerry had the stove tied down up front and everything else stacked on plywood pallets that we could combat offload at the airstrip and forget about. The field we were flying to was supposed to be spare on support.

We were flying to the edge of the Petén, the huge northeastern panhandle of the country. My map showed there wasn't much in that area.

The locals felt differently. The Guatemalan government had sold the U.S. on a plan to "stabilize" the area. To them that meant making it less like a far-away planet and more like something that belonged to the rest of the country. This included improving the few roads in the area, all of which were the axle-busting kind. It wasn't a bad goal. The Petén was flat and wooded, unlike the mountainous majority of the country. It was remote and sparsely populated. It had untouched forest and hidden Mayan treasures and was a naturalist's and archeologist's dream. There was potential for everyone to benefit if it could somehow be preserved yet exploited, finding profit in its beauty that didn't destroy what made it beautiful to begin with.

Unfortunately, because of its remoteness the Petén was also a haven for people who wanted to escape government control, a group which included thieves, drug runners, idealistic foreign entrepreneurs, and members of the URNG rebel group and their sympathizers. For that reason the area attracted attention from the capital. An American hostel owner had been killed in Poptún the previous summer, and even though responsibility for the murder was unclear President Serrano Elias and the military were using it as a pretext to crack down on people they didn't like. The rebel movement wasn't concentrated in the region but there were still groups that harassed army patrols with homemade bombs and sniping. The URNG stashed weapons on farms and sometimes mined roads to the caches. Drug traffickers used out-of-the-way strips as refueling points before heading on to Mexico. Bandits regularly held up travelers on the Rio Dulce – Flores road. Even nature hikes in the northern "eco reserve" were sometimes held up and robbed en masse. A university group was ambushed there the summer I arrived in Panama: four women were raped and two killed. The Petén just wasn't a safe place to be.

Our destination was a dirt strip called Cubilhuitz low in the foothills of the Chama Mountains, the last chain of ridgelines that descended out of the continental divide to the north. Cubilhuitz actually showed up on the only map I had of the area, a 1:500,000 TPC that depicted a hollow blue circle resting on yellow terrain twenty miles north of the town of Coban. It sat a thousand feet above sea level, high enough to enjoy the misty air of the mountains rather than the parched heat of the lowlands. January was the first month of the dry season everywhere in Central America and even though I appreciated the drop in humidity the ever-present scorching sun was uncomfortable in its own right, enough to make us wish for an occasional cloud. The tropics at sea level were hot even with the barometer in the low double-digits. "It's a dry heat," everyone said. Well, true, but it's a dry heat inside my oven, too, and I don't sit in there for twelve hours a day.

There was nothing about Cubilhuitz to recommend it except its location. For that Bob was as excited as he could ever get, for besides being in the mountains Cubilhuitz sat inside the borders of a region called the Alta Verapaz. The Alta Verapaz was known for cardamom, a kind of ginger seasoning that Bob had developed a passion for. He hoped that wherever Cubilhuitz was, there was a town nearby where he could stock up on bushels of the stuff. I knew he was excited because he bothered to mention it at all. For him, volunteering personal information was the equivalent of a joyous leap into the air.

The day of our flight we had a late start out of Panama due to a problem confirming diplomatic clearances. Garb Taylor fought a running battle at Group with embassies and Defense Attaché Offices (DAOs) throughout the theater over bureaucracy and its limitations. The battle wasn't with personalities so much as process: all too often one person in a country's government gave approval for a flight without talking to another person in a different office, who was the guy who needed to approve landings, for example, or take-offs or personnel clearances or whatever else. Or the DAO was used to dealing with one official but that guy was on vacation this week so the replacement cancelled whatever the DAO had lined up. Or, most often, the embassy and DAO used separate back-door channels to fill all the squares in their paperwork, and then those channels didn't touch base with each other. There were any number of reasons why our approval to fly in someone's airspace might fall apart. It was common for us to launch an aircraft somewhere and then have to recall the plane halfway through the flight because the diplomatic clearance – the official permission for the plane to be within a country's borders – was denied. It was also common for us to show up someplace and have no one there know we were coming. I'd already been in trouble for that in Peru and was willing to wait on Garb if it meant avoiding the problem up north.

But eventually Garb worked his magic and got us the clearances we needed. We finally took off and headed west and then north to Guatemala. Our plan was to hit Cubilhuitz, drop our load, fly on to La Aurora airport at Guatemala City to refuel, then return home.

Three hours later there wasn't another soul in the air as we descended south of the Petén. We approached the strip from the east where low hills gave way to open forest on our right and mountains on our left. Clouds sat over the mountains but only at their peaks. They rested on ridgelines, the air above them clear as glass but the land below never having a clue that anywhere in the world had anything but gray, drizzly skies.

"You have the field?" I asked Harcourt who was flying.

"Mm-hmm," was his somnolent reply.

"Is it that patch with the cows on it?"

"Mm-hmm-mmm."

The only open area I saw was a giveaway yellow slash of dirt tucked neatly into the V formed by a stream and a dirt road. Scattered black dots moved around on it as we approached: I thought they were cows but a mile out it became clear they were goats. There were people on the road and some shacks by the strip but even with the animals nothing about the place looked permanent. The one solid structure in the region was a farmhouse. I guessed it was the reason the strip was there at all.

"Low approach," said Bob matter-of-factly. That was his landing brief. I took it upon myself to drop the gear.

We buzzed the strip a hundred feet up to look at it before landing. The goats ran in every direction. That was helpful since normally they ignored airplanes. While horses and cows usually scattered when we flew over, goats, gypsies of the quadruped world, more often looked at us with a "Who the hell are you and why do I care?" expression and kept on doing whatever they were doing. Sometimes they were territorial and aggressive, as in Bolivia once when a herd attacked my plane. Sometimes they were just weird, like the time TJ backed onto a runway in Ecuador and blew the roof off a nearby pen – where every goat inside fainted, dropping on its side as though bopped on the head. The one thing goats were not was predictable.

Bob pulled up into a left downwind while I completed the landing checks. The field was on his side but as we pulled abeam I saw the people on the road again. Some had guns. As far as I could tell it was a group of soldiers but Bob watched them and shook his head. Jerry Miner leaned over Bob's shoulder to look down through the bottom window.

"Got somebody," he pronounced indifferently, and slid back into his seat.

We landed and rolled to the end of the dirt. Nobody came to meet us. The road was out of sight behind the shacks and head-high cane plants that grew in a tangle at the edges of the field.

The goats that were on the strip trotted into the brush when we landed but re-appeared as soon as we turned around. They stood for a few minutes in the grass they'd already eaten down to nothing and watched us with scornful eyes. Eventually they wandered back onto the dirt as though daring us to chase them off.

"Ramp," Bob called. "Let's get this stuff out."

Jerry dropped the ramp and raised the cargo door. I hopped out to help him release the straps that held our pallets in place on the rollers. When they were clear, Bob ran the engines up and released the brakes. We rolled forward with a jolt and three plywood sheets of tools slid out the back. Each landed with a *fwhupp!* on the soft ground.

The asphalt cooker was trickier. Since no one appeared to collect it, Bob set the brakes and came back to help ease it down the ramp. It was while we were doing that that the people from the road showed up.

There were maybe twenty-five men, eight of whom were soldiers in Guatemalan Army uniforms and the rest peasants, all Mayans in clothes suited for work in open fields. Cotton pants, faded shirts, bandanas tied around their neck, and towels – *toallas* – draped on a shoulder. The soldiers escorted the locals, walking behind them with rifles pointed at their backs. Everybody in the group was short. Bob was only five-ten and nobody in the group stood higher than his shoulder. We knew that because as they walked up the field one of the soldiers waved and Bob went over to talk to them. The crowd stopped in the grass by the shacks.

The locals looked nervous, as I would have if someone had been pointing a gun at me. They had flat, hard faces with coal-black eyes mostly cast down. The soldiers were a mixed lot. A couple looked pissed off and kept ordering the peasants toward the shacks but others found the plane more interesting than the prisoners. A couple even waved to us.

Jerry and I lugged the cooker away from the plane. He then leaned on it and lit a cigarette while watching Harcourt's back. I put a foot on the ramp and got ready to dash inside and take off.

I hated being around people with guns. I hated especially being around people I didn't know with guns because I had no idea what they were thinking or how they would act. And I hated most of all being around people from Third World countries with guns. Their lives already sucked by my standards and it stood to reason they valued my existence on a similar level.

I didn't mind guns themselves. I was wearing one, as were Bob and Jerry. We all had the standard issue 9mm Beretta semi-automatic. Mine was in a shoulder holster underneath my flight suit but Bob and Jerry carried theirs in nylon-and-velcro holsters strapped to their leg. We had the AR-15s on board but nobody bothered yet to take them out of the hell-hole. We expected civil engineers to greet us, not a Guatemalan army squad.

Harcourt talked to the soldier in charge for about five minutes. The man looked young, with an impassive brown face and flat features that suggested he might have Mayan in him, too. From markings on his sleeve I guessed he was a sergeant.

At first the conversation didn't go well. Despite our bringing supplies none of the soldiers looked happy to see us, probably because they weren't there to build roads. The one in charge kept peering around Bob to look at me and Jerry, making sure we hadn't moved. He gestured a couple of times at the airplane and seemed to be arguing. It occurred to me that we were standing in drug-runner country and this low-level soldier had just watched a plane land and kick stuff out the back. I promised myself I would kill Garb Taylor when we got home.

But Bob spoke good Spanish. His wife was a first-generation Mexican immigrant to the U.S. and she'd taught him well. Better, his implacable calm made him the perfect choice of the three of us to serve as liaison in this situation. I would have been too nervous and Jerry would have blown smoke in the soldier's face.

All the while Bob talked, the two pissed-off soldiers kept trying to force one of the peasants toward the shacks. The closest shack had an entrance facing down the runway, a broken door of dry slats hanging from rope hinges blocking the way. The soldiers prodded him over to the door but he refused to go inside. They poked him some more and when one of the other peasants protested they kicked both men to the ground. That prompted a round of yelling from the sergeant who cursed out everybody, his own soldiers as well as the locals.

"What the hell is all this about?" I muttered out of the side of my mouth.

Jerry exhaled at length and squinted through the smoke.

"I don't know. But we should go before the ethnic cleansing starts."

The tussle at the shack ended Harcourt's conversation. The sergeant finally agreed with whatever Bob said and waved him away. Satisfied that we weren't ferrying coke – what kind of trafficker drops off a pot-bellied stove? – he decided our plane was no business of his.

But then the soldiers shot two peasants. I wasn't looking at them when they did. I was looking at Bob who was halfway back to the plane when over his shoulder one of the pissed-off guys just raised his rifle at hip level and fired two shots into one man and one shot into the other. The first peasant was already on the ground and just flipped backward to lie flat, smoke rising from his chest. The other man fell into the arms of his friends who dropped him and started yelling in fear.

Bob spun around. Jerry jumped up off the cooker.

I ran inside and grabbed an AR-15. I didn't know what I was going to do with the rifle but it gave me something to do. I'd just watched someone die. When I got back to the ramp Jerry Miner held up his hand to stop me and in a no-argument voice ordered, "Don't start a land war, lieutenant." I put the gun down.

The sergeant yelled at the peasants. He grabbed the man who'd protested earlier and shoved him over the bodies to the soldier who stood by the shack. Then he turned toward the plane and shouted at us to leave.

Bob backed up at the same rate he'd been walking earlier. When he reached the ramp he said, still looking at the soldiers, "Time to go."

"Fuckin'-A," Jerry said. Now that Bob was back Miner threw down his cigarette and jumped up the ramp.

Then the soldier by the shack pushed the peasant through the door and the whole thing blew up.

The door blew out. The roof erupted. I didn't see what happened to the peasant but a plank came straight out at Mach speed and cut the first soldier's head off. A second chunk impaled the troop next to him hard enough that pieces of the wood stuck out his back. Both men fell to the ground and were dead by the time they got there.

I ducked away. By the time I looked back the soldiers and prisoners were in complete disarray. Everybody had been blown to the ground. Several of both groups still lay there, some not moving and others writhing in agony in broken dirt and straw. The peasants who could get up did so. They got up and ran for their lives. Most of them ran straight at us.

They ran around the plane at both the nose and tail and continued running into the cover of the brush behind us. Some passed by where I crouched beneath the ramp, dirt and bits of wood raining down on the tail above. There was indescribable fear in their eyes. The only way they differed from me was that they were in motion.

The sergeant had been knocked flat but was unhurt. He rolled over, grabbed his rifle, and started yelling. He shouted over and over for someone named "Titi" to "stop the rebels." *Titi! Titi! Párelos!* But whoever Titi was, he wasn't yelling back. As his prisoners ran away the sergeant pointed his rifle and shot one of them in the back.

I yelled "Don't shoot!" in English and crawled around and up the ramp. The sergeant could have shot me, I suppose, but he didn't. Instead he tracked the others who were running and shot at them. Soldiers around him staggered to their feet. Smoke rose from the burning shack. Pieces of straw floated everywhere on the currents of heat and what little prop wash came up from the still idling engines.

"Mike!" Bob hauled me to my feet. "Get in the seat!"

"You're not going to get your cardamom," I replied. For some reason that suddenly seemed important. But I jogged to the front of the cabin and climbed into the co-pilot's seat.

"Close the ramp!" Jerry called back to Bob. Jerry was sitting in his fold-down seat by the crew entrance door. Why he didn't close the ramp I didn't know – he just sat there with his arms folded and told Bob to do it himself.

Bob hit the ramp lever as he passed it on his way up front but wasn't about to wait for it to close. It was only when he saw Jerry holding his pistol in his folded arms that he realized what was up.

One of the peasants was hiding in the latrine. He got aboard in the confusion and was now trapped. Unarmed, stuck in a phone-booth-sized toilet on a foreigner's aircraft, scared out of his wits as he listened to the shooting outside, he couldn't even see back to the ramp. He huddled against the fuselage padding, cramming himself into the corner as he balanced on the cargo winch which was jammed between the honey bucket and the emergency hatch. And now Jerry blocked the only escape, his folded arms barely concealing the 9mm that he pointed at the Guatemalan.

Bob sized up the situation at once. He did so just as the ramp locked in the horizontal position – and as the army sergeant jumped up onto it and into the cabin.

"*Hay alguien en el avión*!" he yelled above the noise of the engines. We couldn't tell if it was a question or an accusation but he started coming forward in the cabin, his M-16 at his hip.

Now for the first time and only time I saw Bob get angry. People had been murdered in front of him, a land mine had gone off fifty feet away, his co-pilot had gotten hysterical – and the man hadn't blinked.

But now that an armed foreign soldier was storming his plane his blood was up.

"*Fuera de mi avión!*" he lashed back at the sergeant and stalked down the cabin to meet the man halfway.

"*Hay alguien aquí?*" the sergeant repeated but he hesitated. He was angry, too, and partly in shock. Now the shaking and the noise of the plane unnerved him, as did Bob getting right in his face.

"*No hay nadie aquí!*" Bob shouted. "There's nobody here. You can see the whole damned plane. Now get out!"

The sergeant didn't know what to do. He kept his rifle at the ready but at least didn't point it at anyone. Whether he'd seen the peasant jump into the plane or just thought someone might have climbed aboard we couldn't tell. He tried to look under Bob's outstretched arm.

"*Este avión es la propiedad del gobierno de los Estado Unidos,*" Bob said firmly, trying an authoritative tack. "Do you want to cause a problem between our governments?"

I don't think the sergeant gave a good goddamn about problems between governments. But Bob was red with fury and using his five-ten as much as possible to tower over the man. Jerry unfolded his arms to put his pistol in plain sight. The uncertainty, the noise, the fear, and the knowledge that he still had some of his guys out bleeding in the dust became too much. With what composure he maintained the sergeant decided he didn't need any more problems. He turned around.

Bob let him get to the ramp before offering, "Your wounded. *Sus heridos. Podemos llevarlos al hospital. A La Aurora. Póngalos en el avíon.*"

The sergeant looked back and shook his head. Bob went after him.

"You don't have a hospital here! Put your wounded men on the plane and I will take them to a hospital. It's thirty minutes away!"

Now the sergeant had had enough. No more new things. No more decisions. He pointed his rifle at Bob and shouted, "*No!*"

Jerry got up from his seat. I thought Bob was a dead man. But the sergeant didn't pull the trigger. He just kept his gun trained on Bob's chest as he hopped down to the ground. Then he waved us on our way and walked back to his men.

I sympathized with his dilemma. I didn't need any more new things, either. I pushed the engine condition levers from Ground Idle to Run and bumped on the throttles. In the back Bob hesitated. Then he hit the lever for the cargo door and came back up front.

We dropped the peasant near Rabinal, thirty miles north of the capital, at a dirt strip that was part of the road across a canyon floor. It had a decent surface and a creek nearby, a place quiet enough that a plane going in and out would have attracted attention had there been anyone around to attract, which there wasn't. The short flight gave us just enough time to find out some basics about our passenger.

His name was Xachua. He had a square face with wide eyes and black hair so thick it was impossible to see the scalp. His skin was brown and smooth except for a melanoma on his broad forehead that was the size of a Kennedy dollar. To hear him tell it the soldiers had rounded him up with all the other farmers for no reason. He said he was from the Petén but had come south for work. He named a village that none of us had ever heard of and couldn't find on the map. To tell the truth, I could barely understand the guy. Part of it was because he was afraid of the headset Jerry gave him and wouldn't put the microphone close enough to his mouth to block out the airplane noise. He also wouldn't put earplugs in his ears and kept shouting above the engines, which meant that his already garbled words came at us at full volume. Even then his Spanish was in a dialect-tinted accent that hit more consonants than I could make out. Part of it also was that the guy was clearly not the sharpest crayon in the box; added to that was the experience he had just gone through and now being on an airplane for the first time in his life. He was petrified. We asked some questions but didn't probe for details.

None of us knew how to feel about him anyway. Maybe he was an innocent farmer subject to a random army ethnic cull; maybe he was the ringleader of some rebel group that we'd just plucked from danger so he could go out and set more booby traps that would blow off a soldier's legs. Maybe he was anywhere in between. We talked to him just enough to answer the inevitable questions back home. Jerry never put his gun away.

We were low on gas and had no idea where to debark Xachua where he wouldn't get shot or picked up by the local police the instant he got off the plane. There was no way we could take him up to the Petén. He couldn't read a map and recognized the name of only one town on our far-from-detailed TPC, so Bob decided we would put him as close to there as we could find a landing strip. That's how we came up with Rabinal. Bob didn't want to take the guy to Guatemala City in case we were all arrested the instant we landed. Unfortunately for us, we didn't have the gas to go anywhere else ourselves so were just going to have to chance it.

Xachua got off the plane warily, looking around as though we were dropping him on Mars. The expression on his face said, "If this is your idea of help, please don't help anymore." I felt sorry for him but there wasn't much else we could do. Bob gave him the sandwiches his wife had packed for him and I gave him a bottle of mineral water. Naive fools looking even more foolish. But it was what we had to offer, and it made us feel better. He could have been dead.

He walked clear of the strip in the fading afternoon light and sat down as we turned around to take off. The last I saw of him he was shielding his eyes from the blowing dust and sipping at the Evian.

We didn't get arrested at La Aurora. The station manager had gone home by the time we arrived so there was no one even to report the incident to. No one connected to the embassy, anyway. We didn't want to take our chances trying to explain it to the locals, either – better to do that over the phone from Howard. After all, this was a country in the midst of an insurgency, where kidnappings happened by the hour and where normal traffic accidents resulted in everyone being arrested and held for months until the case could go to court. We agreed that accusing the army of first-degree murder might be worse. So we refueled and took off for home.

8. Farnham

Major Gillian Farnham was our squadron #2, the director of operations. He was chatty and innocuous, a C-141 pilot and lieutenant-colonel select who couldn't hide his surprise that he had gotten as far in the Air Force as he had. Most days he walked around the hangar with a cup of coffee in his hand and a look of happy befuddlement on his face, comfortable in the knowledge that he wasn't the sharpest crayon in the box but willing to ride his talents and the needs of the personnel system as far as the military would allow. If he didn't have coffee he carried a pipe. He didn't smoke but he liked the pipe as a prop and would point with it or tap it against things with what he hoped was MacArthurian emphasis.

Farnham was always around but rarely in his office. We guessed he avoided it because he wasn't sure what he was supposed to do there. If he was at his desk he spent the time playing crossword puzzles or reading a book. Guys like Rolo would pop in on him with no warning just to see him scramble and pretend to be working.

The major was tall and good-looking with boyish hair. He had a pencil-thin moustache that Jimmy Buffet would have envied and a relaxed attitude about almost everything. His strong points were that he liked people and wanted to be a good leader. His weak points were that he didn't understand people and was too lazy to do the work leadership requires. In a meritocracy he would have finished his career no higher than a junior field grade officer but in the real world – where the military is subject to the laws of supply and demand like any other business – he was instead on track to command a squadron, if not a group. In the military the key to promotion is often just to stay out of trouble and hope that enough guys quit from disgust before you do: Farnham had that kind of patience. His career was unexceptional but it was solid. Barring any missteps he could expect to take over the squadron whenever Rasmussen left.

But while he was Number Two we didn't deal with him much. Normally the DO is in charge of day-to-day operations but not in the 155th: Lt Col Rasmussen was aggressive and hands-on and unapologetically overshadowed his subordinate. Farnham didn't object – in fact, whenever Rasmussen was absent he was of two minds about being the boss. On the one hand he was flattered to be in a leadership position. We saw that on occasions like when he sat down in staff meetings and realized he was at the head of the table, or when the first sergeant showed him his own parking spot for the first time, or when the Group had a change of command and he got to yell "Pre-sent...*arms!*" for the various flights. His face at those times was pure joy.

But other times he was confused, overwhelmed by the realization that people now looked to him to know what was going on and make decisions accordingly. When that happened his response was hit-or-miss. On subjects that he knew with confidence he was firm; on others he wavered behind a facade of jocularity. He could laughingly agree with both sides of an argument and then switch his position another fifty times. What he didn't know he guessed at.

And guessing was usually good enough. Our mission wasn't rocket science. So long as you followed regulations and erred on the side of safety you were likely to do the right thing. Sometimes, though, responsibility encouraged Farnham to pretend that he knew more than he did and to try to outguess the regulations. It wasn't unusual for him to run with an idea long after the evidence suggested an about-face. Whenever that happened his success rate was never better than fifty percent – i.e., half of his exaggerations ended up destroying whatever credibility the other half won. He never learned from his mistakes, either, so as a budding leader he ran in place a lot.

Farnham also wanted to be loved, meaning he did things sometimes because he thought they would make him a popular leader. He didn't suck up to the troops but it's fair to say that he relished occasions when one of us asked his permission for something.

It let him posture as a sovereign power granting dispensations to the masses – and he almost always said yes. Lt Col Rasmussen was forever countermanding some of the dumb things Farnham approved.

An example was when he authorized me to go to Ecuador on permissive orders to study Spanish. "Permissive" meant the military authorized me to go but refused to provide funding – it was basically an unpaid vacation. Mystic Pete, the squadron executive officer, warned him that only the commander (out of town at the time) could authorize permissive orders but Farnham insisted no, no, he'd done it in other squadrons and it was perfectly acceptable for the DO to sign the papers. Our ignorance was no defense when Rasmussen returned and tried to task me with something and couldn't because I was a thousand miles away. Both of us received ass-chewings for that.

Another time Farnham counseled Story Earnhardt on his next assignment and encouraged him to put his name in for a C-130 position that Story didn't want. His reasoning was that the way the system worked Story would never get picked for the job but by volunteering and getting turned down it would in fact make him eligible to spend another year in Panama – which Story really desired. But then Story was picked up for the Herc job after all. It took all of Rasmussen's skills to keep Story from being shipped back to Little Rock, Arkansas to the C-130 schoolhouse and a lifetime in a plane he hated. Farnham, meanwhile, could only mumble helplessly that "in all his years" he had never seen such a thing happen...

Still he kept at it. The man had a personality that wouldn't stay down. When we lieutenants became wise to his buffoonery he transferred his attention to the enlisted troops. They couldn't avoid him as easily and he caused several of them no end of grief, like when he loaned Sergeants Clovella and Andrews to the Army for a month-long exercise in what he meant to be a good-will gesture, or the time he misunderstood a conversation at the squadron picnic and publicly offered to marry Clunk and his girlfriend – a girlfriend Clunk was trying to dump. Enlisted men spot idiocy in their leaders faster than horses sense fear in a rider so it wasn't long before our loadmasters put Farnham on their goober list.

There wasn't much they could do to him, of course, but they happily seized every opportunity to point up his gaffes. To document his foolishness they kept a journal of his more egregious acts. The journal was on the ops desk inside a tattered green ledger that said *Vehicle Inspection Log* across its spine and *Major Malfunctions – Document Here* printed on the cover. Jerry Miner promised a week of leave in Mexico to the author of the best story. They didn't need the encouragement. It was common for a load-master to come in after a flight with Farnham and call, "Give me the log!" before even dropping his gear to the floor. The announcement alone said a lot.

Farnham suspected that such a diary existed. He was too proud to ask but looked for it during his frequent meanderings around the squadron. He assumed that one of the senior loadmasters guarded it and could often be seen wandering in the vicinity of Bird's or Jerry Miner's cubicle while they were out. Too honest to search their desks, he would only get close and then, from a foot away with his arms crossed, lean over like someone looking into a well and try to discern from what lay in the open whether or not he was being mocked. It never occurred to him that the book would be kept at the front desk. In all the time he spent there he never bothered to peruse the logs, which was ironic because part of the reason he hung out there was in the hope of surprising someone into revealing its whereabouts. "So, you know where they keep the book?" he would query a new guy casually, his lopsided grin as transparent as the plastic coating on his name tag. No one ever owned up, though. The loadmasters had a code of silence to rival the Cosa Nostra.

In our leadership triad Farnham's hapless persona was eclipsed by the seriousness of Lt Col Rasmussen and the sanguine sociopathy of Major Byron. In some units that would have led to him being sidelined by the boss but not in ours. Rasmussen did in fact consider Farnham a boob but – in a lucky break for the major – he liked Byron even less. Since the commander couldn't sideline both of his lieutenants, the boob thus enjoyed more of his confidence by default.

That's why when Rasmussen had to put someone in charge of enforcing the Jeppesen policy the job fell to his DO.

The Jeppesen policy came about because of a crash.

In late spring a T-43 flew into a mountain in Yugoslavia. The airplane was from a U.S. air base in Germany and just like our T-43 at Howard it was a passenger jet used for carrying around important people – DVs, we called them, or distinguished visitors. It crashed while on approach to an airfield in Croatia because the pilots read the approach plate wrong and ran into a crest when they descended early in cloudy weather. Everyone was killed. It was a tragedy in every way.

The approach plate the pilots used was one drawn up by the Jeppesen Company. There was nothing wrong with it. Jeppesen published approaches for airfields all over the world and pilots all over the world used them every day. Pilots all over the world, that is, except most Air Force pilots. U.S. Air Force pilots usually used approach plates drawn up by the Department of Defense – the Pentagon – because Washington had stricter standards for measuring angles and altitudes and obstacle clearance. At the time of the crash Jeppesen plates weren't illegal for Air Force flyers but we only used them when there was no other choice, when we encountered a destination (such as in Croatia) that the DoD hadn't surveyed yet.

The reason the T-43 crashed was that the pilots were confused reading it, and the reason they were confused was that the two types of approach plates, Jeppesen and DoD, held the same information but were laid out in different ways. For example, on a Jeppesen approach radio frequencies were listed in the middle of the page while on a DoD plate they were in the upper left corner. On a Jeppesen approach minimum altitudes were always written at the top of a page while on a Pentagon plate they were always at the bottom. Jeppesen altitudes were in meters – DoD heights were in feet. Even colors varied: Pentagon plates were black and white while Jeppesen showed terrain in shades of brown that gave the page a jumbled look.

The different layouts carried real hazards since pilots are creatures of habit. Anything out of the norm has the potential to throw them for a loop. Most pilots don't even look at an approach plate until they're just about to use it so pulling out one that's in an unfamiliar format increases the chance they'll miss something important. The competing designs were the graphic equivalent of two models of the same car, one with an automatic transmission and one with a stick shift: even if you know how to drive both, if you're accustomed to driving an automatic you would be careless to leap into a car with a stick shift and pull out onto a busy highway. The T-43 pilots had done just that – the accident investigation concluded they had figuratively pulled out onto the highway and then added bad weather and mountains to the mix. The lack of preparation cost them.

Nevertheless, after the crash the Pentagon responded in its usual way. Since some units in the Air Force had been using the approaches for years without any problem, the generals could have said, "Hey, everybody. These guys made a mistake. Don't repeat it." But they didn't. Instead they immediately banned the use of any Jeppesen product by any Air Force crew anywhere in the world.

That posed a dilemma for us at Howard. Our unit was one of the few that used Jeppesen approaches all the time. We had to because there were no DoD approaches for most of the airfields in our theater. The Pentagon considered it not worth the time to go survey the dinky places we flew into. In that the generals were right – it *wasn't* worth it to survey places like Tacna and Pucallpa and Los Cumbres. Nobody flew there except us and we already had a way to get into them when there was weather – our Jepps approaches, which worked fine so long as we used them correctly.

And we did use them correctly thanks to the harping and good instruction of teachers like Walt and Mike Vaneya and Bob Harcourt. We used the approaches week in and week out and never had a problem. We even flew them during good weather (*visual* flight rules, or VFR) sometimes just to be familiar with their quirks. The Jepps weren't fancy but they were good enough. They were also indispensable during rainy season, when often the fields were covered in clouds (requiring *instrument* flight rules, or IFR). Without them we would have had to cancel every flight where the weather wasn't sunny.

"This is a stupid order," Lt Col Rasmussen told us at a squadron meeting after the new policy came out. "But guess what? We're in the military and we don't get to pick and choose which orders to follow. So from now on if a field is IFR and you don't have an approved U.S. plate, you don't go there. Turn around, divert to an alternate, or hold until the weather gets better."

The irony of the new policy was that arguably it made us less safe in our operations. Before, we had always used Jepps approaches as a last resort for getting into a field. Now since we could no longer fly an instrument approach we tried even harder to skim below the clouds to make it in.

Eventually the Pentagon came out with a procedure for requesting approach surveys but because the requesting process took so long and because our destinations changed so often the policy did nothing for us. We stopped flying Jeppesen approaches on our missions. For the bulk of my time in South America if we wanted to put the plane on the ground we had to guide it there ourselves.

"God, I love to fly!" Farnham exuded as we cruised over Costa Rica at 20,000 feet. He set his coffee down and tilted the seat back to prop a foot on the panel. The leg of his flight suit rode up so the loadmaster and I could see the red socks he wore that ended above his boot but below his pale leg. He sighed in elaborate contentment. When nobody reacted he did it again, gazing out the window over Puntarenas.

There was a cloud deck below us that stretched to the horizon. It blocked our view of the coast but its choppy surface was interesting in its own right, as though the ocean had turned white and climbed up two miles to get closer to our plane. The morning sun skipped rays across the deck's crests with enthusiastic abandon, creating shards of rainbows that burst out of the whitecaps and posed in midleap like the peacock bass we caught by the dozen in Lago Gatún. Farnham studied them with vague recognition, like a gentleman farmer surveying twenty acres that someone else has planted. There were no clouds shown on the worthless weather forecasts we had picked up before takeoff so he had trouble squaring the information he held in his hand with what he saw out the window. After twenty minutes of thinking it still wasn't clear which one he was going to believe.

"We don't see you much out on the line, sir," Airman Tunkelman observed.

Jamie Tunkelman thought Major Farnham was a tool. Part of his dislike was because Farnham had twice cancelled Jamie's leave on short notice and ruined the airman's planned vacation to Cozumel. Jamie had never been to Cozumel but he wanted to go and had been thwarted both times by the same person for no good reason. But even besides that he thought Farnham just wasn't that bright. He told me once the major was proof that light traveled faster than sound since he appeared bright until he opened his mouth.

Still, in all our professional dealings Jaime deferred to his superior with such sincerity that no one except a fellow cynic would doubt he meant it. Farnham wasn't a cynic but every now and then even he detected something in the loadmaster's tone that suggested he was being mocked. He could never pin it down, though, so to be safe he papered over any of his mistakes by turning the situation around and counseling Jamie as often as possible on the bigger picture, to which Jaime invariably responded by saying "Thank you for bringing that to my attention, sir," which was loadmaster longhand for "Go to hell, you dumbass." Their parrying extended to the last word.

"No," said the major. "That's true. I'm just too busy."

"You must be. We hardly ever see you around the squadron."

"What do you mean? I'm there every day."

"No, you're not."

"Yes, I am."

"No, you're not."

Farnham bristled. "If I'm gone sometimes that's because I'm busy," he insisted. "The more you advance in rank the more you end up chained to your desk. You'll see that one day."

What he said was true but in his case it was hard to tell if he minded. For a lot of career men flying becomes inconvenient after a while. A nine-to-five schedule is simply easier to live by. Major Farnham hung around the ops desk a lot but it was to gossip, not to get onto a sortie.

The Nicoya peninsula slid by our left wing and disappeared under the clouds. The whole western third of Costa Rica hid beneath a stratus layer that extended miles out over the water and up into Nicaragua. To our right only the volcanoes of the divide pushed their way above it. Arenal boasted a ribbon of smoke as it fell to our four o'clock. It looked like our whole flight to Soto Cano Air Base in Honduras would be over clouds.

Farnham lolled in his seat and surveyed the world, happy as a dog in a car window. Then he happened to look my way and his back stiffened.

"What do you have there?" he asked.

I looked around.

"Where?"

He pointed to my right. We had clips mounted to the window brackets for hanging instrument approaches in bad weather. Before leaving the squadron I had photocopied the Jeppesen plates for a dozen locations along our route of flight and for a handful of fields in Honduras. With the clouds below showing no sign of clearing, a few minutes earlier I had slid the one for Liberia into the clip. It was only a VOR but it would be better than nothing if all of a sudden we needed to put the plane on the ground.

"It's the approach for Liberia," I told him. "A small field thirty miles off the nose."

"I know what it is," he said sternly. "It's a Jeppesen approach."

"I don't plan to use it," I rushed to reassure him. "It's just that there's no place between San Jose and Managua that has a DoD plate. I carry these, you know, just in case..." I gestured to the deck below, assuming that no more need be said.

"No, I don't know," he glowered, believing that more did indeed need to be said. "Jamie, why don't you go off headset for a few?"

Tunkelman spun the third seat around and hopped down into the cabin, his face registering that with the sudden change of mood he was more than happy to get out of the line of fire.

Farnham proceeded to give me a classic dressing-down, lecturing me on discipline and integrity and the importance of following orders. I was confused, never thinking that I had disobeyed orders. The DoD policy was not to use Jepps approaches to get to the destination – but it never said anything about not carrying them in case of an emergency. After all, people don't light their homes with candles because of the fire hazard but most still keep some on hand in case of a blackout. In the same way every pilot in the squadron still took Jeppesen plates along on trips, policy or no policy. I didn't mention that last part to Farnham. Instead I suggested on my own behalf that not doing so would be irresponsible.

He couldn't disagree more. The more I pressed the logic of my actions the more he retreated to the one thing he understood.

"Jeppesen plates aren't tested by the Air Force," he reminded me. "They're not legal. You can't even have them on the plane and that's not open to discussion." He concluded on a note that he meant to sound ominous. "It troubles me that as an aircraft commander you have this attitude. When we get back to Howard I may have to talk to StanEval."

StanEval in the squadron meant Erich Fetterman. Fetterman's collection of Jeppesen plates was as complete as anybody else's so I wasn't worried about being punished. What did worry me was how we could have such a clueless DO. If he persisted in his reading of the policy I foresaw a lot of white-knuckled flying in the coming months.

At Soto Cano we refueled and loaded pallets of lumber to take up to the north coast. A tropical storm that popped out of the Gulf of Mexico had dumped heavy rains throughout Atlantida province and spawned storms in the rest of the country. The rains brought mudslides that washed out villages and roads. Our job was to ferry up to the region anything and everything to help the locals repair. At San Pedro Sula we gave the lumber to engineers from Task Force Bravo and replaced it with bags of sand and concrete mix to take to La Ceiba, a small town a hundred miles further down the coast.

"Sand?" Jamie complained as he lugged the bags aboard. "We're carrying sand? Is the beach at La Ceiba all out?"

Nobody on the ramp could explain the load but Major Farnham hushed his loadmaster anyway. "Sand is a vital commodity," he lectured. "It's not to be taken lightly."

"Easy for him to say," Jamie whispered. "He's not loading the stuff."

Later, at Golosan Air Base, the small airport on the beach outside La Ceiba, a handful of Honduran soldiers ran onboard and removed the concrete mix to a waiting flatbed truck. The sandbags they carried twenty paces across the ramp and stacked around the nose of an F-5. Jamie watched with his jaw set.

We flew back to San Pedro Sula and loaded more concrete mix, lumber, and all kinds of cleaning supplies to deal with flooded homes. Jamie's day got better when the engineers also gave us a pallet of fertilizer in the form of manure. It wasn't actual manure in the sense of a big stinking pile: it was a pallet of dried compost in commercial bags. Still, it smelled like manure and even the engineers apologized as they pushed the pallet aboard.

"The farms have washed away near La Ceiba," they explained. "They're trying to replant."

Jamie was incredulous.

"So not only do they not have sand at their *beach*," he thundered. "They don't have cow poop *at their farm?!*"

Farnham gave him another lecture, this one on the agronomy of tropical homesteads. Nevertheless, Jamie wasn't the only one praying for a tailwind later as we flew down the coast.

When we got back to Soto Cano it was two in the afternoon and storms were building around the valley, rising out of the thickening deck in the form of thunderheads and reaching below them as rain shafts. A wall of rain entered the northwest corner of the valley and slid sideways across the desert, the force of the downpour creating winds that blew up a cloud of dust before the front as though a giant army was marching past. It was a beautiful sight, nature in its power and glory, and particularly striking because of the illogical aspect of rain throwing up sand and dirt. Standing under the tail and watching the monster approach, I felt unabashed respect.

"We've got maybe twenty minutes!" Major Farnham called to Sam, the ramp coordinator, when he pulled up in his pickup.

"Okay," the captain replied, "I'll tell them to hurry. But you guys are going to love this."

'This' was a mule, a tall, fit, black-brown animal with a proud bearing and a long tail that swished with gusto as he followed the K-loader to the back of the plane. He wore a hackamore bit and iron shoes and carried himself with the cultivated unenthusiasm that city slickers normally see only in teenagers. As he walked, he didn't fight his handler – a slight Honduran soldier – but he still made the man work, like a child who insists on taking small steps while holding your hand.

"What the hell is that?" Jamie asked, stepping around the ramp to put it between him and the mule. Farnham, too, was taken aback. I thought for sure someone was pulling our leg.

"It's a mule," Sam informed us. "It needs to go to La Ceiba."

"Buy it a bus ticket," Jamie said.

The mule regarded our C-27 with scorn. Whatever this is, the look said, I won't like it.

"You're kidding, right?" I asked Sam. "This is a joke?"

Sam held out a manifest.

"No joke. Well, I suppose it is but the mule still needs to go to La Ceiba. The Hondurans are using them to get supplies into places where the roads are gone. This boy's got a mission."

Airman Tunkelman was one of our best loadmasters but he'd never carried a live animal on a plane. He looked at the manifest, then at Sam, then at the mule, and then at the cabin as though it was a temperance hall he had to convince to accept a drunk.

"Sir, I quit," he announced to Major Farnham.

"You can't quit," Farnham replied.

"Then I want to be a pilot. Let the lieutenant here figure out this one and I'll go sit in the cockpit."

"Nope. You've got it."

"I'm a loadmaster, sir, not a backcountry packer."

"So load," Farnham ordered.

Jamie studied the cabin again. "Will he sit down?" he asked the Honduran soldier. The soldier didn't speak English so I translated. The soldier laughed.

"That's a no," I told Jamie, who went back to studying the cabin.

I felt bad that I had no suggestions for him. I'd lived on a ranch for a while and knew a fair amount about horses but nothing about mules. The closest I came was one experience with a jenny. Jennies are like mules in that their parents are a horse-donkey mix but with the sexes reversed. They're smaller and just as stubborn. Once I loaded one up with salt blocks and tried to lead it to some grazing lands at the top of a winding canyon. The jenny didn't want to be led, didn't want to carry salt blocks, and sure as hell didn't want to be anywhere near me. It almost pulled my arm off as I all but dragged it up the mountain. Within twenty minutes I wanted to shoot the damned thing.

I knew nothing about mules then and knew little more now. I certainly had no idea how to position one on an airplane for a thirty-minute flight. My first idea was that we would somehow entice it to lie down and let us throw a handful of straps over it just like we would with any large object. We might as well have asked it to submit to abdominal surgery without an anesthetic. After we coaxed it up the ramp and into the cabin, the mule made clear that under no circumstances would it be doing anything but standing up.

"Can we sedate it?" Jamie asked, frustrated.

"With what?"

"I don't know. Hit it over the head with a frying pan, for all I care. There's no way I can have a live horse in the cabin while we're flying."

"It's a mule," Sam reminded.

"Then there's no way I can have a live mule in the cabin while we're flying. He'll fall over or something, or go crazy."

"No, he won't," Farnham insisted.

"Why not, sir?"

"They're very sure-footed."

"Sir, with all respect you're from Albany."

"Nevertheless, Airman Tunkelman, mules are sure-footed. I rodc onc once at the Grand Canyon."

"Oh, my..." Jamie paused and contemplated his fingertips. If you looked closely you could see his lips move as he counted to ten. "Uh-huh. Well, sir, then if he doesn't fall down he'll go deaf. Just the sound of the engines will make him freak."

"No, it won't."

"And how do you know that?"

"They're calm animals. Look at him," Farnham reached up to pat the mule's neck. The mule swung his head around in warning and stopped the gesture halfway. Farnham settled for a nervous wave. "Sure, look at him. He knows he's got a job to do. Once we get underway he'll be as happy as a baby in a crib."

I remembered the jenny kicking and braying its way up the canyon while trying to separate my arm from my shoulder and wondered what kind of babies Farnham had experience with. Still with no useful suggestions of my own to offer I stood at the ramp and kept quiet, watching the storm approach.

The shades of gray in its face swirled purposefully like practice strokes on a painter's palette.

I convinced Farnham to join me for a while and leave Jamie alone to do his loadmaster thing. That worked for a few minutes, time that Jamie used to work out a method with the Honduran for hobbling the mule's front legs. But as the wall of rain neared the base, Major Farnham felt he needed to push the issue. A flash of inspiration hit him and he hurried back into the cabin.

"Alright, come on, now, Jamie, it's not rocket science. What about the Chindits?"

"Sir?"

"The Chindits. Air commandos in Burma in World War II. We learned about them in Air Command and Staff College. Their motto was 'Anytime, Anywhere, Anyplace' and they carried mules."

"Sir, first of all, that motto is redundant. Second, it was their motto, not ours."

"All they did was tie the mule's halter to a rail and stuff socks in its ears for the noise. I tell you, mules are tough and they know how to stay on their feet. Like cats they are. They won't fall over and they'll put up with anything."

Jamie almost had the hobble figured out and wanted to argue but we were pressed for time. The storm was just outside the base. With Farnham pushing him on, he lashed the halter to a tie-down ring and then gave the handler a pair of rags which the soldier promptly shoved into the mule's ears. That made one of the weirder sights I've ever seen in an airplane – a truculent donkey with pink towels popping out of its head like deranged pigtails. The mule didn't seem to care. He seemed to guess he wasn't the first jackass we had carried. Nor would he be the last.

"Hurry up!" Farnham called.

We offloaded the K-loader and slid a stack of pallets and crates behind the mule. None of us gave them more than a cursory glance. It was clearly more material for mopping up from the floods along with dozens of bags of real fertilizer this time for the washed out farms. Jamie ran back and forth positioning the load, his practiced hands placing ropes and chains where they would make the most difference in keeping the goods in place. Major Farnham took one last look at the advancing rain, then leaped aboard and shooed me toward the cockpit.

"Let's go," he urged. "The storm's about to hit."

To our surprise the Honduran soldier trotted down the ramp. His job was over.

"What the hell? Who's going to watch this beast?" Jamie yelled to Sam as the #1 engine started to turn. Sam hopped into his pickup and pointed back at our airman as his answer.

The sky was turning black as we took off to the south. The wall of rain and its accompanying wind loomed behind our tail as we raced down the runway. The full effect of the storm was too late to cause us trouble but it was impossible to ignore its power as a tailwind pushed us an extra third of the way down the strip on our takeoff roll. We climbed out straight ahead, hoping that the worst of the weather would pass by the time we returned to the base in two hours.

The clouds contracted their circle around the valley. Rain shafts clustered like bullies. We lost sight of the ground climbing through five hundred feet but at this end of the valley the showers were light and there was no turbulence. The clouds off the nose were bright, too, suggesting that if we continued straight ahead we might even break into the clear.

"Well, I'm surprised," Jamie's voice came over the intercom. His tone was cautious but relieved.

"How's that, Jamie?"

"The major was right. The mule's being really calm."

"I told you," Farnham replied.

I looked over my shoulder as we climbed through two thousand feet. The mule's head was up, alert, and his ears stuck out in contrast to the rags that drooped past his jowls, but he was still. Jamie had him tied forward in the cabin only a few feet behind the loadmaster's own fold-down seat. Behind him were the boxes of cleaning supplies, then pallets of urea in paper and burlap bags. The mule seemed to be studying his surroundings, wondering if anything in the vicinity was worth complaining about. We could only hope that the lingering smell of cow pies from our previous load helped him to acclimate.

I wanted to keep going south at least to the end of the valley before looping back toward the coast but after only five miles Major Farnham decided we had deviated far enough. He turned east and then north to get us pointed toward La Ceiba.

Immediately the sky out front grew dark. The C-27 began to bounce around.

It wasn't the worst turbulence I had ever felt but it was enough to make me uncomfortable, enough to make me ask myself, "And the reason we couldn't have kept going south was what, exactly?" With black clouds out both sides of the plane and the occasional flash of lightning, it was the kind of weather where most pilots stare out the window into the opaque void and feel the engines whine and the turbulence bump them up and down and think to themselves how much this sucks and how much they really want to break into the clear any second so as to quit worrying about dying. It was the kind of weather where most pilots stay quiet, their mouth twisted into a thoughtful wince.

"Yup, you get weather like this down here a lot," the major announced breezily as though his experience in the tropics was any longer than mine. "Big blustery storms, lots of sound and fury signifying not a whole lot." An updraft shoved us into our seats just then as though to dispute his point. Farnham interpreted it the opposite and shoved right back. "See, nothing but..." Another updraft tipped us right and he lunged on the controls to bring us level. The maps he put on the dash fell into his lap. "...nothing but a lot of blow with nothing behind it. Heh-heh," he chuckled. "It's good experience for you young guys. Good to be out here..."

He babbled on. I prayed we would break through the line of storms before they shook our plane apart.

A few minutes later my prayer was answered as the billowing forms around us split and we popped into the clear.

"See?" Farnham exulted. "Told you. You can always get through if you're not afraid to try."

Airman Tunkelman took one look out the window and cast me a glance that made clear he thought lieutenants like me gave the major too much benefit of the doubt. He threw off his shoulder harness and climbed down into the cabin. The cabin is a loadmaster's happy place. How much time he spends there is a good indication of what he thinks of his pilots, and for a while we droned without seeing Jamie.

Our clear air was temporary. We crossed over the mountains to the east of Soto Cano with Tegucigalpa back at our four o'clock, but almost immediately we had to deviate further east to avoid a line of storms.

The mountains were hidden in the deck below us. The updrafts off their crests pushed thunderheads into the sky that built and stretched in the same direction we were flying. As quickly as we popped out of the clouds we went back into them.

"Whoa!" Farnham exclaimed as we bounced against our shoulder harnesses. "Hold on!"

Whereas the first turbulence had been a steady rumble this time it was unpredictable wallops. Great thrusts pushed us up or down every few seconds. Behind us in the latrine the fire extinguisher fell off the wall.

"Holdin' it...steady..." the major spoke to himself as our instruments bounced on the panel and the turbulence chopped his sentences. "Nothing you can do...but hold...it...steady."

And he did a good job holding it steady. I suggested to him twice that we deviate more to the east to get ahead of the storms but he refused. That had logic to it – we were already in the storms so we might just as well fly through them as turn around and deviate. But the problem was we didn't know how far they went. I started to worry that maybe the coast was socked in.

WHAM!

An updraft slapped the bottom of the plane and shook every rivet in the fuselage. Then a downdraft came behind it that gave us the falling elevator effect. Jamie slid into his folding seat by the crew entrance door just in time as we all rose off our cushions to float in the humid air. For a moment it actually felt pleasant.

CRASH!

The mule didn't think so. How much he got airborne I didn't see but the instant he came down he decided that enough was enough. Light turbulence was one thing; getting tossed around the cabin was another. He hit the floor with a clank on his shoes and immediately reared and kicked with both hind feet. The crate behind him exploded as though hit by a cannon ball.

"Hey! Whoa, hey there bossy, calm down! Whoa!"

Jamie threw off his seat belt and jumped in front of the mule waving his arms. The mule didn't calm down. He kicked again, sending gallons of bleach flying across the cabin. Then again, sending a can of whitewash crashing against the wall of the cabin where it burst open and splattered everything from the rescue litter down. Jamie fought the urge to spontaneously combust. He tried to pat the mule on the head but the animal jumped around too fast for him to get close.

"Here, here," he pleaded. "Come on, damn it. There's a good horsie. Behave now and I'll give you a treat. Coo, coo." He fumbled in his pockets for a granola bar and held it out to his passenger.

The mule ignored him. We hit another updraft that shoved both of them off-balance. The mule staggered sideways against the wall of the cabin and knocked the broom and the first aid kit to the floor. When Jamie reached to pick them up the mule staggered back and broadsided him, throwing him into the latrine. Then he stomped on the broomstick and broke it, and scattered the kit contents over the floor.

"Now that does it!" Jamie wailed, emerging from the latrine. "Calm my ass, you long-eared bastard!..." He leaped for the mule's halter to rein him in. The mule lunged in turn and bit at Jamie's arm, causing our loadmaster to retreat to the cockpit and leave a piece of his flight suit behind. He threw himself up the steps as the mule strained at his harness to reach him.

"What's wrong?" I asked, preoccupied with the clouds.

"What's wrong?!" he repeated, cowering at the center panel. "Look! *That's* what's wrong."

He pointed into the cabin but didn't have to. The noise of the mule's havoc climbed above the din of the engines. The animal also began to bray with a vengeance. For a few minutes that preoccupied him but when a bolt of lighting lit up the clouds in front of us and glazed the air in the cabin, his eyes almost popped out of his head. He braced himself with his forelegs and began a new assault on whatever was behind him. Crates, bags, and barrels went flying. The targets varied because with each new jolt of turbulence the mule pivoted with the bump and kicked in a new direction.

The padding on the walls from the latrine back to Station 280 separated and shredded under the onslaught, throwing up ticking that floated in the cabin like snow. The cleaning supplies on the first pallet disappeared – containers of paint and gallon jugs of bleach lay broken and leaking all over the cabin. The pallet itself – the wooden one that we tied down on top of the larger steel mat – was in pieces.

Jamie watched the destruction and scowled. He counted his fingertips again and considered his words carefully.

"Did your trip to the Grand Canyon end on a happy note, sir?"

Farnham had yet to look over his shoulder to see the damage but his tone was parental.

"Now, Airman Tunkelman, don't get upset."

"No, really. Did you get lots of nice pictures? Did your kids dip their toes in the Rio Grande? Did you have lunch at the lodge and get to pitch tents along the rim?"

"Now you're being sarcastic..."

"You said he would be quiet!" Jamie barked. "You said they put up with anything!"

"They do," Farnham replied, holding us as steady as he could on an altitude close to 15,000 feet. "You must have tied him too tight."

Jamie reached for the nav table, intending to grab one of his Popular Mechanics magazines and roll it up to beat the pilot about the head and neck. But just then the mule started kicking the fold-down seats by the door. Since the seat frames were aluminum and would bend in a strong breeze, now Jamie saw his own real estate under assault. He grabbed the broken broom and batted it against the mule to force him back to the center of the cabin

As he fought his battle we popped out of our cloud bank and saw that our weather problems weren't over. Another line of storms stood between us and the coast. Worse, our radar showed cells out over the ocean as well, moving inland. We might get to La Ceiba and not be able to land.

"Take the controls, will you?" Farnham asked me, mopping his brow. "This is wearing me out." I did and immediately turned parallel to the storms. Almost certainly we would have to go back to Soto Cano.

The major looked back into the cabin and his jaw dropped. The cargo hold was a shambles. Paint was everywhere and there was a strong smell of bleach. Worse, his loadmaster was in hand-to-hoof combat with our only passenger. "Airman Tunkelman," he cried, "what are you doing?!"

Jamie backed off from the mule and retreated to the cockpit steps. He struggled to be calm.

"Sir, I want that mule off of my plane."

"No, Airman Tunkelman. You need to get him under control."

"Under control?! Are you insane? *You* get him under control. *I* didn't want him on my plane in the first place!"

"He's excited. Calm him down somehow."

"How? Sing to him? Tell him a story? Every time we hit a bump he wigs out. In two seconds I'm going to open the door and airdrop his ass. There's no way..." He stopped speaking and sniffed the air. At the same moment my eyes began to burn. Maj Farnham rubbed his nose and glared at us.

"Did one of you fart?" he asked.

I glanced around the cockpit. There was an acrid smell, usually a sign of an electrical fire. Tiny bits of ticking drifted in the air but now there was something else, too. A haze...

"Circuit breakers?" I asked.

We scanned the panel behind my head but none of the breakers was popped. Then the mule brayed anew and brought our attention back to the cabin. He'd stopped kicking and was panting for breath. From the pallets behind him a yellow steam rose and filled the top half of the cabin.

"Smoke!" Jamie repeated. We all grabbed for our oxygen masks.

Our masks were of the quick-don type, designed to throw over our headsets and cover the whole face. By the time I got mine in place my eyes were tearing so I flipped the switch to Emergency. That blew pressurized oxygen through the mask until it leaked out the sides, blowing away the fumes but making me feel like a fat man sucking on a balloon. For a while I couldn't talk.

"Smoke and fume elimination checklist!" Major Farnham gasped.

I pointed to him since I was flying. He fumbled for the checklist and called out the steps.

I turned us back toward Soto Cano while he read, curving east to avoid the storms we had just passed through. The Tacan needle pointing to the base fell to our three o'clock.

"We need to depressurize," Farnham advised. "Jamie, I'm going to dial our altitude up and then pop the cork."

Jamie didn't answer. He swapped his mask for the portable oxygen bottle and stumbled down the cabin to see what he could do about the smoke. The mule, now shaky on its feet, let him pass.

"Slow down," Farnham directed, his voice muffled by the rubber mask even though he was still speaking into a mike. "We might need to open doors."

I slowed to 180 knots but kept a bank in to circumvent the worst weather. Off to our right where the air base lay, a thunderhead climbed higher than any of us would ever fly. Through the roof window I saw an anvil form. Anvils only form at the top of the worst thunderstorms, and this one looked very bad indeed.

Jamie pulled the fertilizer bags apart with the idea of separating them. His first thought was that one or more of the bags had caught fire somehow so he dragged one after another off the pallet and onto the floor. Then he grabbed what was left of the broom and swept away pellets from the broken ones so they wouldn't burn. Loose urea spilled into the pools of bleach. More chlorine gas filled the air and he soon realized his mistake.

"Oh, damn!" he hooked into the intercom and reported. "It's not a fire, it's gas. And I just made it worse. It's World War One back here."

We descended to 10,000 feet and de-pressurized, then opened the troop doors. With the doors cracked the fumes were sucked outside but there was no way to stop the fertilizer from making more as long as the bleach lasted. Jamie wanted to start throwing bags overboard but Major Farnham nixed that: we were back in the clouds and there was no way to know what we would be dropping them on. Then came the bad news over the radio from Soto Cano.

"We're socked in, sir. The rain's just sitting on the field. I've got no viz outside my door and I'm only fifty yards from the ramp."

That left Tegucigalpa.

"We have 2000 feet ceiling and five miles visibility," the never-reliable tower controller in the capital told us when we called him. *"Explain your emergency again, please?"*

I turned us south in a broader arc around the storms. We were twenty miles from the city but had to maneuver to get to the instrument final approach on the other side of the airport. That gave us time to set up for the landing. It also gave Farnham time to swallow his pride.

It was silent in the cockpit as he chewed over the situation. For once I was glad to wear the claustrophobic blue rubber mask – it hid my smug look.

In the cabin the mule fell to his knees. Jamie knelt by its side for a while in sympathy but finally admitted he wasn't concerned enough to share any of his oxygen and so came back up front. He climbed into the third seat and looked over our shoulders.

"So what's the plan?" he asked when neither Farnham nor I spoke.

Farnham looked away out his window at the swirling mass of gray that hid the mountains around Tegucigalpa, regarding them much as he had the more benign stratus layer earlier in the day. When he didn't say anything I answered in as neutral a tone as my ego would allow: "We'll be flying an approach into the city."

Jamie nodded, the hose on his oxygen mask flopping like the dewlap on a rooster. He understood immediately what that meant.

"An approach, eh? Would that be an *instrument* approach?" he asked, his voice muffled but all the sarcasm making it through the wires nonetheless. "In that case, colonel, here...let me go through your bags and find that officially-sponsored Department of Defense plate for you so you can fly it. Oh, wait...I just remembered, we don't *have* an approved approach for Tegucigalpa..."

Farnham's mask twitched as he chewed his lower lip.

"This gas is getting worse back here," Jamie continued. "I don't think this donkey's going to make it. The Hondurans may have to eat him when we land 'cause he sure doesn't look healthy enough to carry anything. But we can't land, can we? There's no way to find our way through these clouds. We'll just drone around up here in the weather until we run out of gas and crash. Oh, and I'm so young..."

We curved around the southeast corner of the city and crossed the lead radial for the approach. I intercepted final and then pulled the photocopied plate out of the holder. Handing it to Jamie I motioned for him to prop it below the weather radar so all three of us could use it. He clapped his hands together in feigned shock.

"What's this? Forbidden fruit? Oh, thank the lord! Praise the heavens above someone had the courage to break the rules. Someone kept his thinking cap on and brought along a copy of this forbidden, prohibited, untested, dangerous...”

“Alright, alright!” Farnham snapped. He didn’t have his mask on Emergency so some of the mustard gas seeped in and his voice was raspy as though he was fighting an allergy. “I get it. I get it already. Yes, it’s a good thing we have this approach right now. But you have to understand that in a world-wide operational environment, a sound strategic decision has to...”

I held up my hand.

“Sir, could we talk about this later? We need to fly this course.”

He agreed but reluctantly, tapping his hand rapidly against his leg in frustration. For his part Jamie’s anger was up so high that he bounced with adrenalin in the third seat and punched a fist into his other palm as though warming up for a bout. Farnham took that as a victory dance of some sort. I flew down final to the minimum descent altitude thinking that at any moment the two of them would jump on each other and start grappling.

We broke out at a thousand feet just after crossing into the bowl around the city. A couple of civilian airliners sat at the terminal and a swarm of vehicles drove in all directions around the ramp but none of the activity seemed geared to greet us as a declared emergency. It wasn’t until we landed and turned off at the end of the runway that two cars approached:

one was the Follow Me truck and the other was a blue sedan with an Andy Griffith patrol car light on the roof. Neither was in a hurry.

I parked and shut down the engines. Major Farnham signaled for everyone to get out but put a hand on my shoulder as we headed for the ramp.

"Lieutenant Bleriot, we'll need to report this, of course, but I don't think it's necessary to get into the discussion over approach plates. I'll have a quiet talk with Capt Fetterman and recommend that maybe all of our crews should carry some emergency plates, you know, just in case, but other than that I don't see a reason to bring it up, do you?"

I used my face mask as an excuse not to respond and waved him toward the clear air outside.

Ten minutes later we had all the doors open and as much of the urea as we could shovel off the plane outside and in the grass by the side of the ramp. Chlorine gas still drifted out the doors like a persistent fog. The mule lay on its side, unconscious. To get it into fresh air we had to unload everything else, then Jamie hooked tie-down straps to its feet and backed the Follow Me truck close enough to lash them to its hitch. Once we pulled the animal into the grass, though, we didn't have a clue what to do. I didn't, anyway, and neither did Major Farnham.

Jaime, however, knew exactly what to do. The driver of the blue sedan was the airfield manager and in lieu of medical support he'd brought a clipboard and an instamatic camera to document our emergency. Jamie bought the camera from him for ten dollars and immediately started snapping pictures, dashing around to make sure he got Major Farnham and the mule in the same frame as often as possible.

"This is for the investigation up north," he proclaimed when Major Farnham protested. "You know, so the Air Force can do another study and ban something else from now on. Like compasses, maybe, or oxygen bottles or anything else we don't need. And," he pointed at his boss, "this is definitely going in the log! Yes, there's a log! And it's a BIG one, too damned big if you ask me. And we keep it right where everyone can see it!"

He scampered away as Farnham grabbed for the camera and chased him across the ramp.

"I'm going to Mexico on this one!" Jaime called to me over his shoulder as they raced down the taxiway. "Me and the mule, we're going to Mexico and there's a good chance we're not coming back!"

9. Griswold Beckett

THERE WERE A lot of people Lowell Hendricks didn't like and Griswold Beckett was at the top of the list.

Getting on Lowell's list wasn't hard; you just had to do something to tick him off. That could mean listening to the wrong music, driving too aggressively, not driving aggressively enough, surfing like a queer (Skinny Steve's transgression), or showing up at a party with whores when there were already host-supplied whores there – which Lowell's own roommate Kurt did on a regular basis. But to get to the top of Lowell's list you had to do something really out of the ordinary, something really incredibly moronic or obnoxious or dangerous that would catch Lowell's attention. Griswold had tried to kill him.

He did it the standard way, by almost crashing the airplane in which they were both flying. Griswold was the aircraft commander and Lowell the co-pilot on a re-supply trip they made to Araracuara, far off in the eastern lowlands of Peru. Like Site 3, Araracuara was a radar site perched on a hill deep within the jungle. A sliver of an airstrip between the trees served as its only link with the outside world. At one end of the strip was the camp, at the other a deep ravine. There was a berm at the lip of the ravine but otherwise nothing to keep someone from driving off the edge into the abyss were they so inclined.

Lowell knew Araracuara already. He'd flown there once with Papps as his aircraft commander and Junior Flats as the load. They picked up a trio of pallets that the Army guys in the camp assured them weighed 2,500 lbs apiece. In fact the pallets weighed almost 4,000 lbs each. On take-off the C-27 hit its acceleration targets and clawed its way into the air but then couldn't climb out of ground effect, that generous cushion of air half a wingspan from the surface. It wouldn't accelerate, either. Unable to stop, Papps and Lowell saw themselves cruising at 100 mph toward the berm, the ravine, and the sea of trees beyond it.

"Up! Up! Up!" screamed the normally talkative Papps, now reduced to monosyllables.

Lowell, who was flying, fought with the controls. When he pulled back, the wings shuddered in a stall and they fell back to earth, bouncing on the dirt.

"Uuuuupppppp!!!! Goddammit, uuuupppppp!!!"

Lowell shoved the power levers to their stops, over-torqueing both engines but getting the aircraft airborne again just before they plowed into the berm. The berm skimmed the gear...and then the ground disappeared beneath them. With it went the ground effect. The aircraft dropped like a tired elevator.

"Ahhhh!!!! Down! Down! Down!"

That wasn't hard. Lowell pushed over. The nose tilted its way into the ravine. They had 600 feet to get airspeed that would keep them from crashing.

By Lowell's reckoning they needed 540 of those feet. He pulled back late enough to have the accelerometer spike at 4Gs but with an airspeed of 160 knots, good enough to raise the flaps and gear without sinking into the river bottom. Papps slapped the dump switches. Fuel cascaded into the pristine water below, helping them lose enough weight that five miles later they were able to gain a 200 foot-per-minute climb and exit the ravine before it narrowed and snapped their wings off.

Lowell didn't like that kind of excitement. He liked the kind where it was rush hour in Panama City and he could pull into the Circle of Death in his pickup and drive around it again and again in order to keep Panas from merging into the inside lane. Or the kind where he walked into the Strac Club on Saturday night and threw a fistful of dollars into the air just to watch local girls scramble over each other to get at the money. Almost crashing into a river in Peru wasn't his game. For a long time he was depressed over that day, keeping to himself and not the drinking buddy he'd been before.

But by the time he flew into Araracuara with Griswold, Lowell was past all that. He had more experience under his belt. He knew enough not to trust the Army. Now if someone in BDUs told him the sky was blue, Lowell demanded proof. If a sergeant-major produced three pallets of Styrofoam that would blow away in a light breeze, Lowell insisted they drag out the scales and demonstrate the weight to the last ounce. If a stick of twelve Rangers hopped onto the plane for a parachute jump, Lowell stalked through the cabin and counted them three times just to make sure they hadn't hidden an extra battalion somewhere in their rucks. He didn't trust the Army, he didn't like the Army, and he wouldn't hang out with the Army. He'd learned his lesson.

So when they almost crashed on take-off the reason had nothing to do with the Army. It was all Griswold.

In the C-27 when the co-pilot makes the take-off the pilot still controls aircraft steering below 60 knots using the nose wheel. The ailerons aren't effective yet below that speed; so, since the nose wheel steering grip is on the left side of the cockpit by the pilot's elbow, it's all his show. At 60 knots the co-pilot calls, "Co-pilot's controls," whereupon the pilot releases the grip, the nose steering deactivates, and the co-pilot handles things from there on out.

Except that Araracuara, as mentioned, is a short runway. The trees press in close on both sides. The actual landing surface is narrow and the drop-off at the end is steep. It's an intimidating experience to sit at one end of the clearing and look at the other and wonder if you'll make it airborne by the time you get there. Especially if you're an idiot.

So Griswold didn't let go of the nose wheel steering at 60 knots when Lowell called for it. Instead he gripped the joystick like it was the railing of a ship whose deck he'd just fallen over, the white knuckled, bone-cracking grip of a man who is staring death in the face and rendered immobile from the act.

"Hey! Leggo!" Lowell yelled as they hurtled down the runway and Griswold, shaking in fear, pitched them from one side of the strip to the other.

"Uhhrrrrghaa..." Griswold replied. Skinny and stoop-shouldered, he leaned in his seat like an anxious bowler, perhaps trying to will the plane onto a straight takeoff roll or maybe fear just robbing him of normal balance. Wherever he leaned the plane went with him. The grunts watching their takeoff must have figured they were drunk.

"Let go of the steering, goddammit!" Lowell shrieked.

At seventy or eighty knots the ailerons were no good to Lowell yet, not enough to override the nose wheel, anyway. He needed the nose wheel grip to steer but that was on Griswold's side of the cockpit. Lowell wrenched the flight controls to no avail. A wing clipped leaves. The plane tipped up off its right gear. They passed their acceleration checkpoint, nowhere near their numbers.

"Leggo, leggo, leggo! ABORT!"

Lowell yanked the power levers to idle and stomped on the brakes as hard as he could. Everyone flew forward against their harness.

The C-27 skidded across the dirt, gravel rattling the underside of the fuselage like a volley of small-caliber shells. The tires grabbed at the ground. Great, curving tracks marked their progress as they fought the plane's momentum every foot to the precipice, the left pair finally sinking into a patch of soft sand that dragged the nose ninety degrees to the left and let the plane slew sideways to a stop against the berm. A cloud of trailing dust caught up to the plane and enveloped it.

For a few minutes the soldiers back at the camp couldn't tell if the C-27 had gone over the edge or not. Some ran to help. Others stood and listened, awaiting an explosion.

In the cockpit nobody moved. Until the air cleared for all they knew they were teetering on the edge, ready to plummet to the river. When it did and they could see, the sight wasn't much better. The right wingtip hung over the ravine. The berm touched Lowell's window. Without craning his neck he could see down into his favorite canyon. That jolted him. He pried his feet from the toe pedals and exploded.

"What were you doing!" he screamed across the cockpit. The fact that Griswold outranked him was suddenly irrelevant. "What the FUCK were you doing? What the fucking, mother-fucking, sonofa-bitching goddamned fucking hell were you doing, you stupid motherfucker!?"

Griswold hunched in his seat, his tiny head tilted toward his lap with eyes shut tight. He breathed heavily through his mouth, each exhalation a prayer. His hand clutched the steering grip so tightly his fingers could have warped the metal.

"You shithead! You stupid shithead! You could have killed us!"

Lowell started crying. He beat his fist on the dash.

"You can't fly! You can't steer! You can't even get off the ground! You're a useless sack of shit! How did you ever make it through pilot training? How are you a captain? You were going to kill us!..."

Griswold's eyes opened. He looked up, waking from his bad dream and trying to put reality into context. He was never an intelligent man but now, gazing around the cockpit as though taking things in that others had missed, he collected himself. The basics made it through the fog: crisis situation...hysteria...no one in charge...something wrong... You could almost see the pages of the officer's leadership manual turning in his mind, the professional hamster climbing back onto the big blue Air Force treadmill and trotting away. Must assert control, he thought. Must lead...

"Lieutenant," he held up his hand for silence. He frowned. "Why did you abort the takeoff, lieutenant?

That was dangerous. We might not have stopped in time."

He twisted in his seat to level a calm if confused gaze on his crew, reassuring them that things were back in control.

"I recommend that we..."

Lowell hit him. Punched him straight in the mouth so hard it broke Griswold's lip. Blood flew up to mix with the floating dust.

Fortunately for Beckett, Leonard Mondavi was their loadmaster that day. As big as he was, it took all his strength to pull Lowell out of the cockpit before the young lieutenant beat their aircraft commander to death.

However, the great thing about Griswold Beckett was that he was, in fact, an idiot. Not the kind of guy who was inconsistent, who some people liked and respected and who others felt was lacking upstairs. No, Griswold was universally acknowledged – at least in our squadron – to be a moron and a bad pilot. He flew alright in the pattern, on sunny days when the winds weren't strong and the goal was just to make takeoffs and landings. He wasn't bad on instruments, either, so long as he had plenty of time to set up and the weather was cloudy but not dangerous. But sunny landings and long radar patterns don't make a pilot. Ugly days do, the ones that have the potential for turning scary but don't because the guy in the cockpit knows what he's doing. As Walt reminded us when he learned to quote Seneca, "You learn to know a pilot in a storm." Griswold just wasn't there. He wasn't at that level. It wasn't a particularly high level but he still wasn't there. A rule in flying is, never let your plane get someplace your brain didn't arrive at five minutes earlier. Griswold couldn't do that. Somewhere in his world, deep in the recesses of his inadequate brain, he might have felt comfortable flying a Cessna around the pattern in a rural part of Kansas where there was nothing to hit and there were lots of places to land. But in the C-27 he was out of his depth.

Sadly, he knew it. He wouldn't admit it but he knew it, enough that he often weaseled out of flights. Major Harmon called Griswold a pigeon. As the squadron scheduler Harmon had to get everyone up in the air regularly to keep current in flying events like instrument approaches, airdrops, assault landings, etc. Griswold came up with so many excuses why he couldn't fly that Harmon claimed he needed to throw rocks at the man to get him airborne. Griswold desperately wanted the Wing Safety job where he could sit and write reports all day, talking about flying without actually doing it. Most of us sincerely wanted him to get it.

"You know, he's religious," Josh told me one day.

"He ought to be the way he flies."

"No, I'm serious."

"So am I."

"He's a God-fearing Baptist."

"You say that like it should count for something."

"Goes to church every Sunday and holds Bible study in his house on base. I guess he's friends with the wing commander that way."

"That's right," I remembered. "Heidl's a nutcase, too, isn't he?"

Josh bristled. "Just because he believes in God doesn't mean he's a nutcase."

"No," I agreed. "Believing in God doesn't make him a nutcase. Wearing it on his sleeve and talking like the Second Coming is around the corner makes him a nutcase."

"Does he do that?"

"Have you ever been to the weekly wing stand-up?" I replied, referring to the commander's staff meeting. "I had to go once last month to fill in for Rasmussen. First, we started with a prayer. Not one led by the chaplain – Heidl led it himself. He went on and on about how we were all blessed to be stationed in Panama, how he was blessed to have everyone show up for the meeting, how his family was blessed for blah-blah-blah, and how he wanted us all to turn to the person sitting next to us and thank them for their service. Then after everyone had briefed him on what was going on on base he said, 'Well, with the Lord's help we'll prevail in the face of these afflictions.' What the hell is that? Potholes on the main road aren't an affliction, they're a job for the civil engineers. Panas sneaking onto the base aren't an affliction, they're a security issue."

"Maybe he just takes his job to heart," Josh demurred.

"Julia Childs takes her job to heart. Heidl takes his job to church. Or rather, he takes his church to his job."

"There's nothing wrong with a little religion in your life," he insisted.

"Uh-huh. You know how to make God laugh?"

"How?"

"Tell him your plans."

"What's that supposed to mean?"

"It means if there's a god up there somewhere, do you really think he cares how many times you get down on your knees or bow your head or say bless this and bless that? Just do your job well – he'll worry about the translation."

"That's sacrilegious," Josh sniffed.

"Don't pray in my school and I won't think in your church."

"You're close-minded."

"Whatever. There's a time and a place for everything. If someone wants to believe in gods, fine. Just keep it to yourself."

"Maybe he can't," Josh suggested. "Maybe he thinks his meetings need a little...guidance."

"Josh, I don't want my military commander to be a starry-eyed Bible-thumper. I want him to be a cold, callous, no-nonsense, just-the-facts military professional who likes to kill people and blow things up. Listen, at that briefing I wasn't the only one in the room who was uncomfortable. All these lieutenant colonels and unit commanders were exchanging looks while John Brown up there was praying. They listen to him because they're afraid for their careers, not because they think he's a competent general. He's a nut."

Josh wanted to argue. He thought for a moment, eyeing me as a case study.

"You know, Mike," he suggested, working hard on a patient, didactic tone, "at some point in your life you start thinking about more than just the here and now. You wonder if there isn't more to the world than what you see in front of you."

"Grasshopper," I sighed, "that's called a midlife crisis. For now I'm 26 and still busy making mistakes so I have something to feel insecure about later."

"Don't you ever think about religion? About the future?"

"Sure, I think about religion every time I see something on TV about Jim and Tammy Faye Baker, or read in the paper how the Jews and Arabs are blowing up each other's kids because God gave a piece of land to one of them but forgot to sign the title. As for the future, to get there, Josh, I have to worry *right now* about ham-fisted Elmer Gantrys who can't fly their way out of a paper bag trying to kill me whenever I climb into the cockpit. And so do you, I might add."

"I've flown with him before. He's...slow."

"Slow?"

"Alright, he sucks. But he doesn't scare me."

"You've flown with him around the flagpole, Josh. Just watch him if you ever go down south. Beckett can pray all he wants. I just wish he would spend less time reading the Bible and more time studying the Dash 1 so he knows how take-off and landing data can kill you if you screw them up."

Josh gave up.

"Whatever," he waved his hand. "Maybe he does suck. What surprises me is how close-minded you are."

"About what?"

"Religion."

I laughed. "Dude, when I was twelve my parakeet died after I prayed for him to live. If that doesn't close your mind I don't know what will."

He shook his head.

"You should be careful," he warned.

"You, too. Don't fly with Beckett."

There was a rumor – just a rumor – about certain aircrew in the squadron considering murdering Garb Taylor shortly after the C-27 arrived in Panama. Garb, our permanent representative in Group Current Operations, was much like Griswold

Beckett in that he was almost thoroughly incompetent in the air. He made so many basic mistakes that could have resulted in catastrophe that within weeks of the initial cadre coming to Howard some were musing about taking things into their own hands if the leadership didn't find Garb a desk job. The rumor blossomed when Vince, one of our crew chiefs, casually told a story to some of the co-pilots about a civilian contract crew he knew who'd been faced with a similar situation of a dangerous flyer that the higher-ups refused to ground. Vince, a kind, professional, and ruthless man, knew how we felt about Griswold and didn't miss a chance to offer his crafty two-cents worth of subliminal influence. The contract crew, he said, took a page from the Chilean dictatorship's book and made the flyer "disappear," knocking him out and dumping his body over the ocean. "Pretty extreme," he shrugged, "but got the job done. Nobody's crashed in that outfit."

Griswold had once flown B-52s, the strategic bombers that plane-for-plane could carry more destructive firepower than all the bombs dropped by all sides during World War II. That fact alone would cause the Dalai Lama a year of sleepless nights. But flying the Buff gave Griswold a lot of flight hours. Hours were what counted when it came time to move up the ladder from co-pilot to pilot to instructor. What really got some of us thinking about aerocide was when Griswold's name popped up during an instructor meeting about future instructor pilot candidates. I wasn't in attendance but Walt informed us later that no one from the squadron had mentioned Beckett's name. It was broached by none other than Brad Giverson.

"Why?" Lowell asked Walt. "Giverson's a hammer on check rides. Why would he want to see Beckett moved up to instructor?"

Walt shrugged. "He probably doesn't. Knowing Giverson, I don't think he gives a rat's ass about anyone but Giverson. But there are two reasons he might throw Beckett's name out: one, he hasn't flown with him and so doesn't know how bad he is; two, Giverson briefs the general every week. The general is chummy with Beckett – so I hear – and may have mentioned something to Giverson. Giverson *wants* to be chummy with the general so if the big man says Beckett should be an IP, than Brad's going to make it happen."

"What was the reaction of the other IPs in the meeting?" I asked.

An impish smile crawled across Walt's face.

"About what you'd expect. Charlie said, 'The guy's a moron' and left it at that. No corporate man, Charlie. Fetterman said he'd think about it but then when Giverson pushed the issue he dug in his heels and said that Beckett didn't have theater experience yet so wouldn't upgrade anytime soon. Which, of course, was the wrong thing to say because he and

Brad don't get along anyway so if Fetterman's against the idea of upgrading Beckett then Giverson's going to push it even harder. Everyone else – Flutie, Bob Harcourt, Mike – was pretty negative on the idea."

"As they should be."

"How about you?" I asked. "What did you say?"

Walt gazed upward.

"I prayed to the Lord my God for guidance."

"Uh-huh. And what'd He suggest?"

"He said not no, but hell no."

"Damned straight," Lowell nodded.

"On the other hand, Lowell," Walt suggested, deliberately provoking him, "maybe's there's a bigger picture than you see here."

"Uh-huh. And maybe you're a handsome man and your wife married you for your looks. That bastard almost killed me. There's no bigger picture than that. There's no way they can make him an IP. I'm not kidding, he'll kill someone."

"Or a bunch of someones," I added. "What if he loads up a bunch of hoo-ahs out at Araracuara and pulls another 'Allah will provide' stunt on take-off?"

"He's Baptist," Walt replied. "I don't think you have to worry about Allah."

"Whoever. You know what I mean."

"Yeah, I do. But," he held up his hands. "We had our meeting. We put in our votes. It's up to the leadership now to decide."

The leadership compromised. They decided to make Griswold a 60-1 instructor. A *sixty-dash-one* IP was one who could teach on local sorties but not on tactical flights. In other words, in Panama Griswold would be able to impart his wisdom to the rest of us but on flights north or south he was still a line pilot. This didn't sit well with most guys in the squadron but it was a clever move on Lt Col Rasmussen's part given the situation he was in. Heidl wanted Beckett to be an instructor; Rasmussen made him one while creating minimum risk to the rest of his flyers. Walt, his perspective and humor intact, promised us quietly that as scheduler he would make sure Beckett never got out of the pattern.

However, the god I didn't believe in showed his own sense of humor the following week. Walt got an opportunity to go to the Advanced Instrument School and left for a two-week trip to the States. Major Harmon, standing in for him at the ops desk, scheduled me and Josh for a three-day LNO swap down in Colombia. Then, seeing the long days we would fly, at the last minute he threw Beckett onto the crew as well.

All was fine for the first two days. We flew into Bogotá and hooked up with Fast Eddie and his girls. The first day we did a quick shuttle down to Apiay and Villavicencio. Josh was the aircraft commander so Griswold and I took turns playing co-pilot. The weather was clear during the day and we always managed to land before it got dark when the thunderstorms preferred to form.

On day two we were tasked with a long triangle of flight that took us to Buenaventura on the coast, Florencia in the south foothills, then to Leticia in the southeast before returning to the capital. Except for Florencia all the airfields had paved concrete strips. Brian Wilson, our taciturn loadmaster whose dream was to leave the tropics and get an assignment up to Alaska where he could frolic in the cold and snow, hopped out at each one and frowned.

"Hmmph!" he said at Buenaventura. "Looks like a C-130 strip to me. Runway's so wide we could land cross-ways."

He was right but that happened sometimes. Not every flight Eddie coordinated took us into the sticks. Sometimes we just moved troops from one big town to another because that's what the Colombians wanted. Eddie traded favors like that for things the U.S. wanted like flexible flight clearances and intelligence on the drug runners. If it meant we occasionally did the job of a Herc, I didn't mind. Flying was flying. Even places like Villavicencio and Leticia were closer to the middle of nowhere than most.

Florencia certainly was. It was nothing unusual, a medium-sized town on the edge of the jungle halfway between the Apaporis and Caqueta rivers. There was little around it for miles besides farmland pushing up to the foothills and a dark brown airstrip one-half mile south. The strip was flat. Narrow but flat and almost a mile long. The only obstacle was a fence running along the west side, outside our wing-tip but close enough to keep an eye on. We needed to drop off four Colombians there to do god knows what. We would be in and out in five minutes.

I had wanted to be in the seat for the leg into Florencia precisely because it was the only rough surface on the schedule for today. Josh and Griswold flew to Buenaventura where we picked up the first troops and at that point Griswold and I should have swapped. However, on the ground I had to run into the terminal to clear up a flight plan misunderstanding with the locals. By the time I got back Josh had the engines running and was impatient to go. I jumped in the door as they were taxiing and settled into the back.

"Well, I guess I'll hop out," Griswold said after we climbed to our cruising altitude.

"Nah, it's a short flight," Josh said. "Stay in the seat and we'll get Mike up here for the trip to Leticia."

The pause on the microphone was pregnant.

"Uh, I think Lieutenant Bleriot wanted this leg," Griswold persisted.

"Oh, well then, let's ask *Lieutenant* Bleriot," Josh replied sarcastically. "What do you want to do, Mike?"

I wanted to fly but the hint of nervousness in Beckett's tone suddenly made me change my mind. He was afraid of the dirt strip.

"No, no, not at all," I called cheerily. "It's all you, Griswold."

Sergeant Wilson made an O with his mouth to signal his amusement. Griswold hated it when lieutenants called him by his first name – he preferred 'Captain Beckett.' It was perfectly alright for lieutenants and captains, all company-grade officers, to be informal. But just as there were guys like Fetterman who wanted to be reminded they were a 'Major-select,' there were guys like Griswold who wanted lieutenants to remember he was a captain.

"I don't want to take the lieutenant's leg," Griswold resisted. "He needs the experience. I'll get out."

That did it. *He needs the experience?* I could fly rings around this clown. *He* needed the experience, not me, though I doubted it would do him any good.

"No, no, stay up there," I insisted through gritted teeth. "I did a trip down here two weeks ago. You should get your turn."

Wilson knew exactly what was going on. He'd flown with both of us before and was laughing freely behind his microphone. Josh figured it out, too.

"Alright, ladies. Forget it," he said with disgust. "Griswold, just stay up here. We'll swap out on the ground like I said."

I wouldn't leave it alone.

"I agree, Josh. I think that's the best decision. Griswold can get the landing into Florencia, then I'll get one later in the day."

"No, no!" Griswold jumped back in. "I don't need the landing. You have it, pilot."

Looking up toward the cockpit I could see Josh shaking his head, no doubt wondering how he'd gotten himself into this situation.

"Griswold, when was the last time you flew into a dirt strip?" he asked bluntly.

Beckett shrugged.

"Last week."

"Where?"

"Fort Sherman. I shot approaches there all day with Captain Vaneya."

"That's NOT a dirt strip. I said a *dirt* strip. Is there any dirt on Fort Sherman?"

In the cabin I punched my fist into the air, much to Wilson's delight. Josh was so wonderfully un-subtle.

"Well, no," Griswold explained. "But it's an assault strip. I thought that's what you meant."

"No, I meant a *dirt* strip. Fort Sherman's tight but it never changes and we go there all the time. A dirt strip in Colombia isn't so predictable. You do the approach to Florencia. It'll be good for you."

I couldn't see Griswold's face but imagined from his silence that it was pained. He was a small man with a slight build and one of the smallest heads I'd ever seen on an adult. When he was under stress he winced and pursed his lips and drew deep furrows in his brow that made his whole face scrunch down to two-thirds its already small size. If the prayers hadn't started already, they would soon.

In southern Colombia the eastern range of the Andes is forbidding. Forbidding but not downright scary the way it gets further south in Peru and Chile. Its menace is real but it hides a beautiful alpine landscape, one that while not friendly is at least user-tolerant. From afar the terrain looks dry and jagged but close up it's green. Curving valleys and high mesas lie among the peaks. Sub-alpine forest gives way to scrub brush and grassland which in turn give way to rock. There's always snow on the high ground. In winter it coats the mountains in deep, even drifts and in summer it clings to the ridges and north-south shadows. Sunlight reaches where it can and pushes water down thin cracks in the canyon walls, letting isolated farmers and distant villages exist where one would think they couldn't, sharing space with goats and sheep and llama in crisp cold air that leaves visitors gasping to breathe.

Flying over the range we usually went as high as we could, 20,000-22,000 feet. That allowed us to receive the navaids along the coast for as long as possible and also gave us more time to glide in case we lost an engine. But even at that altitude we were often only three to four thousand feet above the terrain. Dormant volcanoes like Puracé and Huila, silent and poised, watched us pass. We kept a wary eye on them always, knowing how easy it would be to smack their sides if there was bad weather or it was night and we had to descend due to icing or low power. In turn they watched us through heavy-lidded, igneous eyes, biding their time, knowing they could toss us from the sky with a moderate belch of sub-surface power and never note the effort. Sometimes they hid in the weather, their cones wreathed in a mantle of white cloud. Sometimes they thrust up gray-and-white summits against the blue sky, every notch and ridge along the plunging *faldas* visible with startling clarity from miles away in the high thin air.

Normally one who likes to fly low, I loved looking out the window when we flew over the Andes. I say loved, but it was love with a hint of masochism, the way one loves going faster and faster on a motorcycle knowing that any second it could all end in disaster. From my pressurized cockpit I could admire the beauty and power of the mountains and enjoy feeling nervous at the same time. Awe at nature's strength and size mixed with an acute awareness that only the most tenuous silken strands held me suspended above it all. The Andes were the gate-keepers to the jungle, the border between the coastal desert and the inland garden, a wall thrust up from the earth to keep lesser mortals from mingling between the two. My nervousness came from knowing that we were cheating the system, using technology to vault the wall and defy nature's guardians. I knew the mountains knew it, too. I could see it in the ponderous, supremely confident way they went about their business, shouldering the massive responsibility of being one of the world's largest ranges. They knew that in the age-old struggle between man and the world, you always bet on the world. Given the chance, given one tiny mechanical malfunction of either of my engines, they would pull us from the air and show us just how puny we really were.

Maybe Griswold was in awe, too. He started his descent late, way late, so we arrived over Florencia still at four thousand feet. We approached the town from the west and circled south looking for the airfield. Finding it we saw that the strip ran mostly north-south. Josh directed Griswold to set up for a left base to final. His plan was to overfly the field once, then come around and land.

Griswold worked his way to final but leveled off when Josh turned his attention to the checklist. The result was that we were still two thousand feet up when he banked toward the runway.

"Uh," Josh observed with unsuppressed sarcasm, "we're not going to see much from up here, are we?"

"Oh, well, I didn't want to descend too low while you were head's-down with the checklist."

Josh sighed.

"Well, then take us around again. Fly over no higher than five hundred feet."

We circled and rolled out on final again. Josh saw smoke from a cooking fire at a nearby farm and pronounced the winds calm.

"Five hundred feet, Griswold."

"Well, I was thinking a thousand would give us a better view..."

"No, five hundred will give us a better view. That's why I said it the first time. Get down."

We descended some more. Leaning over Brian Wilson's shoulder I could see the fence on the left side of the strip. A dirt road that wasn't on the map paralleled the fence. There was no traffic on it.

"Couple of holes," Josh noted. "The surface is rutted but nothing serious. The fence is short enough. Might be dusty toward the end where the grass peters out. Looks like we're good to go."

Griswold pulled up and right toward a downwind leg.

"Maybe you should do the landing," he suggested. "I think you were able to see more of the runway than I was."

"That's because you flew down the right side of the strip instead of the left. Most guys who are doing the landing will make sure they can see it themselves. Now you'll just have to take my word for it. It's good. Nothing out of the ordinary. Take a look out your window on downwind if you want to see more."

We rolled out at a thousand feet facing south. Griswold slowed and Josh lowered the gear and flaps. Griswold briefed the speeds he would fly on final but delayed his turn to base until the airstrip fell way back to our five o'clock. When Josh finally said something he turned reluctantly, as though hoping that by continuing to fly away from the strip we would all forget about Florencia and just continue on our way. I began to wonder if it had been such a smart move to put Griswold on the spot.

"Okay, how does this picture look to you?" Josh asked when they had rolled out on a three-mile final.

"Uh...," Griswold hesitated. "A little low?"

Josh shrugged. "No, it's not low. Well, maybe it is but that's only because we're so far out. This is a bomber pattern. You're not in B-52s anymore, Griswold."

Griswold chuckled nervously.

"I wish I was," he said quietly to himself, but not so quietly that it didn't come over the intercom.

We droned in, the brown gash in the midst of green growing taller and wider in the windscreen.

"Bring it down," Josh prompted.

Griswold lowered the nose but from my position on the cockpit steps I could see it wasn't enough. One beer can was the norm – imagine a beer can sitting on the dash, then put the spot where you want to touch down on the top of the can. Maybe Griswold didn't drink enough beer because he started out with an aim point that was too low. Then he backed off pressure on the yoke and made it even lower. The nose rose again.

"Bring it down," Josh repeated. "We're getting way high."

The nose came down again but without backing off on the throttles Griswold let the airspeed increase more than he made the altitude decrease.

"Hey, what are you doing?" Josh demanded. "Earth to Griswold, we need to descend and slow down."

I saw trickles of sweat working their way down Griswold's cheek. His hands were sweating, too, and every few seconds he took them off the controls to wipe them on his pants. The standard measure of performance for a pilot is how far he stays "ahead of the plane." Right now Griswold looked like he was jogging tiredly somewhere aft of the tail.

Hearing Josh, he pushed the nose over hard but this time pulled the power out, too – too much. For a second or two the picture looked good in the windscreen but then the sink rate carried us below the glide angle. Griswold was forced to raise the nose again. He didn't increase the power with it, however, so when the nose came up the airspeed bled off while the plane continued to sink toward the trees. All of this with the airstrip still a mile off the nose.

Josh barked a warning and then goosed the power himself. The propellers growled their displeasure at the cockpit buffoonery but the C-27 climbed. It caught Griswold by surprise. For a moment he waffled on the controls, rocking us back and forth like a fledgling on its first leap from the nest.

"What'd you do that for?" he said when he caught back up to the present.

"What'd I do what for?" Josh replied.

"You pushed the power up."

"Oh, that? I was just keeping us from crashing."

"I was just getting on glide angle."

"You were going into the trees," Josh corrected. "Remember, pitch controls your airspeed. Power controls your altitude. Come on, you've still got half a mile. Let's get this done."

Griswold grumbled and tried to get his target fixed off the nose. But by this time we were too close and too low. To clear the trees at the beginning of the strip we would have to come in on a steeper-than-normal glide slope. To get to that glide slope we would have to climb and by the time we climbed we would be right over the touchdown point. I knew Josh could do it but Griswold wasn't up to making it happen.

We stayed low until the trees cleared enough to see the end of the strip. Griswold shifted his aim long and started to descend. Maybe, I thought. Maybe, since the runway runs almost a mile. But then he shifted his aim even longer and leveled the aircraft while we were still two hundred feet up.

"What are you doing?" Josh whined, tired of feeling like he was back in pilot training.

"I...I don't think this looks right," Griswold struggled to get the words out as he leaned forward in his seat, trying to keep in sight the landing zone that was rapidly disappearing beneath the nose.

Josh grabbed the controls.

"My controls," he barked. He shoved the power levers up to a thousand foot-pounds and arrested the tiny sink rate we still had. "We're going around."

Definitely a mistake, I thought, sitting back down in my web seat. It was definitely a mistake not to swap places with Griswold. I had wanted to put him in a position where he would demonstrate to Josh-the-unbeliever what a bad pilot he was. Now that he was doing it, however, I felt nervous in my stomach that he might kill us all and prove my point. The Colombians had no idea what was going on and I avoided looking at them. Sergeant Wilson was doing what all good load-masters did, maintaining a poker face to mask what he thought of the pilots he was flying with. But he did turn around in his seat to share the poker face with me. That was enough to tell me his thoughts. Definitely a mistake.

"Griswold, what the hell...?" Josh said once we had leveled off on downwind. He kept the controls while he talked. "What the hell was that back there? What kind of an approach was that?"

Griswold wiped the sweat from his face and struggled to shroud his anxiety in professionalism. He pursed his lips in thought.

"I don't know. I wasn't getting the picture I wanted. I think maybe the winds were playing with us..."

"There are no winds. It's calm. Your picture was fucked up from the start."

Griswold recoiled like he'd been slapped.

"Well, I don't know..."

"You can fly a three-mile final if you want but you still have to get on glide path once you're close. Personally I'd recommend just flying normal spacing. You said you beat up the pattern at Sherman last week? Then fly the same thing here. Turn base, turn final, acquire your angle and land. Don't scare me, damn it, because I get pissed when people scare me. Understand? You ready to fly?"

Griswold wasn't but he nodded anyway.

"Your controls."

"My controls."

We tried again. This time Griswold made his turn to final two miles out. I got up from my seat again to watch over Sgt Wilson's shoulder. Griswold started out high but soon corrected. By one mile it looked like he had the aim point shacked. His airspeed sat on 104 knots, our descent rate was a steady 300 feet per minute, and the beer can had found its home. All was right with the world.

Then a goat trotted across the runway.

It didn't stop. It didn't even look up. Halfway down the strip it merely crossed from the fence side where it had been munching weeds to the open side where it ambled away into the brush. Griswold never noticed. It was Wilson who made the mistake of saying, "Huh, what was that?"

"Just a goat," Josh replied.

Griswold's eyebrows shot up.

"A goat?" he cried. His left hand jammed the power levers forward in a spasm of action. His right hand yanked the nose skyward. The picture out front went from all green to all blue in a heartbeat and I nearly fell off the cockpit steps. The Colombians grabbed for anything to keep from sliding aft in their seats.

"Going around! Going around!"

Josh nearly came out of his seat.

"What the –! Nose down! Nose down!"

He grabbed for the controls and pushed forward before the wings could stall. Even so we went from 700 feet to 1200 feet, so quick were the props to chew their way through the air. The airstrip disappeared beneath the nose.

"Let go, pilot!" Josh ordered.

We weren't about to crash but Griswold still had his left hand full forward, elbow locked, pushing the throttles to above their max limit of 1300 ft-lbs. With his right hand he tugged on the stick, the same one Josh was pushing on to keep us level, while his eyes jumped frantically over the gauges without registering any of them. Any second now, I feared, the two of them would break the elevator interlock that went to both yokes.

"Let go!"

I pushed myself over Sgt Wilson and hit Griswold as hard as I could in his left shoulder, the only part of his body that I could reach. The blow jerked him in his seat and snapped him out of his panic. His hands dropped from the controls.

Josh yanked the power back and leveled the aircraft, the C-27 reining in like a frustrated racehorse. As the engines spun down and the horizon smoothed out across the nose, I fully expected an explosion of unprecedented magnitude from the pilot's seat. But for once Josh was speechless. For several seconds, his face flushed and hands trembling, he ignored all of us and stared at either the instrument gauges or the picture outside. I could see the jaw beneath his cheek clenching and unclenching, the tendons in his neck stiff behind his collar. He ground his teeth so hard it was audible through the intercom. Whose god was he praying to now, I wondered.

Finally he turned halfway in his seat and jabbed a finger in Griswold's direction. His eyes smoldered.

"You! GET – OUT – OF – THE – SEAT!"

That was all he said and it was just as well. I'd seen Josh bitter, I'd seen him sarcastic, but I'd never seen him angry enough to kill someone. That was how he looked now.

Griswold was an idiot but he knew enough not to argue. After a moment or two to get his breath back, look around, and remember where he was, his face moved through its evolution of hurt child to misunderstood professional. He climbed slowly out of the pilot's seat, working hard to stay calm and dignified. Sgt Wilson made room for him, as did I, avoiding eye contact and the standard pat on the back. Once he was clear I scrambled up to take his place.

Locking my shoulder harness I suddenly had a thought and turned to look at Sgt Wilson. Pointing to him, I then pointed to my eyes and finally to Griswold who was lowering himself into a web seat in the cabin like a tired old man. 'Keep an eye on him,' I was saying, and Wilson understood. He rotated his seat sideways in the cockpit, able to look forward or back.

Josh needed time to calm down. That was clear. He stayed on the controls and flew us north for a few miles, then turned east out over the jungle. The endless green was a calming sight. We flew that way for a while, soaking in the visual sedative that was the Amazon Basin at mid-day. Trees, trees, trees. An unbroken, uninterrupted canvas of thick, dense, jade forest as far as the eye could see. It stretched to the horizon. Even at 300 feet we were looking to the curvature of the earth and beyond.

Neither Wilson nor I bothered to ask something stupid like where we were going. We were going to the jungle. The jungle fixed everything. The three of us had been down there long enough to know that.

When the Caqueta River came into sight we turned south and then curved around bit by bit to the west. I watched our gas but we had plenty. The only thing that would suffer today was our timeline. Because of Griswold's buffoonery we would now get back to Bogotá after dark. But the delay was worth it to fly around now and calm the nerves, to re-shuffle the cards of life and get the deck back how it belonged. By the time we turned to a long final the world was again as it should be: the jungle below, the sky above, and guys who loved to fly sailing smoothly along between the two.

Josh made a perfect landing in the first two hundred feet of the strip. In the time that we had been out collecting our nerves a white flatbed truck arrived at the field and sat waiting in the high grass for our passengers. The four of them who were getting off did so with enthusiasm, practically running off the ramp and plopping themselves onto the back of the truck with wide eyes and visible relief. The six Colombians who remained watched their comrades go with envy, then turned pitiable eyes back to the front of the cabin like lab rats who know the experiments aren't over. I felt bad for them and hated Griswold all the more.

Josh also did the takeoff. We lifted into the air after a thousand-foot roll and turned immediately toward the southeast.

It was a long haul to Leticia, two hours' flight time, and that was good because it allowed everyone to calm down and put the incident at Florencia behind them. It was bad for the same reason. For Josh was a conflicted person, a stern, sarcastic cynic who nevertheless had a good heart and wanted to believe that people weren't as bad as his brain kept telling him. When we landed at Leticia he was still mad at Griswold but was starting to think that perhaps he had set him up somehow to fail. By the time we took off again he was thinking that a good instructor wouldn't have allowed his co-pilot to put us all in a dangerous position and that Griswold almost crashing was really Josh's fault. When we finally leveled off at 18,000 feet, on the leg home and with the sun dropping below the horizon, he had convinced himself that Griswold deserved another chance.

"Did you hear that?" I asked, turning up the volume on the HF radio.

"Hear what?" Josh asked. He was still flying, as he had done all day, though now it was simply a matter of keeping the aircraft trimmed up for straight-and-level flight.

"Chatter on short-wave. The commercials are calling thunderstorms forming over the mountains. I guess there's a fair amount of lightning."

Josh pulled up the HF peanut button on his comm console and listened to distant airliners trade weather observations for a while. He sighed and shrugged.

"They only said "isolated storms" in the forecast," I mumbled, knowing it was an unhelpful comment.

"They *always* say "isolated" storms," Josh pointed out. "Always. It's nothing but the weather guys covering their ass because it's easier for them to say "isolated" than to admit they haven't a clue what's going on beyond the view from their window. *Forecasts*," he muttered. "They're to weather what Florida swampland is to real estate."

We droned for a while. Then, picking up the discussion again, Josh made his decision.

"Nothing to do about it. It's clear enough. We should be able to avoid them."

The good thing about thunderstorms in this part of the world, as powerful as they could be, was that most of the time they weren't embedded. "Embedded" meant they hid in bad weather, which sounds strange because thunderstorms are themselves examples of bad weather. But the heat and moisture of the tropics usually caused thunderstorms to form quickly independent of any larger weather system. The storms eschewed hiding and thrust themselves up in clear air, displaying the same machismo that prevailed among the people below. As a result, almost always we could see a thunderstorm while it was still fifty to a hundred miles away. During the day it was a massive white mushroom- or pod-shaped boomer, the worst ones developing the tell-tale anvil at the top and the mottled gray shading in the center. We could see them coming and avoid them with ease. There could be dozens of them spread across the horizon but we just picked our way through them like a wary ball inside an arcade machine.

At night avoiding storms was trickier. If the sky was clear we could see the storms against the stars and moon. If it wasn't clear their own lightning gave them away, backlighting the cells every few seconds to pinpoint their position. That was good because we always wanted to know where the storms were. When you're flying in the rain *and* can't see outside *and* there are thunderstorms around you, that's the scariest thing in the world.

Last but not least, when all else failed we had our color weather radar to guide the way. Our radar was good, very good, and only bogged down when the rain outside was so intense that water coursing off the airplane's nose confused its returns and gave us a screen full of static like a late-night test pattern on TV. Green blotches on the screen signified areas of light to medium rain and were to be avoided if gas and time allowed. Yellow blotches were heavy rain (and turbulence associated with the rain) and nothing you wanted to fly through if you could help it. Red blotches were the worst. They were walls of rain – no-kidding, flip-you-upside-down, rip-your-wings-off, three-screamer up- and down-drafts that would dope-slap you across the sky and send you to meet your maker. Needless to say, if red blotches appeared in our flight path we ran screaming like little girls.

"There they are," I said after a while and pointed to the horizon.

Way in the distance little flashes of light appeared. We were heading northwest and they appeared all across the horizon from left to right, which meant the storms were exactly where they were supposed to be, over the Andes and spreading east where the heat and moisture of the jungle could sustain them. The flashes were sporadic and separated, like so many artillery duels on a distant battlefield.

"Doesn't look so bad," Josh mused.

"No," I said carefully, thinking that storms were always bad. "They're separated."

"Yeah."

Josh paused, thinking.

"Griswold, are you awake?"

Uh-oh, I thought.

"Um, yeah," came a tinny voice from the back.

"Why don't you climb back up here and get the rest of the leg back into El Dorado?"

My mouth dropped open and I wondered what to say. I knew Josh and knew what he was thinking but all the same stared at him with a look that asked, what the hell are you thinking? He nodded that he understood but held up his hands to placate me. Don't worry, said the gesture. I know what I'm doing.

I climbed out and Griswold took my place. Then because Brian was sleeping in the cabin I took the third seat and spun it around to look out front. After a while I grew bored and borrowed the HF radio to make a phone call to my folks.

Phone patches were something the Big Mac guys did all the time. Flying for hours over the ocean seven to eight miles up you might as well make a phone call. C-5 and C-141 drivers had become masters at the practice and I had picked it up from them. In the C-27 we rarely had the chance but now seemed as good a time as any. We weren't learning anything more about the weather. There was only so much the commercial airlines could tell us given that we were on the opposite side of the mountains.

Short-wave radio operators ("hams") all over the world sit in their basements just itching to talk to someone. Many of them have phone-patch capability. If you knew the frequency of an operator in the States you could get hold of them and have them connect you to a phone line for a call home. Down in South America none of the frequencies I used in C-5s would work for me but Walt had given me a couple that reached the right antennae in the Midwest. Very quickly I got hold of a guy in Kansas who called himself "X-Ray-Mike-Four-Four-Juliet."

"Hi, sir. Wondering if you could give me a patch to a number in Chicago. Over."

"Shore can, son. Always willing to help out our boys in uniform. Over."

I gave him the number. Normally he made the patch on a collect call to the receiver but this time I lucked out.

"Yup, the long-distance carriers are feelin' all patriotic due to Desert Storm so this one's paid for. I'll have you through in just a second."

That made me feel guilty. I wasn't exactly a grunt sitting in the desert.

"*Okay, son,*" Four-Four-Juliet came back in a few minutes. *"I've got your party on the line. Go ahead. And just remember to say 'Over' when you're done talking so I know when to flip the switch."*

"Hey, thanks. Break-break. This is Mike. Who am I talking to? Over."

It was my sister. She thought it was a hoot talking on the phone to someone flying over the Amazon jungle and asked me three or four times if that was really where I was or if this was some kind of joke.

"No, really, that's where I am. I just had a few minutes so thought I'd call and say hello. Over."

"Well, your job can't be too hard if you have time to make phone calls just to talk. Over."

"At the moment it's not. I'm not even flying, I'm just riding along. But I do work sometimes, you know. Unlike some people. Over."

"Uh-huh. Well, Allison went to grab Mom so she can talk to you. I don't really have anything to say. We were having Margaret's graduation party outside with a bonfire but then the neighbors complained and the cops showed up. It wasn't a problem because half the people at the party are cops but then it started raining so everyone came inside. They're all here…there must be thirty people in the kitchen… do you want to say hi to them? Oh, wait. Frederick just showed up. He must have heard we had food on the table. Hey, get away from that, that's for later! Oh, here comes Mom. Although I don't know if she's going to like this talking over a radio business…"

There was silence on the radio.

"Remember to say 'Over' when you're done speaking, dear."

"What?"

"Remember to say 'Over.' I have to throw a switch."

"Who is this?"

"This is Four-Four-Juliet, ma'am."

"That's your name?"

"Not really. It's my handle."

"Your what?"

"Would you just talk, please?"

There was a pause while my sister intervened. Then I heard, *"Hellooooo? Is this my Michael?"*

"Hi, Mom! Listen, we're talking through a short-wave radio in Kansas so you have to say 'Over' whenever you finish speaking, okay? Over."

"You're in Kansas?"

"No, no. I'm in South America. Well, in the air over South America anyway. It's just that there's a guy in Kansas helping to make this call so you have to say 'Over' to help him out. Over."

"Oh." Long silence. *"Maybe you should talk to your dad."*

This is what most HF phone-patch conversations were like. I had yet to hear one that actually conveyed information. That said, I had been privy to one of the calls now legendary in the Big Mac community. One night over the Pacific while I was desperately trying to stay awake in the copilot's seat as the automatic pilot took our C-5 to Japan, I overheard one of our other pilots trying to patch things up with his girlfriend. It wasn't going well. Knowing this, he came up on intercom and asked the rest of the crew – out of courtesy – to punch off their HF peanut switches so he and his girlfriend might have a bit of privacy. Naturally that had the opposite effect as we and every other station around the globe that happened to be listening to that frequency immediately turned up the volume. It was short and sweet.

"It's over. Over." the girlfriend told him.

"Wait! What do you mean it's over? Over."

"I mean it's over. Over."

We had long since passed the VOR at San Jose del Guaviare when the lightning that had been backlighting the mountains appeared suddenly to our left and right. Rain spattered on the windscreen.

"Hmm. Must be a few out here that aren't showing up on the radar," Josh said, unworried. The rain's too light."

But further ahead the radar showed plenty of storms. They stood like chess pieces at the beginning of a game, spread across a line parallel to the mountains and evenly spaced. As we got closer their spacing became irregular. Some merged and others moved forward or back to offer us either safe passage or sucker holes, ours to find out which. We started to pick up turbulence.

"Did Bronwyn tell you the big news? Your dad's thinking about retiring! The board is doing this stupid thing where they turn over control of the schools to the parents and since most of the parents have nothing more than a third-grade education that's really going to make things interesting. What are you doing out there that you have time to talk on the phone?.."

"Griswold, just work us around those cells. Try to keep us at least twenty miles from the big ones."

"You want I should descend?"

"No."

"Well, it might be smoother down around fifteen."

"It might be. Right up until we smack the mountains, that is. Griswold, we've got a wall coming up only fifty miles away that reaches up to 18,000 feet. It's the second highest mountain range in the world. Try not to forget that, okay?"

"Oh, nothing much, Mom. We're just coming back from a trip carrying some supplies to people. We're up over the Amazon jungle. It would look really cool except that it's night so we can't see anything. There's some lightning in the distance that we're watching right now and it's kind of pretty. Over."

"Well, that sounds dangerous to me. I don't know where you guys get it. Your brother Matthew's doing the same thing working on his civilian license. Except he's in these little planes that don't even look like they should fly. I tell you, the two of you are going to drive me to an early grave...."

The rain fell harder, hard enough that you could feel it against the skin of the plane. Josh flicked the landing lights on briefly to get a sense of how heavy it was. The beam from the left wing shot forward far enough to tell us we were in a car wash that was going 250 mph. He should have warned us before he turned the lights on because it briefly gave an unsettling visual illusion of closure. With everything dark outside we just looked at our instruments and never gave a thought to how fast we were going. Suddenly being able to see – and then seeing millions of drops of water and wisps of cloud coming right at you – made your brain think for a split second that you were about to hit something. Or in Griswold's case, more than a split second.

"Auughh! Turn it off!" he shrieked and banked the plane right as though he could avoid the rain.

Josh snapped the light off and looked across the cockpit in surprise.

"Okay, okay. What was that all about?"

Griswold recovered.

"You shouldn't do that without warning me!"

"Alright, I'm sorry."

Josh turned in his seat to share a look of 'what the hell?' I was straining to hear my mother above the crackle in the radio from the weather and just shrugged in response. He's the one who had wanted to put the idiot back in the seat.

"You know, Griswold," he continued carefully. "The rain's still out there even without the lights on..."

"Oh, speak of the devil. Look who just came through the door! Here, talk to your father..."

It was getting hard to avoid everything on the radar screen. Green blotches were popping up everywhere now and some had merged to form thin lines of yellow. There was only one red spot, a small dot far to the north that so far was no factor for us. But the yellow streaks and some of the green had suspicious shadows behind them that Josh didn't like. More and more he was head's-down in the cockpit, concentrating on the map and the radar screen while telling Griswold which way to turn. For his part, Griswold went silent. For a while he mumbled to himself and made inane suggestions about holding until the weather passed (which would be tomorrow) but after a while he stopped even that.

A bolt of lightning up ahead showed us we were exiting one rain shaft and heading toward another. Josh pointed Griswold to the left.

"I don't like these dark spots," he said to no one in particular.

The radar had two weaknesses. While it could show us a cell that had rain in it, it couldn't show a cell where there was no rain yet. It also couldn't show what was behind the rain. The transmitted waves bounced off precipitation: if none had formed yet you could fly right through a towering cumulus of up- and down-drafts with no warning. And if rain *had* formed and was heavy, all the waves might be reflected off the shaft leaving a black hole behind it that for all you knew contained the biggest boomer this side of Galveston. I started half-listening to my folks and leaned forward to watch the radar myself.

"So what exactly are you doing out over the Amazon?" my father asked. The weather and the lightning were distorting our voices in mid-word, causing his pronunciation of 'Amazon' to have about nine syllables and cover four octaves. *"Or can you tell us? Maybe if you tell us you have to kill us. Ha-ha! Over."*

We ran over some turbulence like it was a speed bump. I picked my checklist off the floor.

"Well, right now we're trying to pick our way through some bad weather. It's funny. Usually during the day it's really clear down here but at night you get these big storms

that blow up. It's like the storms you guys get in early summer except they're all over. Over."

"It's funny you should mention that. We've had a lot of rain over the last couple of weeks. One storm came through the other night that we thought would blow the roof off. You know the ash tree to the right of the front porch? Well, it lost a couple of branches that must have just missed the porch by inches...."

The radar screen now gave us no options. The storm cells merged on all sides ten miles ahead of us and left us nothing to go between. Josh was faced with a collapsing multi-colored line that curved in a semi-circle across the scope. Both left and right had yellow streaks mixed into the ranks and even a red blob had appeared out of nowhere to the south, blossoming up out of one of the yellow cells we were avoiding. We had to penetrate the line somewhere. Josh had to decide where.

"We need to descend," Griswold insisted, his voice quavering. Somewhere he'd gotten the conviction that we could go *under* the storms.

"No, we don't," Josh said calmly. He peered at the scope. Five miles to go. Where, oh where to penetrate the line?

"How about if I turn north?" Griswold suggested. "I could turn north and descend."

"We're on an airway, Griswold. You don't just turn off it and try men's free-style because you want to."

"But there's storms up ahead."

"I've got news for you. There are storms all around us. Come right ten degrees. No, twenty."

I peered over Griswold's shoulder. His hands were shaking.

"Twenty degrees, Griswold. Come on," Josh urged as Griswold hesitated. Josh had chosen the thinnest part of the line, a part that at a distance looked like we should be able to fly through it in a matter of minutes. The only scary part was the dark shadow immediately behind it. But that compared to the definite yellow blobs behind the rest of the green line. In this case Josh was choosing the devil we didn't know in favor of the ones we did.

"...biggest one we've had come down in a while. Your brother and I got out there over the weekend to cut it up. We hauled the logs around behind the garage but we're going to leave them there until you come home to chop them up. It'll give you something to do..."

The plane lurched and I grabbed the armrest to hold on. A fly landed on my hand. You picked the wrong flight to be on, fellow, I thought, and brushed him away.

We merged with the green line. As we did the line thickened and the shadow behind it sprouted a yellow mushroom the way heat burns through film in a projector. Josh cursed. He'd been suckered.

"Hey," Griswold said slowly. "We could crash inside of this."

"Oh, quit your whining," Josh ordered. "Just hold it steady."

The rain now hit the windscreen so hard we could see it without any lights. Lightning flashed close by, creating a grey, blurry glow through the windows that told us we were in the middle of something.

"So are you going to be able to come back for the Ridge Run? They're supposed to have a record number of runners this year. It's only six miles. Matt's thinking of doing it. You boys could run it together. Over."

The static from the lightning made it hard to make out what my dad was saying.

"Uh, I don't know...Say, listen, the weather here is messing with the reception. I may have to sign off soon..."

There was a blinding flash outside accompanied by thunder that we heard even above the roar of the engines. The plane dropped fifty feet and for a microsecond our interior lights flickered. The radio buzzed in my headset.

"Jesus, Mary, and Joseph!" Josh yelled. His shoulder harness wasn't as tight as it should have been and he banged his head on the top window.

"Whoa, that was wicked! *Hey, are you guys still there?"*

"Yes, we're still here, over," came my mother's voice. *"You know, tropics or no tropics, I'll bet your weather there doesn't compare to a good summer storm in the Midwest. I'll bet it's pretty where you are... We'll have to come down there to visit so we can see for ourselves..."*

An updraft caught the right wing and flipped us into forty degrees of bank. Even with the shoulder harnesses Josh and I both had to grab the seats of our chairs to keep from getting tossed about. Griswold at least had the control yoke to hang onto.

"Alright, level us out, Griswold. You're doing a good job."

The plane tipped toward forty-five degrees and the nose started down.

"Level us out, Griswold," Josh repeated. "Griswold!"

Griswold was sitting bolt upright in his seat, eyes wide. Both his hands rested on the yoke but he wasn't making any effort to move the controls, probably because he was hanging on too hard to keep from falling over to the left. He wasn't even looking out front anymore. Instead he had turned his head and was looking quickly around the ceiling.

"How does he do it?" he asked as the nose came through the horizon.

Josh tried to follow his gaze.

"Who? What?"

Griswold stared up in deep thought.

"How does that fly keep up with us?"

"What?"

Josh reached for the controls but the storm outside beat him to it. This time an updraft caught the left wing and pitched us back to almost-level. We lurched in our seats like a trio of bobble-head dolls. The updraft also thrust the whole plane upward so that even though the nose was still below the horizon our vertical velocity indicator registered a thousand foot climb. Imagine tripping and falling forward but going up instead of hitting the ground. The barometric altimeter climbed back through twenty thousand feet.

"How does he keep up with us? You know, we're flying over 200 knots. That's like 240 miles per hour. How does a fly keep up with us?"

Griswold let his left hand slip off the power levers so he could point upward, tracking the progress of the fly which had entered an elliptical holding pattern over the center panel.

"What the hell are you talking about?" Josh barked. "Fly the goddamn plane!"

"...it's the heat that I'm not sure we would like. Your father hates that hot weather and the way you talk about the humidity I'm not sure it'd be any great shakes for me, either. Though the rain must be a welcome break for everyone down there, don't you think?..."

"Hey, I'm getting water back here," Sgt Wilson called. "It's just seeping in around the door but wow, that's unusual. There's no reason we should be getting rain inside a pressurized cabin. Is it coming down that hard?"

On the windscreen it looked as though every fire department in the world had its hoses directed at us.

"He should be smashed against the back of the cabin..." Griswold mused. His eyes tracked the fly with dreamy abandon. "That's just not right. Something...Someone...is helping him..."

The VVI wobbled at 1,000 feet per minute then dove back down to three hundred. The nose hovered its way above the artificial horizon and we slowed down. With our airspeed dropping below 160kts the p-factor on our temporarily floating plane caused it to yaw left. At the same time the slipstream off the left engine pushed on the tail and we slowly began a bank to the right.

"Hey, you freak!" Josh shouted, looking up from the radar. "What planet are you..." He leaned over to slap Griswold but mid-strike re-prioritized and grabbed the controls on his side.

"Are you still there, over?" my mother asked. *"I don't like this talking on a radio stuff. Why can't you just call us on a phone?..."*

I could picture her voice traveling its sine wave through space, going up to bounce off the ionosphere and then down again to reflect off the ground before finding its way to my tiny plane in the middle of a storm over the jungle. Standing in her kitchen in Illinois looking out over the back yard, listening to cicadas chirp from the trees and watching fireflies wink their flight paths over the grass, she radiated calm and common sense – two traits that were completely absent from our cockpit.

"Yes, I'm here. I think..."

My world came apart. Earth and sky split as a lightning bolt shot across the nose, level with our aircraft and taking the place of the horizon we couldn't see. As it lit up the sky the cloud we were in parted. Billions of volts of electricity burned their way through miles of storm. The bolt shot from nowhere in particular but judging from its size it could have started in Canada and was now on its way to Tierra del Fuego. It appeared without warning, far enough out to miss us but close enough that it scorched the intervening vapor and let us count its electrons one by one. Before it did the cloud, an opaque comforter, had pressed against the glass. Now that same cloud disappeared. For a microsecond it burned with brilliant intensity and then evaporated. We might as well have crashed into the sun. The air turned from grey to white to a shattering yellow. No spotlight in the world could compare. This was God's circuit panel and it had just arc'd. I shut my eyes and tensed, expecting an impact, thinking instinctively that I'd just died.

The simultaneous thunder shook the plane. Josh ducked. Griswold screamed and pulled the controls, hunching over them in sheer panic. The air smelled of ozone.

"Aauugh!" Griswold shrieked. "Down!"

He wrenched the yoke hard right and threw himself against it. The nose pitched over hard as the plane reacted. All of us were thrown up against our restraints. For a moment Josh couldn't even reach the dash. I keyed the mike – the only thing I had my hands on – on the short-wave one more time.

"Gotta go!" I called. *"Out!"*

"Griswold!" Josh cried, his voice fearful for the first time, pleading. "Griswold, let go!"

He managed to get his left hand on the yoke as his right still tried to pull himself down to the seat. We were forty degrees nose low in a right bank. The turbulence and our increasing airspeed – over 280 now –threatened to shake the C-27 apart. Josh pulled hard, straining against Griswold's entire body, and brought the nose up ten degrees.

For a few seconds the positive gravity plopped me down into the seat. Not knowing how long it would last I didn't hesitate. Throwing off the seat belt I lunged forward and for the second time in a few hours brought a clenched fist down hard on the co-pilot. This time it hit the back of Griswold's head.

Stars appeared as pain shot up my arm. It was a poorly-aimed blow, most likely doing more damage to my hand than it did to Griswold's cranium. However, it knocked him face forward into the instrument panel where his forehead broke the glass over the HSI. He visibly deflated.

"Brian!" I yelled.

Sgt Wilson appeared behind me, looking as frightened as I felt. Sitting in the back he no doubt heard the blast from the lightning bolt and thought the plane was breaking up. Together we hauled Griswold's inert body straight out of the seat. With no ceremony, he went out over the center panel, the jump seat, and head first down into the cabin.

Josh pulled us up as we descended through 12,000 feet. If anything the air was more turbulent at that altitude, lurching us laterally as Josh twisted the controls to level the artificial horizon. I fell behind the co-pilot's seat and got jammed there. Sgt Wilson had to help me climb out, whereupon I fumbled to take Griswold's place.

"Where are the mountains?" I yelled to Josh, having lost my headset.

"I DON'T KNOW!! Where's the map?"

He ignored me. His attention was focused on the gauges and outside, outside presumably because he was watching for mountain goats to appear in the mist.

I dropped into the co-pilot's seat and cinched the belt down hard. Sgt Wilson tried to hand me a headset but just as he leaned forward the plane bucked and he ended up slamming it into my face, bloodying my nose.

"Sorry!"

Goddamn Griswold, was all I thought.

Clumsily I put it on, blood trickling over my upper lip. My hands shook so bad that connecting the cord to the intercom panel was near impossible. Then I panicked because I couldn't find anything.

The lights were still on but everything that had been loose in the cockpit was strewn all over. Josh's kneeboard, a water bottle, the approach plates for Bogotá. I felt around and found the TPC under the seat.

Josh turned us straight east.

"Are we climbing?" Brian asked.

Josh gave him a withering look.

"I'm *trying*!"

He was. And we were. The Chuck was struggling like a salmon through the falls, swimming against the current of the downdrafts but still going up. Back in the direction we had just come from. It occurred to me that meant we were headed right back into the cell that had just kicked our ass.

"We're still over the jungle," I said after a few minutes, feverishly working the INS.

"How far?" Josh didn't turn. We passed 16,000 feet and kept climbing. The mountains went higher than that. The radar showed a test pattern.

"I..." I fiddled some more and then realized that with all our yanking and banking the INS was miles off. "I don't know."

"Well, find out!"

We had been closing in on the mountains. For all I knew we had flown far enough west to get above them. That meant Villivicencio had to be somewhere within 30 miles. I dialed up the NDB station there and watched as the needle spun furiously with every flash of lightning.

"Damn!"

I tried the VOR at Apiay. The needle bounced and then settled at our 7 o'clock – behind us. Since we were now flying east it was the most beautiful thing I'd ever seen.

"They're behind us. Come left."

"How far?"

"Come left and I'll tell you. There's no DME at Apiay but if you come left I can time the radials. Probably ten miles," I guessed.

Josh didn't like it but passing 19,000 feet he wanted out of the weather. He hesitated thirty seconds then turned left.

We timed the movement of the needle as it dropped, trying to continue pointing at the station. Rough wag, 20 miles. So I wasn't even close. But 20 miles was better than 10 so neither of us complained.

Josh turned to home on Apiay. We bounced our way through more rain with lightning all around. I suggested landing at Apiay rather than going on to the capital until Josh reminded me that Apiay had no lights. Right. In a storm, low on gas, to a field with one shoddy instrument approach and no lights. Not so much.

Brian climbed down into the cabin to strap Griswold to the floor.

"There!" Josh yelled in excitement just as we entered the mountains.

The cloud we were in broke. Weather clustered around us but for the first time in two hours we could see stars again. A narrow canyon of air stretched twenty miles in front of us, flanked by cells that sparked and sputtered with electric life. One last jolt from behind bounced our tail up. It let us see a ghostly white peak barely visible at our ten o'clock. *Level* at our ten o'clock. Josh turned right and climbed another 500 feet.

The cockpit was silent for a while. We all expected the clouds to close back in. They didn't. They threatened to, teasing us by squeezing together than backing off, but always left us a narrow passage where we could see lightning dance in the distance. It was like sailing up the Thames in a wicked, angry fog.

Eventually I couldn't take the quiet anymore.

"God," I breathed. "I have never been so happy to see clear air."

Josh's face did his talking for him. It twisted through the gamut of anger and fear. Finally, passing over the lights of Las Conchas, he said, "Can you fly for a minute?"

I looked over and said sure, never expecting after all that drama that he would give up the controls.

"Co-pilot's controls."

"Co-pilot's controls."

He pushed back in his seat and loosened his seatbelt. The map that was crushed under his leg he removed and folded carefully. His headset came off. He hung it carefully on the armrest. Then he put his head down into his hands and stayed that way for a long time.

The airfield at Bogotá was deserted. We saw it intermittently through the clouds while miles away, a dark patch on the far side of the city. The lights of Bogotá came and went as a broken deck below us tried to hide them from view. The approach controller was surprised to hear from us, to hear from anyone coming in from the east. He didn't answer me at first and then asked us three times for our position. *Put the coffee down and step away from the doughnut,* I thought, but he told us we could have any approach we wanted. When a big hole appeared in the clouds over the downtown area I told him *straight-in* and dove for the green-and-white beacon. Josh never said a word.

As we turned base I asked if he was okay.

He pulled his head up, hands sliding down his face as though reluctant to let him see the real world again.

"You want the landing?"

He shook his head.

"Okay. Gear down."

He pushed the gear handle down with supreme effort as though on his hundredth push-up.

"He's a nutcase," he said, on the verge of sobbing.

"I told you."

"He's a nutcase."

"Nothing you can do about it."

"He almost killed us."

"I know."

"He almost *killed* us."

"I was there."

"He *could have* killed us."

"You couldn't stop him."

"I can kill *him.*"

"Okay."

"I'm serious. Open the doors and throw him out. Brian!"

"Sir?"

"Open the door and throw Capt Beckett out."

"Okay."

"We're over the city," I pointed out. I looked over my shoulder to see if Brian was actually going to commit murder.

"They'll think it was a drug hit." The effort of talking left Josh hunched in his seat. I couldn't see if he was crying but he sounded like it. We all needed a stiff drink or five.

"Turning final," I announced.

The city lights shone brighter through the mist. One rain shaft swept in from the right and tried to cut us off before getting to the runway but I dodged left and angled toward the captain's bars a thousand feet past the threshold. No one else was in the air and Bogotá had long, long runways that let me do that. The rain sprinkled briefly against the fuselage but then gave up, like a kid with a hose trying to spray a biker. It was the sky's last effort to get us.

"*Shark 18, you can turn right at your first taxiway,*" the tower called as we touched down.

"*Wilco. We're going to CATAM ramp. Comando Aéreo de Transporte Militar.*"

"*Shark 18, roy-er.*"

We coasted a long way down the runway and watched lightning dance over the city. The taxiway was flooded and waves that rolled across its surface flickered reflected light from the sky, but we turned onto it anyway and drove up the parallel like a boat cruising along a levee. The Colombian military transport ramp lay over by Fast Eddie's hangar, north of the parallel in a black hole that at night looked like an abandoned yard. With all the water it was hard to see where the pavement ended and the grass began so I taxied slow, feeling my way along.

Josh squirmed in his seat.

"Hey."

"What?"

He had something to say but didn't know how to say it. He fumbled for a while and then gave up.

"I'm sorry about your bird."

"Huh?"

"Your parakeet. I'm sorry it died."

I didn't answer, trying to remember what it was like to be twelve years old. Probably not a lot different in some ways than being twenty-six.

The ramp outside Eddie's was dark but as we shut down the door below his office opened. A triangle of light spilled across the ramp. Angela, wearing an exquisite black slicker, walked through it to meet us.

"You know, it's Saturday night," I commented.

"So?"

"So maybe we could go to church tomorrow before we leave."

Josh raised a tired eyebrow. "I'm Jewish and you're a heathen," he reminded me.

"So you pray in Hebrew and I'll keep quiet."

He stared at the instrument panel and thought about that.

"Okay." He dropped his headset into his lap. "It can't hurt."

10. Pub

One thing we didn't have in Panama was a place to hang out. A bar, that is, or a restaurant or cafe or club where people met just to relax and spend time together. Panama wasn't that kind of place. No doubt the locals had their hangouts but there wasn't a shared sense of belonging between them and foreigners to allow for a neutral setting where we could all go. Maybe the Union Club was like that back in the '30s and '40s – for the wealthy – but for us even places with great ambiance like the Yacht Club turned into crowds of cliques once they filled up.

To be precise, people didn't go to the Yacht Club because it was the Yacht Club, people went there because it was a bar – a quaint bar on the Canal but still just a bar. Whether it was the Yacht Club or Pavo Real or the lounge in the Punta Paitilla, the cliques stuck to themselves, ignoring each other for the most part so that one location was the same as another for as much interaction or identification anybody had with it. Sahara, Patatus, Dreams – you could have swapped their names around and nobody would have noticed. We didn't have a *Cheers*, a place where "everybody knows your name."

Maybe that was good since it made us substitute our own houses and apartments for the local venue we didn't have. We threw parties instead at the Pinheads', or Kurt and Lowell's, or Rolo's and my place or wherever else we gathered and shared adventures. It was as though we had a movable club of our own. But the bad part about that was it was always the same people who came. We were our own clique.

Years after I left South America I lived in England and learned to appreciate pubs. Or rather, I learned to appreciate the good ones. Describing a good one – the requisite character, tradition, clientele, location – is hard to do, except to say that it helps if it's in a small village or quiet backwater of a neighborhood. It's easier to say what a good pub isn't. A good pub isn't a bar or a tavern or a club or any other lazy manifestation of man's desire to drink somewhere other than his own living room. It isn't loud, doesn't have television (unless a soccer game is on), doesn't prohibit pets, and doesn't allow just anyone through the door. It doesn't serve food unless it's the heavy, filling kind, the kind that'll keep you warm as you stagger home through fog and Norfolk drizzle. It doesn't take its patrons for granted, doesn't tolerate fools, and doesn't close for the night until the proprietor himself shuts the doors.

By those standards the Spratley Arms was a good pub.

The Spratley was in Peru. It sat on Calle Atahualpa in Miraflores, half a mile from Spaghetti Alley and walking distance from our usual hotel. I learned about it on my third trip to Lima when I was stuck with a boring crew: Luz Gonzalez (of the Puerto Rican loadmaster mafia) and Sam Povenich.

Luz could normally be counted on to seek adventure but only when we over-nighted in the middle of nowhere. In Iquitos, for example, he was the honorary mayor given his popularity with the ladies and willingness to drink and dance until dawn. Lima, though, was too modern for his tastes. The moment we got to the hotel he locked himself in his room with a tray of Pisco sours and watched Peruvian game shows until he dozed off.

Since Luz was short, fat, and balding I figured that in a cosmopolitan city like Lima he feared the competition. But Josh saw things differently. Competition or not, he claimed, the key to popularity in places like Iquitos was novelty – for some people money and looks aren't as important as the opportunity to experience a part of the world beyond their usual horizon. In the jungle horizons were small. Therefore anyone who came from beyond them was welcome. There was also something about being where nobody knew you that brought freedom. Luz, who could be gregarious, suave, and a wicked salsa dancer when he wanted, awoke a dormant personality whenever he hit the Amazon town. He was the new kid on the block and he loved it.

And the novelty worked both ways. In Lima a club was a club was a club and Luz was bored. In Iquitos it was a club in the middle of nowhere, populated by people less jaded than those in the city. They were simply more exciting and more fun. There Luz was in his element.

Our normal routine when we landed in Iquitos to spend the night was to park the plane in the grass and change clothes before looking for a moto-taxi to take us to the El Dorado. Sometimes Luz was in such a hurry that he put on his civvies before we touched down. He would jump out to install the chocks wearing his best loafers, a silk shirt, and gold chains dangling into his chest hair. *"Venga! Venga!"* he would urge us. "The Latin Lover has arrived!"

But that was in Iquitos. In Lima Luz hid in his room, the biggest stick-in-the-mud in the squadron.

Except for Sam.

Sam Povenich was a good guy. Stable. Reliable. *Steady*. Not stable in a good way, like Manny who could be counted on to be professional in all things but who could still party with the boys after hours, but stable like a church deacon is stable, or like a dean of discipline who chaperones the school dance by standing against the wall with a glower on his face. The man was boring.

Even Big Bud, another staid member of the squadron, was a frat boy gone wild compared to Sam. Regardless of which town we were in Sam didn't go out once we checked into the hotel. He didn't mix with the locals. He didn't party. He didn't smoke, didn't drink, didn't dance, didn't carouse or gamble or swear or chase women or tell off-color jokes or explore the local boulevards or try to make deals with local businessmen for whatever commodity the country was famous for. He didn't even buy souvenirs. He regarded Luz's party antics in Iquitos as behavior from another world. Loud music irritated him, the locals (whichever locals they happened to be) made him suspicious, and native cuisine scared him off.

And he wasn't that way only when he was abroad. On trips or at home there was a Puritan quality to Sam that made even fellow captains call him *sir.* His haircut was always within regs. His boots always had a shine. He walked straight enough we could have balanced books on his head. In the squadron he worked through lunch. He wasn't known for joking with the guys. He was smart and a bit of a wordsmith: he knew the difference between *historic* and *historical* and how to use 'myriad' as a noun. He did great paperwork, too, and through sheer practice became the squadron editor of all trip reports and performance reviews. I hated seeing him come to the operations desk because more often than not it was to have me correct something I had written and sent up the chain of command. In sum, he was responsible and mature – *steady* – everything you don't want to see in someone your own age.

The annoying thing about Sam's seriousness was that he wasn't weird about it. Whereas Big Bud was quiet and thoughtful because he was an absent-minded genius pondering Fermat's Last Theorem – a situation we could raise an eyebrow at but still accept – Sam was quiet and thoughtful because he lacked personality. He had a sense of humor but it was too cerebral to be on display. The only time he laughed was when he observed something dumb, usually while editing our trip reports: he loved to find malapropisms, as when Paul detailed an incident during an airdrop by writing, "After using the latrine, I tied a gunner's belt around my waste and went to the ramp..." But the idea of *doing* anything fun was foreign to him. His only ambition seemed to be to do a good job in the squadron and maybe get promoted. He reminded me of the legend that General Robert E. Lee passed through four years of West Point without receiving a single demerit. Except that Sam was from New Hampshire he and Lee would have gotten along well.

The only stain on Sam's otherwise spotless life was his wife, Lucy. She was everything he wasn't. On top of that she couldn't handle the confines that came with being a military wife. She partied like a rock star whatever the occasion, got drunk at the drop of a hat, used marijuana when he was away on trips, and generally raised hell whenever he wasn't around to absorb her wildness in his depthless sobriety. It was a wonder to us that the two of them ever hooked up. They loved each other dearly but otherwise had nothing in common. She told Laura Berne once how they met in college, at a campus showing of *Reds* where Sam laughed through the preachy liberal parts and she tracked him down in the lobby afterward to give him hell. Instead they fell in love. Opposites attract, they say, but this was someone to the right of Rush Limbaugh falling for a creature of Woodstock. It was odd.

It was also inconvenient for me because when I was being paid to spend the night in a foreign country I wanted to go out and see the sights. Since our squadron policy was to observe the buddy system when we were away from Panama – never go anywhere on your own – without my crew I was imprisoned in our hotel. Sam was another homebody.

One night after staring at the walls and prowling the lobby I couldn't take it any more.

I called a girl I had met on a previous trip and caught her just as she was heading out the door. Anna Lisa was excited to hear from me but had plans already: she suggested I meet up with her and her friends later at a club across from the Parque del Amor.

Instead I went for a walk, intending to honor the intent if not the letter of our squadron law by ambling through the park across the street. Then I strayed past the park, my sense of guilt fading the further I got from the hotel. I wandered down wide sidewalks and tree-lined streets, enjoying the bustle of coffee stands and sidewalk vendors and stores with bright windows that stayed open after dark.

After an hour I ended up at Spaghetti Alley. By then I was hungry but something about the lane didn't appeal to me that night so on the spur of the moment I waved down a cab and asked the driver if there was a pub in town.

"Un pub?" he repeated, confused.

I explained what I wanted. He nodded, then shook his head and said he would try.

It took a while. First he took me to a two-story chrome-and-glass tapas bar near the Parque Bolognesi. It wasn't at all like a pub. It was more the kind of place where up-and-coming stockbrokers met to discuss mergers and compare neckties. My first thought when I saw it was that the building was a terrorists' dream house: floor-to-ceiling windows with nowhere for the customers to hide when a bomb went off.

Next we stopped at the dance club on the Parque del Amor. It was the opposite of the tapas bar: all brick with nary a window in sight. A thumping base reverberated through the walls and made the cab tremble when we pulled up. A bouncer monitored the door. The patrons who passed by him were solemn and attired in black. The driver assured me that the club served food but I signaled for him to keep driving. Notwithstanding Anna Lisa's later presence, it wasn't what I wanted tonight.

He made two more good-faith efforts to find something pubbish. Each took us further from Miraflores and deeper into gritty neighborhoods. The first was a shack on the beach and the second doubled as a tire store near the Oreo cookie factory. Both resembled a pub as much as *ceviche* resembles fish-and-chips.

I tried again to explain to the driver what I pictured when I thought of the word *pub*. Nothing registered until I added, "In England there's one in every village."

"*Ah!*" he exclaimed. "*Inglaterra. Una club brittanica!*"

"*Sí,*" I agreed. "Britannica."

He dropped me off at the Spratley Arms.

The Spratley looked like a pub – which meant it looked like a house – but it was the kind of establishment that made me wonder how zoning laws worked in Lima. It wasn't anywhere near the commercial district. Atahualpa was a residential street lined with two-story homes fronted by gardens and security fences. It was also dark, a victim of either the rolling blackouts or a recent attack by the Shining Path on the district's electrical supply. Dark and deserted. When the taxi dropped me off I felt further than a mile from the Parque Central. The fog that lent a London atmosphere to the busier streets made the road outside the Spratley feel like an abandoned lane. It drifted around the one working street lamp two blocks away, a lamp whose only purpose could have been to make Jack the Ripper feel at home should he have been out for a stroll. It certainly didn't illuminate the street. It barely revealed the bricks at its own base and never came near the dark building that the driver assured me was a pub.

"Está abierta?" I asked him.

"Sí, claro," he replied as though my question was foolish.

It sure didn't look open. When I knocked on the door I expected someone inside to tell me to get lost.

The girl who opened the door didn't tell me to get lost although if she had I would have complied. She was six-feet tall and had a farm-girl frame that suggested if I put up a fight we would be evenly matched. We didn't fight. When I told her I was looking for a pub she welcomed me inside.

The place was packed. At least sixty people filled the cramped house. I say sixty but it was hard to count because the interior was divided into small rooms clustered around an oval center. The rooms were accessible by short hallways and had cutouts in the walls so people eating could see out to the bar. The oval was near the bar but had no tables. Its floor dipped so anyone standing there was like a groundling in an Elizabethan theater, heard but almost hidden from sight. In the back of the house a brace of windows hid behind velvet drapes. Before them two men wearing Springboks rugbys threw darts at a board.

The crowd was animated. Everyone talked at once, drowning out the rumble of a diesel generator out back. There was no music but that was alright because any noise that rose above the chatter was dampened anyway by thick carpet and heavy paintings on the walls. The sole welcome sound that broke through the conversations was the *thock* of a pint glass being set on the bar. Smoke pressed like a cloud deck against the ceiling, thick enough that I had to duck to see under it and making me wonder not for the first time if short men in Peru had a lower incidence of lung cancer than the rest of us.

"Tienes hambre?" the girl asked. Her Nordic looks made Spanish out of place coming from her lips.

"Sí."

"You are English?"

"American."

"*Qué bueno!* There is an American here tonight. Do you want I should find you a seat?"

"May I sit at the bar?" I asked.

"There are no seats at the bar. Have you been here before?"

"No, never."

"*Bueno, bienvenidos.* I will tell my father you are here."

"And who are you?" I asked before she could get away.

She smiled. She wasn't gorgeous but she didn't have to be: she was tall, she was blond, and she looked strong enough to shag a man all night and then chop wood all day. I would have let her throw me over her knee if she'd asked. Probably she guessed that.

"I am Lorena."

"Hello, Lorena. I'm Mike."

She smiled again and ducked away.

I made for the bar. People looked up as I squeezed past, their expressions friendly. It was a typical crowd for Bogotá – dark faces as well as white with the sound of Spanish, English, British-accented English, and the inevitable German chatted in a corner. I smiled at a pretty girl with black hair who met my eyes. She laughed and looked away. Yup, a typical crowd.

"You're thirsty," a voice informed me. A meaty hand appeared in front of my nose clutching a pint of Guinness.

I accepted the glass. "Thank you."

The hand belonged to an equally meaty man with a large head and a red face that came from the exertion of belonging to its owner.

"Angus Durban," he introduced himself and held out a pint of his own to knock against mine. "I'm the proprietor. Welcome." Then he turned and held up a hand. "Ladies and gentlemen!" he bellowed. "We have a visitor. Welcome him, please!"

Everyone raised their glass and yelled something by way of greeting. I lifted my glass in reply.

If Lorena wasn't enough to make me like the Spratley then Angus was. Establishments where the owner says hello are a notch above the rest.

He gave me a lightning tour. Then because all the tables were taken he set me down at a bench with a handful of other recent arrivals who were cooling their heels and quaffing ales as they waited to eat. I thought we were in a holding pen but after a while Angus reappeared carrying one end of a thick oaken table to place before us. Lorena had the other end. I jumped up to help her but she put a hand on my chest and pushed me back down into my seat – without setting the table down. Angus laughed.

"My daughters are beautiful but they are strong!" he boasted. "Aren't you, Madeleine?"

His daughter flexed her biceps, then blew her father a kiss before dashing away.

"I thought her name was Lorena," I said to Angus.

He shook his head and pointed across the room.

"That is Lorena over there," he corrected me. I followed his gaze and saw to my amazement that Lorena was indeed on the far side of the bar serving another table. Then who...?

"I have twin daughters!" Angus bellowed. "Twin daughters who are beautiful *and* strong!"

Beautiful and strong and busy. Whenever anyone left the house another person arrived to take their place. The twins shuttled food and drink all night, pausing to chat, joke, and flirt with every table.

"You'll have another pint," Angus declared and slapped a new glass before me.

"Oh, thanks," I told him, "but one's enough. I'm a light drinker."

"It's on the house."

"No, no, you can't do that."

He scoffed. "It's my pub. I can do what I want."

"You'd better do what he says," a round-faced man across the table advised. He had curly hair and wrinkles across his forehead that pressed together when he spoke. "He told me that if I don't drink at least two pints of beer he won't let me leave."

The others around the table – two couples and a fellow in a tweed jacket who cheerfully admitted that he was buzzed – were relieved to hear the round-faced man's confession. Angus had told them the same thing.

Madeleine came round and asked who wanted to eat. The menu was two items long: we could have fish and chips, or shepherd's pie. We ordered and she was back in ten minutes, putting down platters that would have stopped a bullet even without the food piled on them.

At nine o'clock someone yelled, "Here now, make room!" The bartender unlocked a closet and motioned to the fellows playing darts. They interrupted their game to carry an old Zenith television out of the closet and set it on a table by the bar. When Angus turned it on, a soccer match had just begun.

"Uruguay and Argentina," a local at the next table explained. "The Copa America."

"Wasn't that game yesterday?" I asked, confused.

"Yes, but this is a re-broadcast. The FARC blew up a relay tower on Montserrrat Tuesday so only half the city had reception during the match. You weren't here? You should have seen it – we almost rioted. Colombians will tolerate car-bombings and kidnappings but take away our *fútbol* and there will be trouble."

The game began but the volume was kept low. A handful of people gathered to watch it while the rest of us glanced over from time to time. At intervals the serious fans announced a goal or good play, at which point the rest of us looked over to see the highlight and cheer. Then we went back to talking.

The round-faced man was from Argentina. He wore a wedding band but introduced his companion as his girlfriend. She was small and delicately pretty with the look of an urban princess who knew her way around a Gucci store but not much else. Still she was pleasant and an enthusiastic listener. Next to her was a couple from Capetown by way of Brazil. They told us they ran a restaurant in Rio de Janeiro and were thinking of relocating to Bogotá – they were in town now to assess the business climate and the violence first-hand.

The fellow in the tweed jacket was Russell, a happy drunk with a library of tall tales in his head. Young and rakishly handsome, he hailed from Vanuatu and spoke in a delightful Australian accent that flowed off his tongue as smooth as the Guinness heading the opposite direction. When I sat down he was already two sheets to the wind and looking for a third.

"Here, love," he told the Argentine girl when she finished telling us how she couldn't walk down tree-lined boulevards for fear of crickets falling out of the trees and landing on her. "A cricket is bonzer. At home we've got the drop bears."

"Drop bears?"

"*Yeeah.* Drop bears. Crazed marsupials, they are. Like koalas but with fangs – and great claws that'll tear a man's arm off. They hang up in the trees and wait for you to walk under. They like children the best which is why where I grew up all boys and girls carry shotguns to school."

The girl from Buenos Aires hung on every word, so intense was his tone. The South Africans, too, albeit with doubt in their eyes. They were about to ask if he was serious when Russell interrupted.

"Of course, they don't compare to the screaming bunyips," he continued, stretching his arms out to describe a mutant strain of carnivorous rabbits. "Four-foot-long when they're born, and then they grow..."

At half past ten the game ended. The dart players were away and Angus was busy so before anyone could get to the set a news program began with a story about Alan Garcia. A scattering of boos greeted the president's face.

A lady near the groundling pit threw a handful of Intis at the screen. The Inti had replaced the worthless sol in 1985, shortly after Garcia was elected, but five years on it still wasn't worth the paper it was printed on. Inflation ran at thousands of percent. Workers' wages were stagnant which meant that one's ability to buy anything decreased with each passing day. Many employers let their people go home on payday the instant they received their checks so they could shop for food before the bills lost value. There were rumors of a new currency in the works, another government attempt to deal with the country's grinding poverty and inefficient economy by lopping zeros off the legal tender, but no one saw that as anything but a stopgap measure. What the government really needed to do was stop running a deficit, crack down on corruption, and lower the barriers to foreign trade but those steps required political capital that Garcia hadn't had since the day he was elected. Everyone in the room understood the woman's willingness to shower her president with the contents of her wallet.

But the government had its defenders. Garcia had been a young and romantic figure when he came to office, Peru's own JFK, and some people were loathe to let go. A bearded fellow in one of the dining rooms now poked his head out the little window to chastise the critics. They responded with catcalls, whereupon the man came out to the bar and began to lecture everyone on the politics of the Socialist International and what it could still accomplish. The booing increased.

Our Vanuatan smiled. "The man's got spirit," he said appreciatively, thumping the table. "Here, here!"

"He's a blithering idiot," the Capetown woman corrected him. "The Socialists are just as bad for the economy here as they are in Brazil."

"Of course they are," said the drunk. "And this bloke's a witless prat if he thinks Garcia is worth anything more than a doorstop at the palace. But he's got spirit! We like that Down Under. Here, here!"

The bearded man continued to speak. Someone offered him a pint to sit down but that inflamed his outrage. He raised his voice, his cadence rolling as in a sermon. My favorite line was when he thundered, *"No se puede machacar a los trabajadores debajo de sus montones de dinero!"* which I translated to mean that no one could crucify the working people upon a cross of gold – or in this case crush them under a pile of Intis – a quaint Marxist channeling of William Jennings Bryan. Like Bryan, the speaker was firm in his convictions, firm enough that he felt we all needed a tutorial in the politics of the Peruvian left. But reality worked against him. The locals had already had their lesson in what the socialists could accomplish. With inflation soaring and blackouts in the city, he had his work cut out for him convincing our crowd that President Garcia knew what he was doing.

At a signal from Angus, Lorena approached and offered to escort the speaker back to his table. The smile as she did so would have melted my heart and relegated politics to a far corner of my brain but this man was made of sterner stuff. He waved her away, shouting that true Peruvian patriots understood that their problems were due to Argentina and Brazil, not to the government.

Lorena may or may not have been a true Peruvian patriot but she knew how to control her customers. With one hand holding a tray, she gripped the bearded man with the other hard enough that he winced, and repeated her offer. The two Springbok fans reappeared by her side.

"Bueno," she told the man sweetly. "Enough politics. Time for you to go home."

He might have argued had the two rugby players not been there. While the rest of us applauded, they rescued the man from Lorena's grasp and escorted him to the front door. He tried one more appeal to our national pride with a shout of "Long live President Garcia!" but the reply from a wag was immediate: *"Don't get lost on those dark streets!"*

Throughout the evening there was a small but lively crowd in a corner by the kitchen. Noise there picked up after the Garcia supporter left. Some kind of a drinking game was going on – when he heard that our companion from Vanuatu excused himself to participate.

The evening wore on. The South Africans bade us good night and went home. The cooks shut down the stoves. Angus rang Last Call at eleven but announced it a pro forma exercise and said everyone could keep drinking so long as they behaved.

More shouts rose from the drinkers. One of the voices sounded familiar. I guessed Russell was doing well so I drifted over to check his progress. Soon everyone felt the urge and we stood several rows deep to watch the half-dozen hard-core tipplers compete. I could see Russell and a trio of others, and the backs of the remaining two. He sat at the foot of the table with a devilish grin and a pair of empty pint glasses before him.

"Right, another round then!" he called.

"What's this?" I asked the man next to me.

"It's called *Copia*," the fellow explained. "A drinking game."

Lorena appeared with a pint of Cuzqueña for each player. Russell set his before him, cleared away the empties, and readied his hands like a gunfighter.

"Right," he repeated, and looked around at his opponents. "Ready?"

They nodded.

"Here we go, then."

He reached up with his right hand and brushed his cheek. The man to his right immediately did the same and then each of the other players in turn. When it came back round to Russell he repeated the move but then added a gesture with his other hand as though wiping his nose. The sequence swept round the table. Each time the turn came back to

Russell he added something else until very soon he looked like a spastic first-base coach sending a catalogue of signals to the pitcher. After four circuits I realized this wasn't a game I could win sober – even if my coordination held up my short-term memory wouldn't. The group at the table didn't suffer the same weakness. They kept up with Russell and if anything their motions grew faster.

In the eighth circuit the fellow to Russell's right finally screwed up, scratching his nose when he should have tugged his ear. The crowd roared and he chugged his beer as penalty. In the next round he began the sequence with an invention of his own and at first seemed to have an edge over the others with a series of tricky facial moves including winking in sequence and wiggling his nose. In the end, though, his own complexity tripped him up and he bobbled the maneuvers. Another pint went down his throat. Thus began a vicious cycle of inebriation that two rounds later made him wave his hands in defeat as he was too tipsy even to see the table.

The signing and drinking continued. Any slip-up was perilous. A mistake led to guzzling a pint, which in turn made it that much harder to maintain coordination. Only laser focus and – presumably – a passing familiarity with alcohol allowed players to survive. Russell more than held his own. Ensconced at the end of the table he watched his opponents like a patient yogi, acknowledging their efforts but batting down all challenges without breaking a sweat. He copied others' movements with smiling aplomb and initiated his own with a throw-caution-to-the-wind assurance. His beer sat before him untouched so long that he requested an extra pint from Lorena just to satisfy his thirst *("Here, love. Toss me a butcher before I blow away!")*

Others weren't so gifted. Within half an hour the group was reduced by half. The latest to go was a German who seemed indomitable until Russell upped the ante by making one of his moves include standing up and slapping the soles of his shoes one after another while shouting *Oy-oy!* Everyone mastered that once but on the second time round the German got as far as *Oy...scheise!* before stumbling backward into the crowd.

It came down to three. I still couldn't see either of the faces at my end of the table but when they leaped up for Russell's move it was clear the person closest to me was a girl. She had black hair and a curving figure that begged for closer scrutiny. I squeezed deeper into the crowd.

"Más cerveza!" the girl called.

"Bollocks!" Russell replied. "Time to get stonkered. How about something stronger?"

"Pisco?" the girl asked.

"Vodka," the man next to her grumbled.

Russell smiled and eyed his opponent appreciatively. He'd found a soul-mate.

"Vodka!" he called.

Madeleine brought shots and set one before each of the players.

Now the varsity team went to work. The girl began the next round, passing her right hand over her head as though dodging a missile. Russell and the other man copied her perfectly. When it was her turn again she followed up with the same move by her left hand. Each move after that was a variation on some wave so that pretty soon it looked like the whole table was engaged in a disco-ish, Hindu dance. They went round and round until I completely lost track of who was mimicking whom and couldn't guarantee that any of them hadn't screwed up already. For all I knew they were making it up on the fly. But they weren't. The drinkers knew what they were doing and they were all good enough to tell if each other was staying honest. Each boasted a steel-trap memory, good enough to get them at least nine circuits into the round before Russell bobbed up when he should have gone down and the opposing pair called him out. The crowd roared. He smiled, acknowledged his fault, and held his shot aloft for everyone to see.

"To the Queen!" he toasted. *To the queen!* the crowd replied. He downed the shot with ease and eyed us mischievously. "That's my cat," he explained. "I call her The Queen."

He transferred his attention back to his opponents.

"You're good!" he announced, pointing at the girl and bowing. Then his eyes narrowed. "But are you this good?"

He launched into a routine that again had them rising from their chairs. That must have been his secret weapon, the constant up-down, up-down, for only six circuits into the round the girl lost track. She leaped up and then hesitated, lost. Russell raised a fist in triumph. We cheered.

And so it went. The rounds continued and the victories and losses piled up for each of the players. Russell did well but every now and then he lost and had to suck down an ounce of Smirnoff. He did it nonchalantly, relishing the glow that came to his cheeks and never letting his insouciant smirk leave his face, but after a while the effort showed. The pair opposite him lost their fair share of rounds, too. Soon all of them were moving slower, looser. I would have been under the table in a coma for the same amount of liquor but these three fought on, competition keeping them upright. It wasn't until the sixth round of shots – when Russell told a bad joke about a kangaroo and a compact car and all three of them laughed far longer than it deserved – that their utter drunkenness showed through. The crowd sensed a finale.

The girl crashed first. For a while I thought she had the men licked. The wavy moves were working for her and the one time she turned toward me

– after four shots of vodka and I don't know how many beers – her eyes were still focused and her gaze steady. Then suddenly on a round that her companion led off, after only the second motion – a rolling gesture that might have preceded a courtesan's curtsey – she fixated on her own hand and froze. She rolled it out in front of her just as he did but then stayed in that position, studying her fingers as though trying to remember how many were there when she started the game. There was a long silence as she stood, tree-like, her black hair draped in a lovely crescent across her upper back. Then she toppled face first into her palm.

Russell was on his feet in a flash and caught her before she could crack her head on the table. That was no mean accomplishment given that his brain should have been as pickled as hers and she seemed to acknowledge it with a grateful wave. He rolled her over and helped her to stand. The two men then steadied her but even though she managed to get upright it was clear the gig was up. Her balance was no longer sound and her eyes wandered – they seemed to pick up the earth's rotation for the first time and found it wanting. To respectful applause she allowed Angus to help her through the crowd to where she could get some fresh air.

It was as she staggered away that I saw what a looker she really was: a Latin beauty, maybe Brazilian, with a model's face and full breasts that made me envy Angus' duty. It was also as she left that she leaned over to kiss her companion on the head and wish him luck, and he patted her reassuringly on the butt.

Sam.

My jaw dropped.

He didn't see me. Instinctively I wanted to shout his name but the shock of recognition was too much so I just stood there mute. Before I recovered the game resumed and I lost my chance. He and Russell sat back down and the crowd closed around again. I was stuck two rows back, peering over the Spratley regulars to see the conclusion of the duel.

Sam looked different. It was Sam, no doubt: square jaw, neat hair, perfect posture at the table even as he locked eyes with Russell's carefree smirk. But there was something about him that wasn't Sam, something out of place with the reactionary martinet we knew in the squadron. It wasn't obvious – I had to study him for a couple of rounds to figure it out. One round he lost and drank a shot but the next he tripped up Russell with an uncharacteristic hula motion after leaping to his feet and climbing onto his chair. The suddenness caught Russell off-guard so even though he repeated the action perfectly, when he came down he laughed so hard he missed Sam's next move completely. The rest of us roared in approval and Sam himself burst out laughing.

That's what did it for me: *he burst out laughing.* I'd never seen Sam laugh. Hell, the only time I'd even seen him smile was once when Clunk on a whim decided to re-enlist and asked Sam as aircraft commander to read the orders in the back of the plane at a dirt airstrip in Brazil where brush fires threatened to engulf the field any minute. Sam had raced through the official script and then leaped back into the cockpit so we could take off, but as we taxied into position he grinned at the absurdity of the event. It was an odd grin then, strained, almost as though his face was trying it out for the first time. Now there was nothing strained about his emotions. He was having fun.

"Royght!" Russell slurred, holding up his hands for silence. "You're a tricky one, ace. A regular dinky-di. You might even have me. But we'll see. We'll see."

He drank his shot, not bothering to toast anyone this time, sucking it down and still throwing his confident half-smile across the table. Sam stared back warily, leaning on the table to keep from falling over.

The final round began with both men on their feet and no one in the crowd sure which of them was more crocked.

Russell began. He started with an I'm-a-little-teapot sequence, slapping one hand on his hip and stretching the other one out to the side, then transitioned to a couple of hops and a few head wags. He followed those up with the *oy-oy* routine again.

Sam followed, trying to hold his gunfighter stare but having a hard time since Russell was just plain too funny to watch. It was clear the two men enjoyed each other's company. Neither wanted the game to end even as the number of moves stretched into the double digits for the first time and it became harder for either of them to stay upright.

The head wags in particular were dangerous. When the world is fuzzy already, shaking up your brain is never a good idea. After a few rounds of that both men wobbled on their feet and the rest of us gasped in anticipation. But they recovered and persevered. It wasn't until Round 14, the longest stretch of the match, that Russell shoved them both over the edge. He finished his 13th move by pounding his chest like a gorilla and then spun around in a complete three hundred and sixty degree turn to face his opponent with a "Top that!" glare. A woman near him *ooohhh'ed* in admiration.

But the spin was too much. Though he got his hands back on the table Russell's balance now deserted him. His feet moved under him like a green sailor on a pitching deck. His smirk disappeared and he fought to stay on his feet.

Sam didn't notice. The instant Russell completed his spin he launched into his own attempt to repeat the fourteen moves, wanting to do it before their memory faded. The result was that while Russell was on one side of the table staggering like a newborn calf, Sam was on the other wagging, slapping, and pointing until finally he, too, reached the last move and threw himself into the twirl. For him it was also a bridge too far. Now both of them staggered like tired boxers, knowing the game was up but trying to stay on their feet long enough for the other to fall so they could claim victory,

The crowd surged and retreated around them. Nobody wanted to interfere but none wanted either player to hurt himself, either, if he collapsed to the floor. We were caught in a *lean forward – no, don't touch!* doubt that made us bob and weave as badly as the players. If a stranger had wandered into the Spratley at that point he might have thought he had stumbled on some weird dance cult.

Finally Russell's candle blew out. He staggered around the corner of the table on what looked like a mission toward the last shot of vodka but then his eyes rolled back and he fell toward his opponent. At the same moment Sam's square jaw dropped for the last time. Mouth open but eyes still alight with more fire than they ever showed in the squadron, he fainted on his feet and teetered into the Vanuatan coming the other way. The two men plonked into each other. For a moment they balanced like poles in a teepee, each holding the other up, the lone shot glass beside them on the table. Then they fell sideways into our arms.

"Seen the captain yet?" I asked Luz the next morning in the driveway of the hotel. We had a late take-off to return to Panama so it was noon when I threw my bags into the station manager's SUV for the drive to the airport. Luz was already there, anxious to get home.

"No, sir. Not yet. But I'm sure he's been up for hours already, probably polishing his boots and doing pushups."

I pictured Sam ten hours earlier when the taxi driver had helped me carry him into the elevator and up to his room. I doubted very much that he had done any pushups since then.

Georgie started the engine and launched into a story about how he had solved the stray dog problem around the hangar by contracting with the owner of a local Chinese restaurant.

"Well, I'll go see if he's okay," I offered.

"No need. There he is."

Luz was right. The elevator dinged and Sam stepped out looking as pressed and trim as ever. His flight suit was even ironed. When he walked to the front desk to check out it might not have been with a spring in his step but it was still as careful a pace as you would see on any parade ground.

"Good morning, crew," he greeted us and climbed into the back seat.

"Morning, boss," Luz replied.

"Morning," I agreed warily, eyeing him for any sign that he remembered the night before. There was none. On close inspection I saw that his eyes were puffy and his skin pale – as though he had started the day bent over the toilet rather than doing calisthenics – but overall he looked normal. The martinet was still in there.

Georgie pulled out into traffic and headed for the Callao airport. Sam pulled out his flight cap and buffed the captain's bars with his sleeve.

"You guys have a good night?" he asked. "Anything exciting?"

His tone was flat. There was nothing hidden in it. Luz talked about a contest he had watched on TV while I muttered something non-committal.

"No, me neither," he said. "Slept like a log." When Georgie lambasted all of us for being lame Sam waved away the objections and added, "George, when I go on a trip it's a chance for me to get away from work and relax. Just rest and recharge the batteries. The grind will be waiting for us when we get home."

He was serious. Absolutely serious. I stole glances to see if he was uncomfortable with the flat-out lie he had just told but his face was an open book – not the slightest indication that he even knew he had been dishonest. Either he didn't remember or he had long since come to terms with his bipolar life. I thought back to the night before as the crowd dispersed and I found myself obligated to see my unconscious pilot back to the hotel.

"He's hilarious," Angus had told me as Lorena and Madeleine carried Russell and Sam outside to wait for cabs.

"You know him?" I asked.

"Of course! Sam's a regular. Comes in whenever he's in town. The funniest sober guy I know. He told a story last time about a blind date that had everyone rolling on the floor."

"Him? He told a joke?"

"Sure. Why's that so hard to believe?"

"Because he's not a funny guy."

"Of course he is. He only gets serious when he drinks – then he tries to do the tough-as-nails bit to psyche out the others in *Copia.* That's why Russell always goes over the top with his moves. He tries to get Sam to laugh. It usually works, too, because normally Sam doesn't drink and so he breaks down earlier. Last night was the first time I've seen him go the distance with Russell. I think it was because his girlfriend was here egging him on."

His girlfriend?

"You'll see him home then?" Lorena asked me, coming inside and pointing over her shoulder to where she had left my charge in the front garden. Sam was propped up against a stone bench while Russell was sprawled on the flagstone path. They looked like a crime scene.

"Do I have to take Russell, too?"

"No. Maarten will get him home. They live in the same block of flats." She indicated one of the Springbok blokes.

"Uh, then yeah. We're staying in the same hotel."

"Good. We wouldn't want anything to happen to him. He's so much fun whenever he comes here."

"Uh-huh."

She leaned over and gave me a friendly peck on the cheek.

"You are so serious!" she giggled. "You should come back with him next time, shouldn't he, Papa? Yes, definitely. You come with Sam. He will show you how to lighten up."

11. Kweasey

Besides Griswold Beckett, the only other person in the squadron that anybody wanted to kill was Dale Kweasey. Dale was a first lieutenant and, in contrast to Griswold, a competent pilot. But he was also a jerk. Or, in Charlie Manson's words, he was a "careerist, back-stabbing, political-maneuvering rectum."

Dale managed to offend everyone just by being Dale. He was intensely interested in his own career, intensely suspicious of other people's motives, and intensely prone to building himself up by putting other people down. Because of those traits he volunteered for additional duties that were completely unsuited to anyone exhibiting them and therefore afforded himself maximum opportunity to insult everyone within a local sortie of the base.

He begged to be our Total Quality Management officer, for example. TQM, like sociotechnical theory and Six Sigma, was one of a series of productivity-improvement business models that the Air Force continuously experiments with in an effort to be more efficient. Most last only a few years, long enough for people to get annoyed and go back to how they did things before or long enough for the person who pushed the idea in the first place to get promoted and move on to other interests. While it lasted, TQM urged the melding of technical skills with an optimum social environment in which to practice them. Dale understood that to mean that his job was to walk around and bark at people, "You're fucking that up! Do it this way!"

I knew Dale because he sought me out after learning that I had passed the Air Force competency test in Spanish. Dale was fluent in Spanish and Portuguese. He confronted me at the ops desk, asked if I spoke Spanish, then exploded with a torrent of questions *en español.* I answered a few.

"Your accent sucks," Dale said. "And you should have used the imperfect tense to describe your studies, not the preterit."

"Is this a test?" I asked. "Because if it is, I already passed the Air Force exam. They're happy with me."

"That exam is bogus," Dale scoffed.

Lowell was behind the ops desk, trying to ignore us as he leafed through a Spanish edition of Cosmopolitan magazine.

"Some would say you're bogus, Dale," he commented without looking up.

Dale scowled and leaned over the desk.

"I'm a linguist," he hissed. "I know what I'm talking about."

Lowell burst out laughing.

"A linguist? Who says?"

"I speak fluent Spanish and Portuguese!"

"So what? My grandmother speaks Norwegian and German. Does that mean she's a linguist? No, it means she's an old woman. And she doesn't run around tooting her own horn, either. So shut up."

Dale tried to retort but Lowell cut him off.

"I won't argue with an idiot, Dale. You'll just drag me down to your level and beat me with experience. Go away."

Our linguist glared at him but Lowell, who fed on glares, flipped him off and went back to reading an article entitled, *"Tu orgasmo, cómo puedes reconocerlo."*

Dale turned back to me.

"I hope you don't have to use it," he advised. "You'll give the rest of us a bad name."

Personally I thought he already had a head start on that.

For a few days I told myself that Dale wasn't such a bad guy and I just needed to get to know him. Besides, he was right. My Spanish wasn't as good as it could be. I certainly didn't consider myself fluent.

But then Declan found out Dale had been badmouthing the two of us to various instructors in hopes of eliminating us as competition in the aircraft commander upgrade. Because of our experience Declan and I were first in line to move to the left seat in the C-27 and Dale, who had come to Panama direct from flight training, wanted to derail our advancement. He reminded anyone who would listen of Declan's incident in Africa and my cockpit mutiny in California, hoping to show we needed 'more seasoning' before we took the controls in South America. So I decided that first impressions were indeed correct: he was a jerk.

Fortunately no one listened to Dale. Declan and I became aircraft commanders while Kweasey seethed. Walt, impish instigator that he was, celebrated by assigning Dale to be our co-pilots as often as he could. That lasted for exactly one ride with each of us, for Dale couldn't take any more.

He was in the right seat on Declan's cherry ride as aircraft commander, a one-day out-and-back to some airfields in Colombia. Nothing was out of the ordinary until Declan flew the approach into Villavicencio.

They were coming out of Bogotá high in the mountains and so were a long way up to start with. Then the snow-capped peaks bid them farewell. The ground beneath them dropped, plunging to the jungle floor where Villavicencio sat at the base of the foothills, two miles below Bogotá and only slightly higher than sea level. Declan slowed down while they were still at 20,000 feet and dropped the gear and flaps. As the flaps came down and the gear increased the drag, Declan nosed over more to keep up the airspeed. It was an efficient way to descend on a steep angle but Dale glanced outside at the trees and cringed.

"What are you doing?" he demanded. His tone was pedantic. Even when he wasn't in charge he acted as though he were.

"It's called landing," Declan replied. "Just as I briefed."

"Yeah, but I didn't know you meant you were going to configure this high. I don't like big approaches like this."

"Big approaches? What's a big approach? We're just descending."

"You're descending too steep. I don't like seeing that much ground out front. It's not safe."

Declan looked at him in horror, as though suddenly finding out that his prom date was his sister. Still carrying a chip on his shoulder for not flying fighters, Declan didn't actually call Kweasey a pussy but the word hung unspoken in the air.

"Hmm, you know, I think you're right," he said. "This angle won't work." He pulled the nose back up which caused the airspeed to bleed off. With his right hand he reached up to the overhead panel. "We may need to increase it."

With the flick of a switch he threw the propellers into Approach mode.

The blades on the C-27's props swung in a vertical arc like three wings attached to a hub. Each 'wing' generated lift that, because it was directed aft, pulled the aircraft through the air. That's what made the plane go forward. We could vary the angle of the blades – how much lift they produced – within three ranges: the Normal range, the Ground range, and the Approach range. The Normal range was just that, the angles of the blades that we did all our usual flying in. The Ground range allowed us to reduce the blade angle to almost nothing so we could taxi around on the ramp at low speeds and not have to be tapping our brakes all the time to slow down. The Approach angle was in between Normal and Ground. It reduced the pitch of the blades well below the Normal range so that instead of producing lift and pulling us through the air, the props instead swung almost flat, creating drag that would make it harder to move forward. It was as though we had swapped two power-producing engines on the wings with two huge dinner plates instead. Or, imagine the difference between jogging into a headwind carrying nothing versus carrying two huge sheets of plywood. What the Approach mode did for us was allow us to keep the engines turning but create so much drag that the only way to maintain our airspeed was to point the nose of the plane at the ground, making us fall so fast that air passed over our wings on its own. This meant we could descend directly over an airfield rather than make a long, angled approach to it. Normally there was no reason to do that but theoretically it would reduce our exposure to ground fire in a combat situation. In Declan's case it allowed him to scare the hell out of his copilot.

"Oh, Jesus," Dale cried, and lunged for the stick to pull the nose back up.

"DON'T touch my controls!" Declan ordered. He banked the aircraft sharply to the left and pulled. Putting g's on the plane while in a 60-degree turn soaked up some of the plane's energy during the dive so he could point the nose down even further.

They could no longer see the horizon in the windscreen. There was no longer any sky out front at all, just green jungle and brown ground spinning around like clothes in a washer. Somewhere in the middle of the spin was the airfield but Dale, pinned to the side of his seat, was suddenly too nauseous to look for it.

"Oh, god. Oh, god," he repeated, his face contorted in pain.

"You know," Declan opined, propping his foot up on the parking brake. "Some would say that if all you can see out the window is ground and all you can hear from the passengers is commotion, then things aren't as they should be."

"Some would say," Bird agreed from the back. He strapped himself into the fold-down seat and hung on tight.

Declan mused while the world spiraled up at them.

"This reminds me: when it's my time to die I want to go like my grandfather did – sleeping peacefully at the wheel, not crying and wailing like everyone else in the car."

Dale reached for the propeller switch but couldn't quite make it. His skin turned gray.

"Say," Declan asked Bird, "doesn't Villavicencio have that woman who sells the enchiladas? The ones wrapped in palm leaves?"

"No, that's Apiay. Fifty miles down the road."

"Oh, you're right. Damn."

"Oh, god. Oh, god."

I was blessed with Dale's presence on a ride of my own in November. It was a three-day trip to Peru to support a joint Colombian-Brazilian push against drug traffickers in the tri-border region. Kweasey lectured me on Brazilian politics for two days, which might have been interesting except for his ceaseless injects of personal experience and name-dropping to illustrate his points.

"One night at dinner in São Paolo, I was talking to a senator from Mato Grosso – I know most of the people at the embassy so he wanted to meet me – and he asked my opinion of..."

He also found opportunities on the ground to advise that I keep quiet and let him do all the talking. When I spoke anyway, he insisted on following everything I said with, "What the lieutenant meant to say is..." He would follow me into base operations to make sure I filed the flight plan correctly and then explain to the officials what I had written just in case they couldn't read. And when the other crew that was already in Iquitos for the hub-and-spoke had trouble with a tower clearance, Kweasey jumped uninvited into that fray, too. He wanted to clear things up, he said, which they might have appreciated except that he did it by bad-mouthing them to the Peruvians. He was, as we say, "all thrust and no vector," so full of energy and self-promotion that it all had to go somewhere no matter the occasion. It was like flying with a malevolent busybody aunt.

Nevertheless, we managed to get along until one morning when we took off from Iquitos, headed for Tabatinga carrying a load of ammunition and outboard motors for some Colombian Riverines. The load was heavy and we took off at max gross weight, just over 57,000 pounds. Twenty minutes after takeoff, at 17,000 feet, the windscreen in front of Kweasey shattered. Everyone jumped at the *crack!* Dale, flying in the right seat, dove for cover as a spider web of fractures appeared in front of him.

This had happened before. Not to us, but to Papps and Mike Vaneya. Exactly two weeks earlier they had been climbing out of Puerto Barrios on the north coast of Guatemala when Papps' windscreen shattered. It scared the hell out of them at first, just as it did to us, but in reality the fracture wasn't as catastrophic as it looked. It was a design flaw with the windscreen. The windows were two sheets of plexiglass that sandwiched a microfilm-thin layer of defrosting filaments. On some aircraft the seal around the edge of the glass failed and allowed rain-water to seep between the sheets. If enough water got in and the temperature suddenly dropped – as it would when climbing to altitude – the water froze, expanded, and broke the outer layer. The experts with Merrill Technologies were fixing the planes one by one. In the meantime they said not to worry, that despite the fractured look the structural integrity of the windscreen was unaffected. The inner sheet of plexiglass was strong enough to keep us safe, they promised. The window wouldn't fly in and decapitate the pilot behind.

But that was hard to believe when it happened to you.

"Aughhh! Descend! Descend!" Kweasey screamed.

My heart rate under control again, I looked over at the right windscreen. You couldn't see through it anymore but the inner layer was solid. Also, the fractures were confined to Dale's side of the cockpit. I thought about it for a second.

"Why?"

From the floor, Dale couldn't believe his ears.

"Why?" he shrieked. "Why?! What do you mean, why? Get down, now!"

I adjusted the trim to keep us level. We cruised lazily between a pair of snow-white clouds.

"Dude, relax. It's the outer layer. You're safe."

"Outer layer? Safe? Who says? Are you freakin' nuts?"

Clunk poked his head up into the cockpit.

"What's the problem?"

I pointed.

Clunk examined the window like a gallery owner inspecting a new painting.

"Is it going to cave in?"

"Not according to Vince."

He shrugged.

"Okay," he said, and went back to the cabin to lie down.

Dale's eyes were set to pop out of his head.

"What the hell was that?!" he demanded.

"Crew coordination," I replied. "Clunk seems happy with it."

Dale crawled to his knees and shouted into my face.

"The loadmaster? The fucking *loadmaster* is happy with it? He's a high school fucking dropout who pushes boxes around! He doesn't know shit!"

In the back Clunk clicked his mike.

"Noted," was all he said. Kweasey had just made enemies of the entire loadmaster mafia.

I tried to be patient. It wasn't easy. On top of his many other charms Dale had legendary bad breath. Now he was right in my face.

"We...have... to... land!"

"Dale, the inner layer is fine. It's the outer one that's broken. Vince and Harry and all the other guys say it's perfectly safe."

"I'm not getting back in that seat!"

I shrugged. Like Declan, I'd always preferred single-seat aircraft anyway.

"Your choice."

Dale was fit to explode.

"Lieutenant Bleriot!" he shouted. "You need to listen to me! I know what I'm talking about. We need to land this aircraft *now.* We are turning around and going back to Iquitos immediately."

I looked at him, not sure what planet he operated on. For some reason the more excited he got the calmer I felt, which infuriated him further.

"Dale, relax. We're going to Tabatinga. Besides, we can't land for another hour anyway. We're too heavy."

We had maximum weights for both take-off and landing in the C-27. Because of the additional pressure put on the airframe by touching down, our max allowed landing weight was 3,500 pounds less than our take-off weight. Since we'd only been airborne about twenty minutes we still weighed almost 56,000 pounds and needed to burn off another ton of gas before we could land. Could we land early in an emergency? Of course, but I didn't see it being necessary in this case. A broken windshield was a minor problem in the grand scheme of things. There were people at Tabatinga waiting for the equipment we carried. There was no way I was going to delay getting them their stuff just because Kweasey was a wuss. The Air Force had enough image problems.

But Dale wasn't through.

"We can dump fuel," he said. "That'll make us light enough to land."

"No. Absolutely not. I'm not dumping fuel."

"Why the hell not?"

"Because it's the Amazon jungle, that's why not! I'm not dumping fuel on it."

My answer made no sense. I was a tree-hugger but if we dumped fuel overboard while at 17,000 feet the gas would evaporate as it fell. Nothing would make it down to the trees. We were creating just as much pollution by flying around and burning the gas as we would by dumping it. But that didn't matter to me. It was the principle. I wasn't dumping gas and we weren't turning around.

Dale stayed on the floor all the way to Tabatinga. He also didn't shut up. For an hour I listened to him vent on everything from the structural limits of the aircraft to my lack of fitness as an officer to the safety reports he would file once we were back in Panama. I was glad he didn't have a gun. Our weapons were all in the hell-hole and Kweasey probably considered getting one out to seize control of the aircraft. But with Clunk in the back I was confident that wouldn't happen. So instead I let him vent.

On final approach he finally crawled back into the copilot's seat, unwilling to trust me to land by myself. He stayed there in a half-crouch, bent over in a wincing, ducking position, expecting the window to collapse at any moment and shoot inward at him at a hundred miles per hour. It didn't. The only excitement came at 500 feet when Clunk leaned forward and shouted "Boo!" in Kweasey's ear, sending Dale into near-cardiac arrest.

12. Rasmussen

BY ALL RIGHTS Lt Col Rasmussen shouldn't have flown as well as he did. As squadron commander he spent his days, nights, and weekends handling the administrative demands of running an operational flying unit that had four models of aircraft and dozens of people to track, train, support, and lead. He didn't have time to fly.

So he rarely did. If he was lucky he got two or three hours a month in a plane, usually flying in the local traffic pattern. That compared to thirty to forty hours a month for the rest of us (sixty in the case of Walt). He almost never got off-station to see what we did down in the jungle or at the remote strips up in Honduras and Guatemala. He had to settle for talking to us and reading our trip reports to know what was going on. He loved being in charge but as a born operator tracking things second-hand was hugely frustrating for him. He wanted to be in the thick of things.

Such was his life and Rasmussen loved and hated it. The competing personas were forever in conflict. For example, nothing pleased him more than going to bat for one of his troops. He loved it when someone disregarded the AOC's instructions in the interests of safety because it gave him an opportunity to *not* punish us as the Group commander directed. But other times the sheer number of things he had to keep track of wore him down. Evan once stopped by to see him after everyone else had gone home for the day and found the commander slumped in his chair, shaking his head as he stared at pages of bureaucracy strewn around his desk.

"Don't ever do this to yourself, Lieutenant," he ordered Evan. "Don't ever become a commander."

Since he spent so much time being a leader and so little being a pilot, Rasmussen could barely keep current in even the simplest flying tasks. If there were any justice in the world he should have scratched his head and fumbled his way around the cockpit whenever he flew the C-27.

But he didn't. While most commanders have to be talked through a flight, Rasmussen's abilities were top-notch. Whenever I had a chance to observe how he flew, he did fine. Maybe a little slow responding to checklists but otherwise fine. He hit every parameter he briefed whether it was on an instrument approach to Tocumen Airport or simulating an engine-out landing at Howard. His touch on the controls was smooth. His assaults were as good as Walt's. He even watched over our shoulders as the rest of us flew, standing on the cockpit steps to critique airspeed control or climbout. He was a stickler for the limits.

"We have these numbers for a reason, gentlemen," he reminded us regularly, referring to bank angles, throttle settings, or any other of the innumerable parameters that a pilot packs into his head.

One day during pattern practice at Fort Sherman he interrupted the sortie after seeing Flutie fly five approaches five different ways.

"Stop, stop," he ordered. "You're all over the sky."

I was in the right seat and Little Bud and Dale Kweasey were in the cabin waiting their turn to fly but Rasmussen made us land and shut down at the end of the strip to emphasize his point. Drawing a rectangle on a piece of paper, he took us on a mental trip around the pattern and told us what he wanted to see. *Exactly* what he wanted to see. For an hour we sat in the wet heat of the empty parade ground as he paced up and down the cabin, lecturing on the importance of "Flying the way you train and training the way you fly." His voice mixed with the drone of insects in the nearby jungle. Palm trees creaked in the breeze. Parakeets gathered on the HF radio wire and chattered with gusto as though to remind us that if we really wanted to know something about flying they could teach us a thing or two.

So although he was rusty the colonel was tough. When I learned that he would accompany me to Patuca, therefore, I was anxious.

Patuca was the hillside encampment in Ecuador where a handful of international observers lived under the pretext of monitoring a cease-fire between that country and Peru. The squadron had flown there for months supplying the troops with food, fuel, and women; then one day the commander decided he needed to get out of the office.

"Mike," he announced. "I see you're flying the next Jungle Express. Lt Hendricks was your co-pilot but I'm taking his place. It's about time I see where my pilots go when they leave the pattern."

We flew south in good weather, stayed off the coast of Colombia, and coasted into Ecuador north of Esmeraldas. Normally we re-fueled in Guayaquil and then pressed inland but today our plan called for the opposite: a quick drop-in to the remote site followed by a flight back over the mountains for gas. The drop-in was due to us carrying an Ecuadorian colonel who had finished a visit to Panama and now wanted to spend a few nights with the observers.

VIPs aside, I didn't like going directly to the LZ because by the time we got there after flying for two hours we had little fuel to play with in the event the weather was bad. Sure enough, overhead the narrow Patuca Valley we looked down and saw two separate cloud decks closing over the field. A handful of rain showers wandered the jungle beneath them.

I'd landed at Patuca a dozen times or more and knew that there was no way to drop into the valley from above – it was too narrow for a spiral approach and the terrain rose so steeply at the south end that any attempt to climb over it had to be started well in advance. Successful approaches started down the valley from the north. Even those were a crapshoot since the constricted terrain meant one rain shaft could mask three or four more behind it and give pilots an unpleasant surprise just when they thought they had landing assured. But we had found that by staying slow and keeping to one side of the valley we maximized our opportunities to turn around or land if the field came into sight.

So that's what I did. We flew over the valley and then turned west to find a hole in the clouds that went all the way to the trees. That took us thirty miles or so from the north entrance.

For a while it must have seemed to an onlooker as though we had gone home. The Ecuadorian colonel certainly thought so. He popped his head into the cockpit to ask if we had changed our mind about landing. Even Rasmussen grew frustrated. Though I explained the plan he fidgeted in his seat as our destination dropped farther and farther behind us.

Over the Mangosiza River I felt comfortable enough for a letdown. We dropped several thousand feet through openings in the clouds and leveled out at a safe distance above the water. From there we ridge-hopped to Manaus. At Manaus the clouds tightened up again but this time we were below them so we could turn south along the Upano River and head back toward the field.

The cloud deck above us stayed comfortably high at a thousand feet. It had long gashes in it leading to clear air above so I wasn't worried about climbing in case of a problem. But the visibility in front of us soon dropped to four miles as mists from scattered showers mingled with steam off the trees. I slowed down and tread cautiously.

Rasmussen followed along on the map but did so with increasing impatience. Several times he looked ready to say something.

Within three miles of the hillside encampment it looked like we would make it into the field. The only obstacle was one last sheet of rain on a half-mile final. It didn't look like a strong downdraft but the sheet was wide so I called for half-flaps and announced that we would delay to let the rain pass down the valley. We would fly slowly over the camp and then pick and weave our way back to final.

At that my boss had had enough.

"Of, for pity's sake, Mike!" he exclaimed. "We're burning gas like you've got an oil well in your back-yard. I have the controls."

He pointed us toward the field and then executed a right turn to reverse course and put us on a downwind to the landing zone. Then he ordered me to fly again but this time with him as a back-seat driver.

"Six hundred foot-pounds," he instructed, pointing at the torque gauges. "Just like in the pattern back home. 200 knots on the downwind until it's time to configure. And...now, now you can lower the flaps. I don't know why you wanted to lower them earlier. *That made no sense.* This is the picture. Slow to 155 now...turn here!"

With no choice but to follow his micromanagement I flew a perfect rectangular pattern – or as perfect as the terrain allowed. Rasmussen talked the whole way. His straight lines took us through clouds – the ones I had tried to avoid – and we came closer to a ridgeline than I would have liked but basically we flew a pattern just as we would have at Fort Sherman: boxed shape, precise speeds, and never more than thirty degrees of bank. The last brought us close enough to the opposite wall of the valley that the Ecuadorian colonel exclaimed *oh-oh-ohhh!* behind us but when I rolled out on final exactly one mile from the runway Rasmussen was jubilant.

"There!" he pointed out the window. "That's the angle we want and we haven't wasted all our gas and half the day getting here."

It was a good angle. The only problem was that as long as we were on it our view of the dirt strip was obscured by the rain shower between us, causing the landing zone to appear above our dash as a wavy line. When we hit the rain even the line disappeared. Water crashed over the cockpit in torrents and blocked out everything in front of us. I fought to hold us steady as the plane bounced wildly. For a few frightening seconds I couldn't see a thing outside – and this while we were only four hundred feet above the ground.

Then the shower passed. The airstrip appeared again off the nose and the bouncing stopped. Seconds later I plopped us into the first puddle inboard of the cliff's edge.

"Gently, gently," the commander continued his lesson as we coasted to the far end of the strip. The gravel ran for only 1,800 feet but he wouldn't let me touch the brakes until the end was disturbingly close. "None of this smashing on the brakes to stop right away. We have to care for these planes – they're the only ones we have and we've got to make them last."

After we parked, the commander of the local detachment asked if we could use our hydraulic winch to assist his soldiers in uploading a water wagon that he wanted taken to Guayaquil. I was on the verge of saying of course when Lt Col Rasmussen cut me off. No, he said, and then explained that the winch required us to run the APU and that used fuel we couldn't afford to waste.

As our loadmaster, Sergeant Clovella, and the Ecuadorian soldiers struggled to push the wagon by hand up the ramp of the plane, Lt Col Rasmussen took me aside.

"Mike, I don't know what you were thinking up there. You were going this way and that, you were all over the sky. We flew halfway across the Amazon just to get in here and then you were going to waste more gas waiting for that rain shower to pass. We lost sight of the runway for two minutes, Mike. Two minutes! You can't *ever* lose sight of the runway, not for a second! Now, of course I want us to be safe," he admonished, wagging his finger as though I had suggested we should do otherwise, "but money doesn't grow on trees. We've got to use our resources wisely. Even more important, we've got to show our customers that we know what we're doing. Precise, measured movements – none of this *hyaka* flying where you just eyeball it and go on in. If they think we're a bunch of cowboys they'll take advantage of us every chance they get." He gestured to the Ecuadorian colonel who fumed as his men labored with the wagon.

"Sir, I..."

"No, no," he interrupted, his voice stern. "I don't want excuses. I have confidence in you, Mike, and in your flying. But lieutenants are anxious to please and anxious to impress. Sometimes too anxious. Remember: the customer doesn't drive the show. You do. Train the way you fly and fly the way you train."

We carried the water wagon to Guayaquil and refueled. But then instead of flying back to Panama we received a message from the AOC telling us to wait on the ground while they coordinated a last-minute trip to Tena.

The delay was enlightening for my commander. The military ramp had no amenities and Rasmussen was surprised by the lack of support. There was no field manager, no one from the embassy, no civilian contractor, and nowhere to get something to eat unless we walked half a mile across the runway and taxiways. The only toilet within walking distance was broken and clogged and exposed to the open air through a collapsed wall. Even the fuel truck we had to coordinate for ourselves and we could only do that because Sgt Clovella spoke Spanish.

"Is it always like this?" the colonel asked. He watched leaves blow down the ramp and under the plane. They had to skip across half a mile of empty tarmac in order to get caught in our gear but they did it, racing down acres of concrete as if they had seen our arrival and wanted to do their part to make our parking spot seem more remote. There weren't even any trees near us. There wasn't anything living at all until a stray dog slunk by and Rasmussen threw a rock at it. It promptly ran into the weeds and joined up with a pack of scrawny partners who then circled us malevolently for the rest of our stay.

Sgt Clovella looked around the broken concrete as though noticing it for the first time. He shook his head.

"Usually there's less," he answered.

The AOC called us over the short-wave to relay our new task. Load up some soldiers and a pallet of jeep tires and take them to Tena, a hundred miles north of Patuca. Then fly home.

By two o'clock we were airborne again. The weather had worsened over the mountains and Rasmussen, who was flying and anxious to teach me fuel management, eyed the storms as if their inconvenience was personal. We cruised north along the front range until finding a clear spot to cross, then dashed between cells looking for the safe haven of the jungle.

Over Tena the weather was similar to what we saw at Patuca. The only difference was that Tena wasn't in a valley – it was a small town on the long downslope of the cordillera, surrounded by trees and with two peaks off its western end that you had to fly between if landing from that direction. I'd landed there once before and remembered a good and bad part to the experience. The good was that we made a lot of friends by handing out pencils to kids who rushed out of the high grass. The bad was that the kids belonged to squatters who lived in a shantytown off the east end of the strip. When a rain squall in that direction made us take off toward the mountains, the blast from our engines blew the roof off the nearest house.

One of the soldiers got up from his seat as we neared Tena. He looked out the front window and shouted something in Sgt Clovella's ear.

"He wants to know if we can fly by the town first," the loadmaster relayed. "It'll let his superiors know we've arrived."

Remembering the commander's concern about fuel I told Clovella no. Our landing at the airstrip would be loud enough to alert anyone nearby. But no sooner were the words out of my mouth than Lt Col Rasmussen spoke up.

"No, no, it's no problem. Tell him we'll be happy to buzz the town."

The soldier beamed.

But we couldn't buzz the town. Showers were splotchy all over the area. It was impossible to find an opening in the decks that was long enough to allow a normal letdown. Rasmussen started toward one hole after another, each time prefacing it with "Ah-ha! Now you'll see that by leaving the power at 300 pounds..." but each time he had to break off the descent and his lecture when closer examination showed that a precipitous drop would be needed to keep us in the clear.

He circled for a while, scanning fiercely for a desirable opening. I kept quiet in the right seat even though each time we faced east I spotted four or five likely holes two dozen miles out over the jungle that we could have used with ease. Whether Rasmussen saw them or not was unclear: what was clear was that he didn't want to wander that far to descend. Finally he couldn't take it any longer.

"Hold on. This will have to do!"

We passed over a drifting gash in the uppermost deck that he had tried and failed twice to angle into. This time he yanked the throttles to idle and tipped us into a ninety-degree bank. The soldier on the steps gripped the railing in terror as our nose sliced through the horizon and Rasmussen spiraled us down ten thousand feet.

"There!" he smiled in triumph as we popped into clear air south of the field. We were still a mile above the ground and another broken deck lay below us but it was easier to make out slices of the countryside underneath. The soldier dropped back into the cabin, fell to his knees, and said a novena.

"We'll probably have to pass on the flyby," I suggested, surveying the scene before us. The thickest clouds were over the town and they barely moved in the calm air. Even better, the landscape on our side of the runway was clear. We could line up to land to the east and be on the ground in five minutes.

Rasmussen squinted in disapproval at the fair weather off our nose.

"No, no," he disagreed and turned us toward the cloud deck over the town. "We'll try a north pattern."

A north pattern? I leaned forward in the hope that getting six inches closer to the window would help me see whatever made him optimistic that a north pattern was even possible. The clouds on that side of the runway were so close together we would have to shimmy between them like a waitress negotiating a crowded bar.

"But don't you think, sir,..."

"No, this will work. This will work. Give me Flaps-Mid."

Half flaps let us fly slower without stalling. They also increased drag on the plane and increased our fuel flow. If we went north we still had twenty miles to go. Twenty miles to buzz the town meant we weren't even close to landing yet...but I lowered the flaps.

"There we go, there we go," he assured everyone. We slowed down and plowed through the air. "Tony, get that sergeant up here to tell us where his commander lives. We'll fly right over the place."

The Ecuadorian soldier poked his head into the cockpit again. He was calmer now and gave us directions where to fly. He had trouble getting his bearings, though, and we made several passes over the town before he recognized even one landmark. Combined with the rain shafts that stalled randomly in our path, that made us fly a sinewy, confused track across the ground. I watched the fuel needles dip from 7,000 pounds to 6,500 and then to below 6,000. If we didn't land soon we would have to go back to Guayaquil for more fuel.

"Allá, allá!" the soldier finally shouted triumphantly. Rasmussen guided us over the spot and performed another spiraling descent. He bottomed at a thousand feet and then shoved in the throttles to climb back out. The engines roared and chugged gas like thirsty men.

"Flaps up," he called.

"Up?" I repeated. "Aren't we going to land?"

"Of course. But I want to get us on a downwind first."

We didn't need a clean configuration to be on downwind but I did as he commanded. Rasmussen curved right, then left, then hunted for a way to get on a straight downwind to the runway while staying clear of clouds. It was impossible. He jinked back and forth across the town and for a while we wandered like lost surveyors. Finally he grew frustrated.

"These stupid clouds," he complained. "Stand ready on the gear and flaps – we'll just go around the damned things."

He curved us north of the town and flew a pattern that resembled a shepherd's crook. The runway sank low on the windscreen and dropped to our ten o'clock before disappearing altogether behind a cloud bank. When it stayed out of sight I wondered if the commander had lost his way. But he hadn't. We dipped into the foothills and continued south until the twin peaks appeared five minutes later. Once they did we curved left between them and saw the runway again, ten miles and almost half an hour from where we started.

"Gear! Flaps!" Rasmussen cried.

Tena was 3,000 feet long and paved. That meant it was four times as long as a C-27 needed to land. Nevertheless Rasmussen hit the beginning of the zone like it was the deck of the U.S.S. Nimitz.

"Reverse!" he called.

The props went into full reverse. The blast they threw in front of us kicked up leaves and straw in a giant bow wave.

There were no buildings on the field but halfway to the end a dirt road cut through the trees and bisected the meadow. A pair of trucks and what looked like half the town waited for us there. They were off to the side and out of the way but the commander decided to stop before we reached them.

"Alright, hang on, hang on," Rasmussen urged as we got close, still decelerating. "Right turn!"

He honked on the right brake. With simultaneous coaxing from the steering grip and some help from the left engine, he spun us to the right as we came abeam the arrival party. The C-27 skidded ninety degrees to line up the ramp perfectly with the dirt road.

"Ha!" Rasmussen exulted. "Shutdown checklist."

Before we finished the checklist, Sgt Clovella lowered the ramp and jumped outside.

"Sir," he called back over the intercom. "These guys are local police. Their chief wants to know if we can leave the engines running for a few minutes. They want to take pictures and think it'll look better if the propellers are turning."

Rasmussen didn't hesitate.

"Absolutely. Tell them to take all the pictures they want. We can leave them running until we taxi out."

I was flabbergasted. I pointed out our fuel situation to the colonel and suggested it could be a while to unload the tires. He waved away my concern.

"Don't be so stingy, Mike," he said. His tone was patient and infuriatingly sincere. "We'll drop 'em to idle. This is a morale thing for the locals."

"But you said,..."

"Now, now, Mike," he continued, his face serene. "There's no template for every operation. You have to learn to be flexible." He unbuckled to climb out of the seat. "And besides," he added. "These are our customers. We have to keep them happy."

13. Farnham 2

ONE DAY I wrote a trip report for a flight T.J. and I made to Tarapoto, Peru. Major Byron read it and sent it back to me wanting more detail. I re-wrote it but then Major Farnham returned it to my desk with the note, "You're not writing a novel here, Bleriot. Cut this down to half a page." I re-wrote it again. This time the report made it as far as the Group before being returned with a request that we include more specifics since "the Colonel wishes to gather the local color of our missions."

We wallowed in paperwork. We were in the military so that was nothing new but the actual practice of killing a forest each time we flew amazed even the jaded among us. Our flight kits contained dozens of copies of every conceivable form that we could possibly use while off-station, most of which no one ever used. We made our charts from new maps before each trip – and then copied them to leave a record at home. Even our training folders had duplicates: every sortie – no matter how short – was recounted on a separate page as if writing all the way to the bottom of one sheet would somehow violate the sanctity of individual flights.

The most notorious example of waste was our travel vouchers. Travel vouchers reimbursed us for expenses incurred while on a trip. When I arrived in Panama we turned in one voucher – just one – after each trip but as the months passed that number grew. By the time I left the country three years later the Finance office required us to submit the original voucher plus *seven* copies. The fascinating thing was that we were never able to learn where those seven copies went, especially as the number of people in Finance shrank by half over the same period. Whenever I asked the question the clerk at the comptroller window returned a glare that threatened an eighth copy would be in the offing if I didn't behave.

The irony of our bureaucracy was that even as it grew the Air Force waged a furious battle against it. Every year I was in Panama a new methodology appeared for making things work better, most co-opted from the corporate world and adapted with varying degrees of success to our non-profit-oriented mission. Every squadron had a point man, too, for implementing these methodologies. Over the years he was known variously as the Total Quality Management (TQM) Officer, the Process Officer, or – ominously – the Facilitator.

Lieutenant Kweasey was our facilitator. He led the charge on all our attempts to improve ourselves, familiarizing himself with each new philosophy just enough to be dangerous and then storming around the squadron trying to cram it down everyone's throat. His efforts to reduce paperwork involved distributing multiple surveys for us to fill out regarding how we did our jobs and then giving endless presentations where he turned over page after page of the flip chart to show us graphical illustrations of what we had just told him. His cubicle upstairs overflowed with notebooks recommending how to cut down on deskwork. He read every book on management he could find and believed every word, even those that contradicted each other. He also refused advice from anyone he knew. Lowell got him a t-shirt that urged *Stamp Out and Eradicate Unnecessary and Superfluous Redundancies* but Kweasey threw it away.

Inevitably Kweasey faced resistance in his efforts to make the world more productive. None was more unyielding than at the operations desk.

Major Harmon ran the ops desk. He reported to Major Byron who reported to Major Farnham who mostly nodded and smiled and let Harmon do whatever he wanted so long as people and things got moved around the theater on time. But Harmon wasn't at the ops desk most of the time so he didn't actually run it. He had his own responsibilities as a C-130 navigator and besides, he spent most of his days in the gym making his torso big and his legs small. Since 80% of the flying in the squadron was done by the C-27s that meant that real power at the ops desk fell to the senior C-27 scheduler: Walt.

Kweasey knew that Walt tweaked the schedule to put himself on as many flights as possible. He also knew that Walt would be a tough nut to crack regarding any reform. Still he was determined. His motives were partly selfish because he wanted to fly more – we all did – but curtailing Walt's empire was also necessary if TQM was going to be taken seriously in the squadron. Ignoring Walt's legerdemain would be akin to Elliot Ness targeting jaywalkers while Tommy guns rattled down the street.

Many of us sympathized with Kweasey's cause. Although we despised him as a person we had each tried our own hand at leveling the scheduling playing field from time to time and had failed miserably. Walt beat back all comers. If a new champion wanted to step up, more power to him.

The challenge was that when it came to flying hours Walt was an evil genius. The amount of time each person spent in the air was tallied in 30-day, 60-day, and 90-day increments so squadron leadership could ensure everyone was getting their fair share of training and missions. It was normal for pilots and copilots to move around on the list from month to month depending on which trips they had flown and what other duties had kept them out of the cockpit. Normal for everyone, that is, except Walt. He was always at the top of each list, always having flown just a few hours more than everyone else. And nobody could figure out how he did it.

But no matter how many times he came out on top of the 30-60-90 list, Walt always had impeccable justifications for it. To listen to him, everyone's schedule was always such that the only pilot available to take an open trip or training sortie was Walt. Even Major Byron sat down once to scrub the data and found that Walt couldn't be faulted: in fact he was often commended for stepping up to the plate and taking lines that otherwise would have been canceled. In other words, Walt was so good at manipulating time slots and numbers that not only was he not punished for being a stick hog, he was actually rewarded for going above and beyond. The Walt, our satiric sculpture awarded monthly and meant to embarrass whoever spent the most time away from his desk and in a cockpit during a given month, sat proudly on its namesake's desk for most of my tour in Panama.

That grated on Dale Kweasey. It grated on all of us but it especially grated on Dale. He saw his duty as Quality officer the way Pope Urban saw the Crusades – a higher power called him to attack the infidel and restore divine order.

So he tried. He wasn't smart but he was persistent so his assaults on Walt's fiefdom came in waves. The first was data-driven and was beaten back decisively when Walt countered with surveys of his own showing customer satisfaction among the Army and the radar sites at an all-time high. The second offensive tried a process-control approach: Kweasey urged Farnham to form the squadron into teams where each had a hand in "problem solving" for every additional duty. That failed when no one understood what they were responsible for and anyway, Walt got himself placed on the scheduling team.

Kweasey's best chance at breaking Walt's stranglehold on the schedule probably came when he proposed a dramatic re-organization of the whole administrative staff. His plan involved putting everyone in the same room in one big circle so that each person's work was open to all – "just like at Microsoft!" he assured the DO. For a while it looked like Walt would lose that battle. Then at the last minute he brought up fire safety and building security issues. He even had an agent from the Office of Special Investigations drop by the hangar to recommend that everyone be kept compartmentalized in the event of a terrorist attack – "just in case." Kweasey almost bit the agent.

It was only when nothing else worked that Dale had his epiphany.

"Contractors," he told Farnham. "Let's bring in a civilian from outside – you know, get a neutral, *corporate* view of our operations. Studies show productivity always goes up when you bring in a consultant."

I don't know what studies Dale was reading but the idea intrigued Major Farnham. He requested a civilian from the Wing. The Wing sent us Helen Krupchek.

Helen Krupchek was efficiency in human form. She was quiet, curt, held an accounting degree from the Stern School, and was married to an artillery officer doing a staff tour on Quarry Heights. She was tiny, five-feet-one at most, with thin lips, no chin, and hair pulled tight as though to streamline her head. Lowell called her "an anthropomorphized mouse." Her eyes were narrow, her expression dour. Pressed about her private life she said she played Monopoly, which we found boring. She added that she and her husband also enjoyed Morris dancing, an English folk dance where expressionless men and women jump around and beat the ground with sticks. That we found disconcerting. No kids, no pets, no further details. But getting that much information from her was an achievement since she talked as little as Big Bud. When she spoke at all it was with reluctance, as though she dreaded any encounter where humans would prove less reliable than her spreadsheets.

At first Walt hoped that Major Farnham would be against having a woman in the office. The last one, an airman admin troop, ended up sleeping with Kurt Nichols so sensitivity about fraternization was high. But then Farnham met Helen. She had a flat chest, pasty skin, and the sultriness of soup.

"She's perfect," our DO enthused.

Looks aside, Helen's arrival at the ops desk was akin to a new sheriff riding into Abilene. The first day she literally swept the place clean, clearing the desk of anything and everything that had nothing to do with work. Old newspapers, books, soda bottles, and half-eaten lunches disappeared into the hopper outside. The loss of such landmarks disoriented those of us who worked there daily. Walt spent half a day searching for his Bambi coffee cup.

Once the initial shock passed, though, he assumed from Helen's diminutive nature that he would have no trouble bringing her over to the dark side. He was a master at getting people to do things they didn't want to do, after all, and was riding high from a recent triumph where he had talked the Fort Clayton Army band into playing the Air Force song at their own change of command. But Helen was no grunt with a tuba. She proved impervious to Walt's subliminal influence, forcing him to turn to more open but ultimately fruitless efforts like bribes of mangoes and chocolate and flower bouquets that grew in size and number as his desperation increased. She was a rock.

Kurt suggested that Helen wasn't really a woman but that remark came from bitterness after she paid no attention to him. I kind of liked her. Her no-nonsense, ego-taming disinterest was a pleasant change to Kurt's bimbo who had worked there before.

Besides, I was flying more. That by itself let me look past easy comparisons to androids and North Korean factory workers.

The only time Helen made me pause was on a quiet afternoon when she and I sat compiling maintenance readiness rates for the weekly staff meeting. The maintenance records were issued on broad green-bar sheets of stiletto flimsies that billowed like topsails when they came off the printer. We were awash in reams of them when suddenly a tiny fence lizard leaped off the wall and onto the table between us. Geckos and other lizards often worked their way into the hangar so this was no surprise. They were welcome, in fact, being harmless and an easy way to keep down the bug population. Helen and I both stopped counting and eyed this visitor, with me at least musing how lucky I was to live where nature would visit me even when I was stuck at a desk. Fence lizards are fast and this one had pleasing blue racing stripes across its back that emphasized its agility.

But it wasn't fast enough. With no warning Helen whirled into action and slammed her notebook down on the creature. She only caught its tail, though, and the lizard quickly left that behind as it streaked away. Helen went after it in a flash, slamming *bam! bam! bam!* and pushing me aside as the two of them raced down the ops desk in a chase to the first opening where the lizard could leap free into the room and disappear among the cubicles.

Helen never said a word. Her face remained impassive even as I was left stammering, *"What the heck are you doing?!"* She finally caught the lizard inches from the ledge and smashed it dead. As I watched open-mouthed, she used her double-entry ledger to sweep its carcass into the waste basket. Then she went back to reading as though nothing had happened.

When I mentioned the incident to Walt it only added to his sadness. He advised me to keep it to myself for fear Helen would turn her ledger on me.

Jokes winged past her. Conversations stalled. Helen lived for order, not sociability, and her face was inscrutable as she studied the computer screen day after day, searching for anomalies in crew assignments that she could level off with the ruthless efficiency of a landscaper killing moles. Because of her intensity Lowell wanted to hook her up with Big Bud but the two weren't as alike as appearances suggested. Big Bud sought order, sure, but in a productive, Japanese auto factory sort of way. Helen's order was more of the Stalinist gulag kind where problems were made to vanish more than they were solved. Walt grew concerned, then horrified. Dale Kweasey was in heaven.

And Walt's fears were justified. Numbers were Helen's friends and they didn't lie. Those months where everyone happened to be busy except for Walt? Gone. Those days where Walt would quick-turn from one local sortie to another? Gone. A month after her arrival the 30-60-90 list came out and the 30, at least, was a model of equity. Walt had 28 hours for the month – 0.5 hours from the average and a good 30% less than his norm. Two months after her arrival he actually flew one hour *less* than the average. Walt turned pale at the news. In fact, while Helen ran the ops desk he began to lose weight. The jovial mischief-maker we knew and loved became withdrawn and gaunt, seeing his long-time playground paved over to build a parking lot.

Major Farnham, on the other hand, was content. Blissful, even. He liked Helen. "She's a good worker," he would proclaim. "Quiet. Steady!"

In truth he probably liked her because she was the closest thing to a mannequin that a human could become and because he could therefore get away with things around her that the rest of us wouldn't put up with, mostly his boring stories and jokes. Because Helen's facial features never changed and she rarely looked up from her computer regardless of who stood by the ops desk, Farnham could loiter there with his cup of coffee and blather on about whatever happened to be in his head that morning and believe that he was actually interesting. The rest of us would have scattered. Helen just blocked him out.

For if Helen's greatest assets were order and efficiency, Major Farnham's were his unfailing good spirit and his obliviousness to whatever was going on around him. We pilots made fun of him behind his back but he still smiled; his wife hated being in Panama but he still smiled; his teenage children were mortified by his fashion sense in civilian clothes – tight shorts that took him back to some happy summer in the 1970s – but he still smiled. The man was an unwavering optimist.

He was such a blithering romantic, in fact, that most of the colonels at the Group refused to talk to him when they called down to the squadron. They demanded to speak to Lt Col Rasmussen instead and if he wasn't around they did everything they could to avoid being transferred to Farnham. The reason was that Farnham would assure them that everything was fine whether it was or not. All the aircraft work, he would promise into the receiver while standing at attention at his desk and wearing a big smile. Morale is high, he would insist. Training is on track and our programmed flying hours are right on schedule, he would say – even if none of that was true. It wasn't that he lied: Farnham just viewed the world through rose-colored glasses and saw sweetness and light where others perceived looming disaster. The hangar could be on fire and Farnham would assure the Group that the 155th was running as smooth as warm syrup. Only Colonel Buncheman, a notorious curmudgeon, called Farnham with regularity and he did so every morning not for information but simply to put himself in a good mood before he started his day.

Farnham's Pollyanna demeanor is what allowed him to miss how Helen was slowly killing one of his best pilots.

He was also oblivious of the fact that we hated him.

Actually it wasn't Farnham who we hated. It was his goddamned dog. Not his dog, but his *goddamned* dog, a mutt who gained the inseparable modifier courtesy of all the schedulers in the squadron who encountered him during Farnham's tour when for one reason or another they had to swing by the DO's house after hours for approval of a crew or mission change. In my own case, time after time I ran up Commissary Hill on my way home to get the major's signature and time after time the goddamned dog – an elderly shepherd named Kit – attacked me.

The first time I ran such an errand Walt warned me about Kit. On meeting her, though, I assumed his admonition was a joke. She lulled me into complacency by feigning disinterest and lying stretched out on the floor of the major's duplex like a sleepy canine octogenarian. It was only when I turned to leave that she leaped off the carpet as if pulled by wires and bit me high on the right leg. (She bit me on the right buttock but after word got out of the incident I maintained the injury was "high on the right leg" because my ego didn't need guys like

Lowell roaring with laughter over how I'd been bitten on the ass.)

That wasn't the only time it happened. Visits to Farnham's house always went the same: I would ring the doorbell and explain there was a mission change, Farnham would invite me inside, I would decline, he would insist, I would point out that he had a vicious dog, he would exhibit shock and assure me that Kit was absolutely tame, I would reluctantly enter, he would turn away to read the document or find a pen...and the goddamned dog would attack. I felt like Charlie Brown except that instead of a football Lucy held a rabid Alsatian.

And I wasn't the only one. Every scheduler was bitten at least once. Walt had a scar on his ankle, Big Bud one on his knee, and even Lowell had a divot in his calf where the animal came close to extracting a pound of flesh when he looked away to answer his beeper. Kit preferred assaults from the rear which explained most of the injuries. She always pretended to ignore visitors at first. Then, skulking behind the couch, low-crawling under the coffee table, or taking the long way round through the dining room she would advance, watching for the messenger's briefest moment of inattention before lunging for a bite.

Farnham, it should be noted, never accepted that his goddamned dog was aggressive. He'd had Kit ever since his days in pilot training and was as attached to the animal as to his own kids. And Kit played her owner like a fiddle. Whenever he looked up she would fall to the floor and lapse into cutesy Border collie mode, all lolling tongue and wagging tail. To him she was always a puppy chasing butterflies on the lawn.

Not to us. The attacks were impossible to avoid no matter how attentive we were. I took to standing with my back to the door while Major Farnham perused the paperwork. Yet at some point I always had to move. Evan's tactic was to stand against the wall and wave a folder in the animal's face. Declan – until he moved to the Group – carried bits of raw hamburger that he surreptitiously tossed around the major's living room, praying the dog stayed hungry until its owner finished reading and he could escape. Walt's tactic – well, Walt's tactic was to send someone else to the major's house whenever anything needed to be signed.

It was a Thursday night and I sat at Sergeant Laurette's desk chatting with Walt. I was killing time while waiting to fly the second half of a night sortie with Bob Harcourt, whose landings and takeoffs we could hear dimly through the walls of the hangar as he practiced assaults with Tommy Goode. Even though it was already dark Walt was hanging around because Helen was still in the seat next to him, typing away on the computer as she built schedules for the next quarter. Walt always played the waiting game with her, hoping she would leave at a decent hour so he could get into the schedule himself and modify whatever she had done that day. Some nights, though, she stuck around long after everyone else had gone home. When that happened their struggle became a battle of wills as each tried to outlast the other. She always had the upper hand as her automaton nature needed no excuse to work late into the night. Walt, conversely, had to keep coming up with excuses why for the first time in his career he felt motivated to give the taxpayers more than their due.

He was about to give up when the phone rang.

"Yes, sir," he said into the receiver. "Yes, we have them right here. Helen was working on them this afternoon." His face scrunched in concentration. "Now? Well, uh...of course, sir. I can run them by on my way home. I was just leaving anyway."

He hung up, his face registering that little was going right for him today.

"Major Farnham?" I asked.

"Yeah."

"What did he want?"

Walt glared at Helen's back.

"The proposals on training sorties. He'll see Buncheman at lunch tomorrow and wants to be able to say yea or nay to the changes."

If Helen noticed the ice in his voice she ignored it. Still typing with one hand she handed the proposals over her shoulder. Written by her, they recommended that our four-hour sorties be cut back to three hours which was much the same as standing over Walt's prostrate body and plunging a javelin into his heart.

Walt took the folder but halfway to his feet he paused. He thought for a moment. Then, watching me out of the corners of his eyes he spoke in Helen's direction.

"Uh, yeah. Yeah, I'll just run them by the major's house. I can finish this other stuff tomorrow. Besides, it'll give me a chance to give him the ops desk recommendation about how he proceeds."

Helen's back stiffened. She paused in her typing. It was well known that when making decisions Farnham usually sided with whoever he talked to last.

"You know," Walt continued to me. "It's good that we have guys like Farnham. Informal types. Straight up. You can sit down with him and hash things out. And hey, maybe his wife will still have dinner on the table..."

Helen quietly turned off the computer and collected her things.

"I've finished for the evening," she announced quietly. "I can stop by Major Farnham's house on my way out the gate."

"Oh, no," Walt assured her. "There's no reason for that. We have to jump when the DO calls but you're a civilian."

"It's alright. I don't mind."

"But he lives all the way up behind the Commissary..." Walt's tone was chivalric concern.

"It's fine," Helen repeated. She accompanied her words with a slashing motion of her hand that we took to mean the discussion was over. She took the proposals from Walt and slid out from behind the desk. "I'll be there and gone in five minutes. You talk with your friend."

Her economy in words and movement were enviable. She didn't look at either of us as she left – her eyes flickered across the floor toward my feet but got no further.

"Thanks," Walt called as she went out the door. "See you tomorrow."

But we didn't see her the next day. Helen came to work in the morning but was gone before reveille had sounded, leaving behind little in the way of explanation and forcing us to piece together the story on our own. The DO didn't return to the squadron until Monday. That was three days after he fired Helen and after a weekend in which he tearfully oversaw the funeral of his goddamned dog.

"She killed the dog?" Lowell asked, his jaw hanging almost to the floor.

"Beat it to death," Walt shrugged, leaning back in his seat and pressing his fingertips together either in prayer or deep satisfaction or both. "With a chair. Apparently Farnham had to pull her off."

Lowell and I stared at each other. Lowell at least tried to form words, his lips mouthing questions even as his mind groped with the image of our diminutive co-worker wheeling on the old wolf and brandishing furniture as her weapon.

"How?...Why?..."

Walt heard our confusion from afar. His mind was already preoccupied with the computer screen where the lines for the next month – highlighted in green by Helen to show they were complete – he was slowly changing to yellow to show they were again "in progress." Even from where I sat I could see his name appear several times.

"She doesn't like animals," Walt explained absentmindedly. His eyes flickered across the screen as he surveyed the calendar, the sorties, and available planes. Pieces of the scheduling puzzle moved apart and came together again under his practiced hands. "Hates them, actually. Short fuse for anything on four legs, especially when it bites." He studied the computer and in the reflection of its green screen we saw the hint of a smile. "Who knew?"

14. Antigua

In November, Rolo was tapped to check out a language immersion school in Ecuador. Charlie Manson got more frustrated every day with the number of problems we encountered on missions that could be resolved quickly if someone on the crew were able to speak Spanish, so he sold Lt Col Rasmussen on the idea of using squadron funds to send crew members to month-long language schools. There were dozens of such schools scattered around Central and South America. After checking around Manson decided that a school in Quito offered the most value for the money. He couldn't go himself since he was already taking a crash course by being married to a Panamanian so he put two co-pilots on a commercial flight to Ecuador and told them to come back in four weeks fluent in Spanish.

Pity the Ecuadorians. Rolo had a facility for languages the way dogs have a knack for the piano. His companion, Big Bud, wasn't much better. Bud rarely spoke in English so god knows what his instructors were able to drag out of him. The two reported to the school and were immediately split up and housed with different families. Rolo spent his month doing a lot of mime and teaching his family how to cook;

Bud – well, no one knows what happened in Bud's home because all he would say upon return was, "It was alright." They came back before Thanksgiving capable of asking directions and describing various pieces of furniture. By Christmas they had forgotten even that.

Manson was persistent. Next he sent Carl Diehrman and Lowell Hendricks. Lowell returned pronouncing everyone in Ecuador "*una idiota*" but Carl had a great time and actually learned some Spanish. He was housed with a family who lived half a mile from the airport. Not only did the parents welcome him into the household but the father worked for a catering company that supplied meals to several airlines. So in the mornings before going to class Carl accompanied his host on rounds of the airport, delivering sandwiches to aircrew, meeting maintenance staff and managers, and getting fluent in the language of airfield operations.

"I even ate free," he commented. "*Fue una experiencia fantástica!*"

Little Bud went to Quito, too, but came home after a week for the oddest of reasons. Nervous, hyper, and annoying like a mosquito, Little Bud was paired with T.J., who he didn't get along with under normal circumstances. That said something because T.J. was the stereotype of the large friendly guy. T.J. was very large, in fact, but he laughed a lot and didn't throw his weight around, so to speak.

He was the jovial chum of almost everybody in the squadron, outgoing and determined to live his life just like anyone who didn't tip the scales at 300 pounds. But in Ecuador that scared Little Bud, particularly after T.J. had a minor accident hang-gliding off Mount Cotopaxi and cut his hand on a llama enclosure during the landing. With T.J. attached, the hang-glider had trouble performing up to its name and slid earthward like an eagle who'd snatched a too-fat mountain goat. At the clinic where a nurse dressed the wound Bud learned of the horrifying coincidence that he and T.J. shared the same rare blood type of AB-. From then on Bud, who weighed 130 pounds only if he was sopping wet and carried a small dog, became obsessed with the possibility that T.J. would hurt himself seriously and require a major transfusion in Quito that would drain Bud dry and leave him limp and wilted on a hospital gurney like a deflated balloon. So he quit the school. Later, back in Panama, he even tried to delay his aircraft commander upgrade just so the schedulers couldn't put the two of them on the same crew.

When later it was my turn the President of Ecuador chose that same week to be kidnapped by members of his own military. For days the government and country were in an uproar. Manson threw up his hands and did an about face on the language program. Literally. He looked north and chose a school in Guatemala for me to attend. And just to make sure I wasn't bored he paired me with Josh.

"Dude, what a scam," Josh exulted. This is incredible! Can you imagine another company wasting money on their employees this way? We are making out like bandits here: free school, free room and board, free flights there and back – this has got to be worth a couple of thousand bucks, easy."

"Josh, it's not a vacation. You do have to study, you know."

"Oh, right. Give me a break, Mike. You're *living* the language, not attending MIT. If I spend the whole time hitting on chicks I'm still meeting the intent of the course. Learn Spanish, that's what Manson said. I can do that."

"You already speak it better than most of us," I pointed out.

"That's because I don't lock myself on base."

"My point exactly. That's why I'm surprised they let you go. You could probably pass the test now."

"Hey, hey, hey, dude! Don't go spreading rumors. You trying to cheat me out of a free trip?"

We flew out of Tocumen on a Saturday afternoon, catching a Copa flight direct to Guatemala City. Copa was the Panamanian national carrier and a decent airline, all things considered. They'd flown a plane into the side of a mountain up in El Salvador the previous year and had one blown up by the drug cartels over the summer but other than that were safe. That's what I told myself, anyway, as the nose gear came off the runway to start our climb-out and the pilot immediately left the cockpit and trotted down the aisle to the toilet.

We arrived at La Aurora airport in late afternoon when oblique rays from a setting sun cast broad shadows across the Guatemalan mountains. The shadows stretched parallel to the ridge behind the capital and clung tight to the ravines within it, causing near night to co-exist beside splotches of sunlight in the changeover hours.

Guatemala City sprawled across a patch of flattened mountains one mile above the sea in the southern reaches of the Sierra de los Cuchumatanes. The mountains were chaotic; the city was, too. It sprawled because it had to: deep ravines prevented straight lines and orderly development. Roads went where they could. Neighborhoods, residential or commercial, sprouted on any piece of land that wasn't too steep to support walls.

The airport seethed with people. White, brown, black, the colors of human skin complemented the blues and grays of business suits and the multi-colored designs of *huipils* and *refagos* worn by clutches of native women.

We collected our bags and walked out to the street where a representative of the school found us within minutes. She was Señora Regina Perera. Her driver was Tomás. Within twenty minutes we were away from the airport, out of the city and climbing into the mountains on our way to Antigua.

Antigua, Guatemala is the former capital of the country. It means, literally, *Old Guatemala* and in fact was the Spanish Empire's seat of government in Central America until late in the eighteenth century. It lies a bucolic hour away from Guatemala City, two square miles of colonial-era buildings and ruins nestled in a bowl between three active volcanoes.

Despite Tomas' skill, getting to Antigua was nerve-wracking. He drove alright but the two-lane highway had hairpin turns going up and down a mountain pass. Usually there were trees flanking the road but sometimes they gave way to steep drop-offs. Those were often decorated with bunches of crosses clustered at the edge, a running tally of casualties on the route.

We drove into Antigua from the east, descending from the mountains into clouds that blanketed the valley. Mist drenched the van windows and cut visibility to a hundred yards.

My first reaction was, "We're here?"

I expected another big town and was disappointed. Antigua was more of an overgrown village. Walls flanked cobblestone streets and hid courtyards and houses behind. Each neighborhood was a serene mixture of those white-washed walls, storefronts, and heavy wooden doors with ornate knockers.

The cobblestones were huge. We trundled as though in a stagecoach, the squeaking of our axles echoing off the walls. The streets were so narrow that all signs were flush against the buildings. The only light came from the occasional lamp that illuminated the fog around it and not much more.

Tomás asked a question. Our guide consulted her list and gave him the name of a family. He nodded. Several turns later we veered onto a dirt road where there were no lamps. Illumination came instead from yellow bulbs suspended over doorways at the street's edge. I began to wonder about the depth of Charlie Manson's research. Josh did, too. Up to now his face had reflected his uncertainty: now it evolved to disbelief. Whatever he had imagined our hosts would be like must have been several tax brackets higher than this.

The van bounced to a halt in front of a low building with crumbling plaster and a plywood roof. The roof sloped so that a curtain of rain dripped onto the van when we parked. There were no lights inside the house that we could see. A ground-floor window had bars that would have swung out on a giant hinge were they not locked with a chain.

Tomás knocked. A lady with sagging jowls opened the door and stood there in her nightgown, her face a mixture of nervousness and glee at the surprise of nighttime visitors. She and Señora Perrera whispered greetings like long-lost sisters and had a low conversation. Then the old lady disappeared inside.

"Miguel," Perrera said to me. "This is your family. The Martíns."

She nodded to Tomás who hurried to get my suitcase from the back of the van.

"Okay," I whispered back, wondering why we were all talking like we were in a library.

I crawled over to the door. Josh grabbed my arm.

"Dude," he hissed. "This sucks."

"Maybe not. Maybe there's a team of Swedish cheerleaders in there on winter break."

"Don't count on it. Where's my place?"

"Probably far out of town," I suggested. "Nothing near so nice as this."

"With my luck, you're probably right. I'll bet it's got rats."

"They're not rats here. They're *ratas.*"

"Then I'll bet they have *ratas.*"

"See you in class."

My lightheartedness aside, it was an odd feeling to hop out of the van and leave behind my only connection to familiar things.

The lady of the house, Señora Martín, came out to meet me. She and Señora Perrera had a conversation that was so fast I caught only a few words of it. It was all "Here's your student – thanks, we'll take it from here" stuff that made me feel like a downed airman escaping through the partisan underground. Then Perrera and Tomás gave me light handshakes and wished me luck. They hopped into the van and drove off, their sole charge gazing morosely out the window as they disappeared into the night. I now belonged to my family.

Dark and deserted on the outside, the inside of the house was lively. The front door opened onto the kitchen where the entire family gathered at a small table. The entire family – and none of them spoke a word of English. There was Señora Rosa Martín, a round woman on short legs; her husband Gabriel; and five children, though it seemed like more than that since they never stopped moving. The maid flitted in and out with an ambivalent smile and averted eyes.

"*Tu habitación está aquí,*" Rosa guided me through the kitchen. The back wall was open and led to a flagstone courtyard open to the sky. Left and right were a pair of rooms, the second one on the right being mine. In the back was a corridor backing up to the neighbor's house where plants in the shelter of a greenhouse cast shadows from the kitchen light.

My room was spartan. Two walls were plaster and stone, including the outer wall, the one with a large square where a window would normally go. The wall to the courtyard was a series of stacked planks unevenly nailed. If I stood back from it, I could get a good picture of everything going on in the rest of the house. Fortunately the wall between me and the next room up was more complete. That was the room the family girls shared; for good measure they'd hung a paisley sheet on their side that blocked light between the cracks.

The open window concerned me. It was high enough that I had to stand on tiptoes to see outside but it was still open. There wasn't even a frame for glass – it was just a hole in the wall. Outside was a yard belonging to the next house.

I hung some clothes in the armoire. Most I left in the suitcase. I pulled out the books I'd brought and put them on the small table underneath the window. That done, I sat on the bed and looked around. Other than the bed, the armoire, the table, and a chair, there wasn't a thing in the room. I looked at my watch. Eight-twenty. Saturday night in rockin' Antigua, Guatemala and here I was sitting in a bare-bones room wondering what the hell to do. For a few minutes I was overwhelmed with loneliness. What a life I led.

Since the family still moved around in the rest of the house I finally figured I'd best go out and be social. There was Spanish to be learned, after all. I went into the courtyard to make the tour.

There wasn't much. The bathroom was the next door down. Then came the greenhouse/garden, then the other side of the yard where there were two more bedrooms. Up toward the kitchen was an open area with the dinner table.

Rosalba, the thirteen-year-old, sat at the table writing furiously. An open textbook and a study guide for some class lay open before her. At first I didn't want to bother her but then figured, why else was I here?

"*Tarea*?" I asked, remembering the word for homework.

She looked up and nodded. "*Biología*." The book before her had drawings of a dissected leaf.

Since she didn't seem to mind I asked her about her school. She started out shy but soon went on at great length about her classes, the other students, and how she didn't mind homework so long as it wasn't math. I understood most of what she said and felt smarter for the conversation.

Leaving Rosalba I joined Victor, the six-year-old, in the kitchen. Señora Martín flitted in and out – she and the maid were washing clothes in the tub by the greenhouse – but Victor ruled the television roost.

"Hola, Victor. Que miras?"

He looked at me briefly as if to say, what kind of a dumb question is that? Then his eyes returned to the screen.

"*Hola*," he replied.

I recognized the show he had on. *Sábado Gigante*, a three-hour Mexican variety show that was a staple of Saturday night viewing throughout Latin America. It was an unapologetically brainless cross between The Tonight Show, The Price is Right, and the Playboy channel. A portly, garrulous host told jokes, interviewed celebrities, introduced musical acts, and shepherded audience members through impossibly complex, humiliating games while teasing them with the chance to win two or three hundred dollars, all the while surrounded by Latin beauties in various stages of undress. The perfect formula for television success.

"*Te gusta este programa?*" I asked Victor.

He munched on a cracker. A clown on a tricycle chased one of the beauties in high heels. It was hard for Victor to break away.

"*Sí.*"

Marlen, the nine-year-old, came out of his room to join us. He'd had homework, too, but was now finished and ready to soak in the jumping, fuzzy screen.

The host of the show, Don Francisco, introduced a new game. He invited a skinny young man from the audience to compete for a hundred dollar prize. Cramming him between two of the show's buxom hostesses, Don Francisco made fun of the guy for a while then showed him an elaborate set containing eight glass rooms, each of which had a locked door. In each room was household furniture. Don Francisco said the game was simple: all the young man had to do to win was unlock the door to each room, rearrange the furniture in a certain order, and then lock the door again. All in three minutes. Simple, no?

"*Listo?*" Don Francisco cried.

The young man nodded. Sure, he was ready.

"Bueno. Entonces, aquí están las llaves!"

Don Francisco handed the young man a key ring the size of a frisbee. It must have contained a hundred churchkeys. He would have to figure out which one fit each door.

Marlen and Victor were on the edge of their seats. The three minutes ticked by as the music played and Don Francisco described the hapless efforts of his contestant. The young man fumbled with the dozens of keys, trying one after another, and finally got the first door unlocked as his time ran out. He never even got to re-arrange furniture. It would have been unwatchably stupid except for the hostesses who hovered around him the whole time, jiggling and cheering and never leaving the camera. The perfect formula.

In the morning, we went to church. I normally didn't attend church but it never occurred to me *not* to go while in Antigua. The ambiance dictated it.

There was no breakfast on Sunday. The family started moving and dressing itself for the nine-o'clock service about an hour before, by which time I'd been up for quite a while trying to keep my growling stomach from waking anyone. I'd been awake so long because at 4 a.m. I learned what the neighbor's dirt yard was for: chickens. Chickens ruled by a rooster with no sense of a diurnal schedule. He crowed long before dawn, his first cry piercing the open window like the loud-hailer on an ocean vessel. So I was up and about, prepared to think of things like when I would eat next, which made me think how long it had been since I'd last eaten, which made me think how long it had been since I'd last showered, which made me think about showering. The experience of showering made me think about going to church.

When I asked about attending mass Rosa and Gabriel were surprised but then insisted I come with them and the children.

Their church was just up the street, a ruin-in-waiting that loomed over the dirt lane like a stone warehouse. Inside there were narrow pews and glimpses of the building's ornate past. Polished brass gleamed wherever there was a rail, candlestick, or crucifix. Statues and gargoyles were oversized and over-styled, their glowering presence putting us in our place from the moment we cleared the doorway. The nave was short and wide, squat like the people who filled it, while the altar was a gaudy hint of the gilded extravagance that had decorated all the town's churches when Antigua was the governor's seat.

I folded myself into a pew and knelt where I could without kicking the people behind me. Marlen sat beside me; Rosa looked over every now and then to see how I was doing. Without trying to I had scored major points by coming to the service. It was a cultural connection, the knowledge that while all her boarders were welcome to believe what they wanted, she felt better having a Catholic along who knew the same prayers she did. Even a lapsed Catholic like me.

Padre nuestro que estás en los cielos…

What Rosa and Gabriel didn't know was what I was praying for. I prayed not to die in the shower.

The bathroom next to my room had a toilet. A small toilet. A toilet with a shallow bowl and little water that inspired nothing but doubt. The shower was in a separate stall, a closet of cement and wood planking between the bathroom and the greenhouse at the back of the courtyard. I discovered it before going to church that first morning, while the rest of the family slept and the rooster next door schemed to reach ever-shriller notes.

"Good lord," I murmured after swinging aside the lath door.

The stall was cement, three walls surrounding a flagstone floor. One of the stones tilted down to expose a hole in the outer wall where the water ran out. Since it was the same wall as the one in my room

I could only hope the water would hit the rooster on the head.

High on the wall was another open window, open again meaning it couldn't be closed until someone installed something to close. That concerned me a little. The window was higher than my head so being exposed was no problem. But it was cold outside!

This was spring, *early* spring, and Antigua was a mile above sea level. It couldn't have been more than fifty degrees and for all intents and purposes I was getting ready to shower in the open air.

But dying of pneumonia took second place as a threat once I looked up at the spigot. The shower head protruded from a pipe that ran along the ceiling. There was only one handle to turn the water on and that was a handle above the shower head itself. Next to it was a hairball of exposed wires that attached in various places to a piece of electrical tape wrapped around the pipe. The electrical cord responsible for supplying the current was jammed into a junction box four inches from the shower head. Under other circumstances I would have checked out of the hotel and called a city inspector. In this case I gazed awestruck at the wires and repeated my prayer.

"Good *lord*."

However, the system worked. I talked myself into disrobing with the reasoning that I couldn't go a month without bathing and didn't have the money to check into a hotel. Squeezing, shivering, into the stall and trying to stand away from under the spigot without pressing too hard against the clammy cement walls, I reached up to the faucet handle like an FBI agent defusing a bomb. Twist, twist, twist... nothing. Twist, twist, twist,...*fwoosh*! There was a paralyzing ten seconds that lasted for years as cold water gushed from the head in a spray much wider than I anticipated. I bit my tongue and stifled a scream that would have curdled the blood of every resident of the former capital.

But the Rube Goldberg-contraption worked. The heating coils, working on a pressure switch installed in the shower head, clicked on the instant the water started to flow. I actually heard it *"tic"* into action. The water warmed. It never became hot but compared to the arctic flow at the beginning I couldn't complain. At least I could stand under the spray and get clean. So I did, taking a quick and invigorating shower right up until my only bar of soap slipped from my grasp, bounced off the flagstone, and slid neatly through the drain-hole to plunk into the dirt some four feet below on the other side of the wall.

"*Coño*," I muttered, remembering the only curse word I knew. I rinsed myself off quickly and reached up to turn off the water.

That was the moment when I got religion. Though I'm quite sure my hand touched the valve and *only* the valve, the proximity of wires, their lack of insulation, the presence of water on, over, and in a puddle where I was standing made me one giant conductor for every amp of current on the only circuit in the house. Fortunately the voltage was high enough to kick my hand like a .45-caliber shell and knock me against the cement wall. My hand jerked free. Had the current held me in place I would have fried standing up.

I stood looking at the tiny scorch mark on my middle finger. Death by shower. Death – naked – in the shower – in the Third World.

Going to church became a better idea by the minute.

The *Proyecto Linguistico Francisco Marroquín* was a small language school just off the Parque Central. I showed up early Monday morning anxious about going one-on-one with an instructor for seven hours. I'd tried it once before, as a fifth-grader taking after-hours instruction from a free-lancing Catholic nun, and the only Spanish I'd taken away from that experience was a handful of personal pronouns and the phrase *No me gusta leche con cocoa* – which made no sense because I did in fact like chocolate milk. My first action on stepping into the school's inner courtyard was to appraise my fellow students and determine if they were all brilliant linguistic loners who would leave me in their dust.

If they were, they were cleverly disguised as college students on holiday.

The headmistress gave me a tour. The entire school consisted of a front office, the courtyard decorated with a fountain, and eight small classrooms that ringed the latter. She introduced me to my instructor, Ramón. Ramón was medium-height and thin with neat black hair and a clipped moustache. He wore an open-collar dress shirt with the sleeves pushed back and the steady gaze of one who knows exactly what he's doing – this wasn't some local the school had hired to make conversation with a gringo for four weeks. He was a teacher. He also spoke no English.

"*Bueno,*" he said. "*Bienvenidos a mi país.*"

With that introduction we were off.

We made small talk for most of the morning, with Ramón doing most of the talking. He told me about himself, how he had been born and raised in Antigua. He was a carpenter by trade but a teacher by training, working in both fields to provide for a wife and a young daughter. He was building a house on the west side of town, just behind the bus terminal, and hoped to have enough money saved up after two more years to invest with his brother in a small coffee farm five miles outside of town. I was his fourth student. He had taught one American, one Briton, and a German before me. The German quit on him early, deciding to go work at a hostel near

Panajachel instead. Ramón said that simply but his tone implied disappointment. I nodded in sympathy, assuming that meant the pressure was now on me not to repeat.

In the afternoon Ramón made me do the talking. I had never realized how much effort that could be, simply talking. Putting one word after another when I had to struggle for each syllable. My brain was a muscle and it got a workout that it hadn't had in a while. Remembering which word meant what, then whether it was a masculine or feminine noun or if the adjective had a special ending or if the verb conjugated in the normal way or was irregular – it was work. For me, speaking Spanish had always meant forming a sentence or two here, carrying on a small conversation there. Now Ramón made me speak paragraphs. Pages. A muscle indeed. Each conversation was like building a wall using heavy bricks. By the end of the day my head hurt. I was mentally drained and had trouble thinking in English.

"*Buen trabajo, Miguel,*" Ramón said when we'd finished for the afternoon. "*Mañana vamos a aprender el pretérito. Hasta luego!*" He clapped me on the shoulder.

The past tense? I barely had the present tense down. My brain wanted to lie down and take a nap. And I still had a month to go.

I met a girl named Amy. She was tall with blond hair and a nervous smile. She sat on the fountain in the school courtyard one day and asked me for help with a phrase she wanted to translate – she said she asked me because I looked like I knew what I was doing. I helped her anyway.

We spent a lot of time together from then on. She was in Antigua for a month but half her program was already over. She came from Alabama and had just graduated from Tuscaloosa with a degree in anthropology. When she got back to the States she was going to work on a dig of Indian mounds along the Mississippi.

"Is there money in that?" I asked.

"None at all."

One night, she and I met Josh at a bar called Fenix. It was tucked away on the north end of Avenida 6, hiding behind a massive door with an enormous gargoyle knocker. The interior was small and elegantly decorated with polished wood and hanging plants. Josh had found it while exploring: the place had beer, bar food, and a pool table that nobody ever seemed to use so he adopted it as his own. He escaped there almost every night to get away from his family who – by his telling – grew weirder with each passing day. Apparently they were trying to starve him, only begrudgingly feeding him breakfast and giving him one bowl of soup with bread for dinner. They also refused to speak to him and looked embarrassed whenever he started a conversation on his own. So he was spending his home life as a starving apostate and a confused one at that.

Whenever I told him how friendly my family was he threw up his hands in frustration. Josh being Josh, he felt he was being taken for the seven dollars he paid in room and board. Only incredulity at the situation kept him from speaking up.

That evening he was a broken man, hunched over a bar table looking for all the world like a puppy that had been kicked. One hand grasped a beer, the other picked at a bowl of pine nuts. From a stereo behind the bar the voice of Leonard Cohen growled about the future. If Josh knew that someone had once described Cohen's work as "music to commit suicide by" he might have asked the barman to change the CD. But he didn't. For his part the barman, also the owner, sat quietly behind the bar and watched his only three customers begin a game of pool.

"The maid uses my clothes to wash the dishes," Josh began, toying with the cue ball.

We weren't sure we heard him correctly.

"No, really. I came home from class today and found her at the sink, using my blue shirt as a dish rag. Apparently she figured it would save time to wash them both at once."

"You're kidding."

"Why would I kid about something like that? I walked in the door and she was scrubbing away, singing. She didn't even stop when I came in."

"Did you say anything?"

"Did I say anything?" he repeated, skidding from apathy to anger. "Are you kidding? I hit the roof! Well, I mean,...what *do* you say to that? What do you say when you find someone doing dishes with your clothes? Huh? I said, 'What are you doing? What are you doing? *Qué haces? Qué haces?*' That's all I could say, I was so mad. She looked at me like I was crazy. Like *I* was crazy!"

He slapped the ball down on the table and looked at me to see if he'd somehow misinterpreted the situation. His face was pure pain, utter confusion at the injustice life had thrown at him. But as quickly as he exploded he calmed down again, crawling back inside his forlorn shell. I bit my tongue to keep from laughing – something about Josh kept me from ever feeling pure sympathy for him. His agony was too entertaining.

Amy didn't know him as well.

"That's horrible," she said. "Why don't you see about changing families?"

Josh noticed her for the first time.

"And get somebody who's worse?"

The poverty, literal and emotional, of his situation made Josh want to leave Antigua on the weekends. Our first Saturday there he talked me into joining him for a trip back to the capital. For him it was a chance to enjoy luxury again, the pleasure of a hot shower, a clean bed, and – not incidentally – beautiful upper-class women who hung out at the clubs in Guatemala City. We took a bus over the mountains and got rooms at the Hotel Camino Real a mile or so from the airport. Five stars all the way for a mere (at the embassy rate) fifty dollars a night.

"Now this is what I'm talking about!" Josh exclaimed after he cleaned up and put on a jacket and tie. "We need to have the language school up here!"

The highlight of that night for me was when we got lost trying to find a nightclub Josh had heard about. He only had an address, not the name of the club, and through a misunderstanding of how the city's zones worked we ended up taking a taxi ride clear to the other side of the city. The cabbie didn't mind. He talked a blue streak the whole way telling us about the local landmarks, pointing out the Civic Center, the university, and the National Palace along the way, driving what I later realized was a very circuitous route to our destination. Josh, however, was uninterested in tourism. He fretted through the long drive, believing that every minute wasted looking at the Torre del Reformador, for example, was a minute he could have spent finding the woman of his dreams. But finally the cab driver dropped us off at the Parque Minerva and Josh's luck reappeared.

As we stood there in the dark wondering where the heck we were, by complete accident we met two girls who were on their way to a dinner in Zone 10, a posh neighborhood of villas and embassies not far from the hotel we had just left. So we hopped into their chauffeur-driven Volvo and let them take us to a birthday party on an estate overlooking the Rio Negro.

The house was a mansion behind security gates and high walls, a beautiful three-story building with expansive grounds and awash in light. No one at the party was older than twenty-five and all had the air of people with access to tremendous amounts of money they'd had no part in earning.

The birthday girl was a twenty-one-year old named Lourdes. She was short and thin with lustrous hair and a radiant smile that was highlighted by diamond earrings and a choker that she kept holding her hand to as though to ensure it was still there. Spoiled as she was, she had impeccable manners. She was genuinely excited that her friends had brought Josh and me along. She took us around the party and introduced us to everyone. Everyone was polite.

The introductions let us take a measure of the crowd. Though it was a party and everyone seemed game to have a good time, there was an air of superficiality that was palpable, a sense of bored luxury which helped explain interest in the two gringos.

We weren't handsome or rich but we were different, a cultural oddity for Guat City's young elite. Josh ended up having sex with a girl in the garden and making a date with her for the following night. By two a.m. Lourdes had kissed me twice and offered me cocaine and something more upstairs in her bedroom. Tempting as she was, the cocaine and the presence of her boyfriend in the kitchen made me think the party had gotten interesting enough. Shortly after that Josh and I thanked our hosts and left.

As a night out it couldn't have been more successful. The party, along with the women and of course the luxury hotel, was exactly the kind of escape Josh was looking for. At brunch the next morning we relived the evening while gorging ourselves on a spectacular buffet.

But taking the bus back to Antigua made me feel as spoiled and superficial as anybody at the party. I liked Josh and thought he was a great guy but we had come to Guatemala to learn Spanish and experience the culture. There had to be a better way to do that than to take advantage of the American dollar and our white skin while partying in Guatemala City. I had spent a night basking in decadence and now was returning to the Martín family who made seven dollars a day giving me food and a place to live. What a boor.

So when Amy asked me to accompany her on a trip to Tikal over the following weekend, I abandoned Josh and told her yes. Although I had doubts about security up north, it would be more interesting than flirting with crack heads in the capital.

Tikal is a Mayan archeological site in the Petén, the northern panhandle of Guatemala. Mayan Indians lived there for over a thousand years before vacating the site around 900 A.D. Their population varied over time but easily got into the thousands and spread over a wide area in what is now an expansive rain forest. Their disappearance was part of a broader collapse of lowland Mayan civilization but late in its history the culture built an enormous ceremonial site at Tikal. There were pyramids, plazas, and carved stone and wood lintels that recorded their history. When the site was abandoned it lay at the mercy of the jungle for nine hundred years. From the 1850's onward, sporadic scientific expeditions went to Tikal to explore the area and unmask what the jungle had had a millennium to cover. Then in the 1970s it had a cameo appearance in the first Star Wars movie. A decade later the tourist industry began to notice the site.

But even when amateurs began to appreciate the romance of a lost culture hidden in the jungle, visitors to Tikal were few. In 1990 Guatemala was still engaged in a civil war. The worst violence was over and most people recognized that peace was the way forward but atrocities still happened. The Guatemalan government still hunted the URNG, the main rebel group, and the URNG still stole from, kidnapped, and murdered those who wouldn't support it. Shortly after I arrived in Panama, in fact, there was a widely-publicized murder of a transplanted American farmer in Poptún. No one knew who did it but there was enough give-and-take between the rebels and maverick government troops that it could have been anyone. Such murders were infrequent but foreigners, tourists, and self-proclaimed peace activists were always targets of opportunity in rural Petén. And that was where Amy wanted to go.

"How do we get there?" I asked.

"There's a bus," she answered. "It runs once a week and only costs $12."

"A bus? But that's got to be two hundred miles!"

I'd driven in Central America and knew that two hundred miles wasn't the same distance it might be in the States. Sure enough, Amy didn't disappoint.

"I know. Someone said it takes 14-18 hours."

Fourteen to eighteen hours on a Guatemalan bus, driving on Guatemalan roads, through Guatemalan mountains, across Guatemalan bridges, and in Guatemalan traffic. Fourteen to eighteen hours of sitting next to someone with a chicken in their lap. Of watching the driver try to stay awake. Of hoping oncoming vehicles stayed in their lane. I thought of all the crosses on the hills outside Guatemala City and of all the stories I had heard of bandits pulling over tourists and robbing – or killing – them outright.

"No," I said. "No bus. Besides, I'm not sure it's all that safe up in the Petén. Why don't you just look at ruins here in town?"

"Because Tikal is an entire lost culture sitting in the jungle," she said patiently. "A crumbled church doesn't compare to that. It'll be an adventure."

"It'll be an adventure, alright. Is it worth riding on a bus for most of the day?"

"Well," she mused, wrinkling her nose at the lack of choices, "we could fly."

That we could. There was an airport in Flores, a town 40 miles south of Tikal. We could fly direct to Flores from Guatemala City and then take a bus to Tikal. That to me was preferable to the all-day bus ride from hell. So Amy and I bought tickets.

That was where the first hitch occurred. There were only two flights to Flores. Both were on Friday morning and both were almost booked. I managed to get the last seat on one plane. Amy reserved the last seat on the other. We wouldn't be flying together but since the planes left at nearly the same time we could meet up again in Flores.

Early Friday morning I woke up and crept out of the Martín household. It was 4:30 am and still dark. I walked past the Candelaria church, then down to Santa Rosa to get over to the other side of town where the road ran north toward the capital. The shuttle bus was to pick me up outside the Baghdad Cafe.

Antigua was spooky in the early morning. The streets were empty and yellow lamps every two or three blocks struggled to spread their glow in damp air. A light rain had fallen overnight, making the paving stones glisten where they could be seen at all.

I walked quickly and at the Baghdad Cafe set my backpack against the wall and waited. 4:45 went by with no bus. Our flights were supposed to leave La Aurora at 6:30 and I worried that the driver had overslept.

Somewhere in town a rooster crowed. Another rooster far away answered, then a third. Then the first crowed again and the cycle repeated.

At 4:50 a pack of dogs appeared a block up the street toward the mountains. They had caught a cat. Amidst much growling and anguished yowling from the cat the pack was trying to rip it apart. An abrupt end to the yowling told me they succeeded.

At five minutes before the hour I heard the whine of a transmission from somewhere in the town. The sound moved back and forth, one minute floating west toward the Volcano of Fire and the next returning toward the Volcano of Water. But exactly on the hour a pair of headlights appeared down Sixth Avenue. When the minivan pulled up I saw Amy's sleepy face looking out the side window, visibly relieved to see me just as I was to see her. Two other students were aboard, hunched against their overnight bags and trying to sleep. As soon as I climbed in the driver roared off, anxious to make up for lost time.

"Hey," she whispered.

"Good morning. You look like you didn't sleep much."

She shook her head. "I was afraid I'd oversleep. Were you waiting long?"

"Long enough. This town's creepy in the dark."

The heat on the minivan didn't work so we squeezed together and tried to sleep during the hour-long ride to the capital. Amy did, I couldn't. The mountain road with its omnipresent crosses kept me awake. I watched our driver as he hunched over the steering wheel and urged our van up the serpentine road. The headlights stabbed the darkness in straight lines that swept around turns in the curving road, slicing through trees in the forests on the hill and illuminating objects on the inside of the turn only at the last moment. Usually those objects were people, workers up before dawn and walking on the road, carrying firewood or market goods. Our driver swerved a couple of times to avoid a dim profile in the road. Against all odds we arrived in the city in one piece, pulling up to the airport just after six.

"Now what?" one of the students asked after the driver dumped us at the terminal and pulled away. Her name was Anne. She was another friend of Amy's and had a ticket on the same plane I was taking. The fourth student was a tall, skinny guy named Warren who I only knew in passing. He hung out at Fenix, never drinking and too shy to talk but content to watch the rest of us play pool and listen to our conversations. He had tickets with me and Anne.

Foolishly we had figured that since planes were scheduled to take off at 6:30 that meant the airport would be open at that time. The terminal was shut tight, however, and the whole length of the street we stood on looked like an industrial area closed for the holidays. I looked around. Despite my many visits to Guat City I had always arrived at the military ramp, on the other side of the runways about a mile away. Nothing here was familiar. We waited for someone to show up but no one did. The only movement on the street was – again – stray dogs.

Then we heard a motor start. Somewhere off to our left, behind the terminal buildings and a chain-link fence, an airplane was revving up.

"This way," I said with a shrug.

We trooped down a street parallel to the airfield until a break in the buildings let us approach where the planes were parked. Out on the ramp was a DC-9 with such a bad paint job I could still see where it said Pan Am underneath the current operator's name, *Aero Transporte.* Next to it was a small Chinese-made twin turboprop that looked like a reverse-engineered Shorts 360. Passengers were walking across the ramp to both planes, bags in hand. The DC-9 people were directed to hurl their luggage into a cargo bay beneath the stairs before boarding. Those getting on the smaller plane carried their bags with them.

I managed to get the attention of an airport worker sitting on a bicycle inside the fence. He confirmed that the planes were headed to Flores. When I explained our predicament he opened a nearby gate so we could enter the ramp.

It was the Chinese turboprop that had already started one engine. Now that we could see company names on the planes our tickets confirmed that Anne, Warren, and I were on the jet and Amy would be riding the Shanghai Special. She and I rushed over to the carrier just as someone inside was closing the door. After a hurried conversation the co-pilot (there was no flight attendant) told us the plane was full but that since Amy had a ticket she could ride in the jump seat by the door if she wished. He handed her a length of rope to use as a seat belt.

"Is this safe?" she pleaded, seeing me as the expert on all things aviation.

Of course it wasn't safe, I wanted to say. Neither plane looked airworthy. Both would probably fall apart at the first hint of turbulence.

"Oh, yeah," I lied. "This plane is a workhorse."

"But it looks old. How can you be sure it won't crash?"

"How do you think it got to be this old?" I told her. "Don't worry, you're safer in this than in the jet. We'll see you in Flores."

I helped her tie the rope around the fold-down seat.

"*No abre la puerta!*" the copilot admonished her before climbing into the cockpit. *Don't open the door.* He wagged a finger in her face like it was important. She looked at me, clearly wondering why anyone would open the door in flight, but I didn't have an answer for her. Maybe the copilot had a history.

"Good luck!" I shouted above the engines. "Think of it as an adventure!"

I latched the door and ran over to the DC-9.

There were only two noteworthy things about my flight to Flores. The first was that the plane's cabin smelled badly of unwashed humanity. There were a hundred or so passengers and the air conditioning was on the fritz. After an hour of flight I was ready to pass out.

The second thing was the relaxed attitude of the flight crew. On takeoff roll – while the plane was accelerating down the runway toward the ravine that I knew contained wreckage of many other aircraft – the stewardess sauntered past me going up the aisle toward the cockpit. She led an excited four- or five-year-old boy by the hand. Up ahead, the door to the cockpit was open and the pilot – the pilot! –twisted around in his seat to motion the boy forward. On his face was a big smile. In his hand he dangled a candy bar.

I looked away and prayed.

We didn't crash. As the sun rose over the mountains behind the city we climbed into the clear tropical air and headed north to the Petén.

The airport at Flores was warm and bathed in sunlight when we landed. The terminal looked new and so did the paving on the runway. Someone mentioned the government was trying to get more people up to the area. Even with the violence more tourists meant a better local economy. If so, the locals had a ways to go. The nearby lake was beautiful but the town was dusty and careworn.

We went through a customs line and then – since the bus hadn't arrived to take us to Tikal – sat around in the morning sun to wait for Amy's plane.

She arrived half an hour after us, looking as she came through the terminal like someone who had gained a new appreciation for life.

"I won't fly on that plane again, Mike," was the first thing she said. "They almost hit a mountain! I'll buy another ticket. I'm flying with you."

I didn't tell her about the cockpit tours on the DC-9. She was upset enough.

In the end there were thirty people from the two planes who came to tour Tikal. Most were part of a tour from the Netherlands. Only the handful of us came from Antigua. Together we waited for our tour bus and guide.

The bus showed up around ten o'clock. The driver looked like he could care less that we had been waiting but the guide bustled around with profuse apologies. His name was Emilso. He was short and stout with a quick smile and a quicker frown that suggested he feared being on the verge of losing his job. He hustled everyone onto the bus and then gave us a hurried speech about how the entrance to the park was an hour away and the Tikal Lodge was thirty minutes after that but that we would try to get to the security of the lodge even faster if road conditions permitted. He spoke in rapid Spanish, eliciting smiles and confused nods from the Europeans.

"What does that mean?" asked Anne, who tried to follow Emilso's staccato proclamation. "'The security of the lodge?' Does that mean the road isn't safe?"

I shrugged.

"Well?" she insisted. "You're supposed to be the expert!"

I didn't like Anne. She had a sourpuss face and complained a lot. I was patient with her because a week earlier she'd had a bad experience on a bus to Chichicastenango where the driver hit an old woman walking by the side of the road. The woman flew up and smashed the windshield but the driver didn't stop – reasoning correctly that he would end up in prison if he did. Instead he drove on, carrying the body a good half-mile before it fell off, then continued another fifty miles back to Antigua with his passengers shrieking in horror all the way. It was a nightmare experience for everyone so Anne could be forgiven for still being a little tense. But tense was one thing and bitch was another. On the plane where we all suffered through stuffy cabin air and body odor only Anne saw fit to make loud comments about it. On top of that, she resented me being along on the trip and occupying so much of Amy's attention.

"Maybe there's traffic," I suggested.

And maybe not. Amy and I were on the other side of the aisle toward the back of the bus. A Dutch couple in front of me talked over Emilso's words so I didn't hear exactly what he said, but from the look on his face if our guide was concerned about something it probably wasn't rush hour. And as we pulled out onto the road, the dearth of cars suggested traffic wouldn't be a problem.

"You know, I talked to the embassy," I reassured Amy. "They said everything's fine up here so long as you don't go looking for trouble."

"I asked at the Rainbow Room, too," she agreed, referring to a coffeehouse hangout in Antigua. "I'm not worried. Nobody there has heard of any problems, either."

"It's a national park," I said confidently. "The only people up here are students and tourists."

She nodded. For a while we rode in silence. Then she said, "You still don't think it's safe, do you?"

"No."

We drove east out of Santa Elena and onto the highway. Our bus was the only vehicle on the road. Emilso sat hunched on a seat behind the driver with a watch and a clipboard that he consulted often. Frequently he leaned over the driver's shoulder to point out turns and give directions. Just as frequently he turned to his passengers and asked no one in particular if everything was going well. "*Todo está bien, no?*" he would enquire.

After a while I saw a gravel road off to the right. A sign pointed to the border town of Melchor de Menchos, forty miles away, on the other side of which was Belize. In the distance were mountains and open countryside, a tableau that the gravel road climbed into and disappeared within. The sight gave us a sense of just how far out in the middle of nowhere we were getting. Miles of rolling hills and forest in every direction with nothing but a sense of optimism to keep us safe.

After forty minutes we were still alone on the road but almost at the park. Emilso announced this with a relieved smile. But no sooner were the words out of his mouth than the driver said something and Emilso's face fell.

We rounded a corner and found a roadblock. A pickup truck and what looked like a topless Ford Bronco stood at angles in the road, blocking both lanes. Half a dozen men stood near them, holding rifles and wearing bandannas that covered the lower half of their face.

The passengers went into a panic. The Dutch woman in front of me let out a long wail and began crying, a reaction that spread to others up front. I felt a stab of fear as I realized that I might have gotten Amy into a very bad situation. I looked to the driver, thinking he might crash through the blockade – our bus was big enough – and make a run for it. But Emilso and the driver looked resigned. Already we were slowing down, rolling to a halt right in front of the pickup.

The door swung open and a gunman leapt aboard.

"You are late!" he accused Emilso, pointing a dirty finger in the guide's face.

"*Bicho,*" Emilso pleaded, looking more disappointed than afraid, "we are almost at the park. Why do you have to stop us here?"

I leaned forward to hear what they were saying, my job made easier by the fact that most of the passengers lapsed into a terrified silence when the bandit came aboard.

The gunman shouldered his rifle but was still angry. With only occasional glances at the rest of the bus he lectured Emilso on how he and his men had been waiting most of the morning and had almost gone home. From the look on Emilso's face that seemed to have been our guide's plan.

While they were speaking a second bandit came on board and yelled from the top of the aisle for everyone to give him their money. The Europeans didn't understand but when he started down the aisle, shaking them down one by one, hands reached out holding watches and wallets. The bandit disregarded the jewelry, pushing it aside and taking only the cash.

"Oh my god, oh my god, oh my god, oh my god," repeated Anne across the aisle as she fumbled in her backpack. Amy's hands, too, shook as she tried to get open the fanny pack she wore around her waist. I had money in two pockets and reached into one, hoping the guy would be happy with whatever I gave him.

It was while I was extracting the money that the bandit turned straight down the aisle and I could see the top half of his face. He had broad, flat features and brown skin beneath impossibly thick black hair. He also had a birthmark on his forehead, about the size of a Kennedy dollar.

It had been a few months but I recognized our passenger from the day Bob Harcourt and I made the cardamom run. Xachua.

Don't make eye contact, I told myself quickly. Recognizing someone who's robbing you is the worst thing you can do...

I looked away but wasn't fast enough. Xachua looked at me just then. He did a double-take, trying to figure out where he'd seen me before. Too late, I looked down at the money in my hand and pretended to be counting it out.

"Ho!" he exclaimed behind his bandanna. Everyone froze. I looked up, pretending to be confused. Xachua stared at me with wide eyes, trying to spur recognition. I glanced around.

He ran to the front of the bus to confer with his partner. Outside the four other gunmen gathered at our window. Xachua hurried back down the aisle and looked at me again, holding his rifle up. Not knowing what the hell he wanted me to do I did nothing. He then pulled down his bandanna to show me his face and a big, toothy smile.

"Hola!" he said excitedly. *"Hola!"*

He held out his hand. I shook it.

"Hola."

He started jabbering in a language I didn't understand. The bandit from up front came down the aisle. He smiled, too, and shook my hand. After a shouted conversation someone from outside reached in the window and shook my hand. They had a conversation in which I understood about every fifth word. Xachua punctuated his description of our first meeting with gyrations in the aisle and lots of hand movements, including mimicking firing a gun at various people in the back of the bus which set them to crying even more, convinced now they would face mass execution. When he finished his story the first bandit nodded approvingly and shook my hand again. Then they both motioned for me to follow them off the bus.

"Where are you going?" Amy whispered.

"I guess they want to talk," I said.

"Do you know them?"

"Not really."

"Don't get off the bus!" Anne ordered me in a hoarse whisper of her own. "They'll kill you!" Then, to Amy, "They're going to kill him!"

She was rigid with fear but had enough composure to put a tone of I-told-you-so in her voice. Her left hand gripped the headrest of the seat in front of her, her right clamped like a talon on Warren's thigh. Warren seemed content to put up with it. He hadn't said a word about the robbery and now slid his wallet back into his pocket.

I shook my head and went up the aisle. What else was there to do?

The robbers gathered around the door of the bus when I got off. Xachua repeated his story for the whole band. If he was speaking Spanish I felt like an idiot because I understood no more of this version than the one I'd heard on the bus. When he was finished, the six men looked at me and waited.

"Uh, *hola,*" I said.

A man with the same square features as Xachua and eyebrows that met over his nose nodded in my direction.

"*Gracias,*" he said. "*Gracias por ayudar a Xachua.*"

There was another round of hand-shaking.

"*De nada,*" I replied.

Eyebrows and his band repaired to the Jeep for some discussion. I stayed outside the bus since nobody told me to move and it seemed prudent to wait for orders.

Emilso had abandoned me on my way outside but now he poked his head out the door to ask, "How much longer?"

Eyebrows came back.

"My name is Ignacio," he said in careful Spanish that at last I could understand. "I am not from the Petén but this is where I live now. I am sorry to inconvenience you. You saved the life of my friend Xachua and we want you to know we are grateful."

I said, "You're welcome," again.

"Are all these people your friends?" Ignacio asked, motioning toward the faces pressed against the window.

"No," I said, "just one."

"Well," he said, looking down at his shoes and tapping the toe of one of them with the barrel of his rifle. "We will not take any more money. Just what we have already."

"Thank you." That seemed appropriate.

He looked down the road.

"You know, I would like to do you a favor. The bus will be robbed again that way, in maybe ten miles."

"Really?"

"Yes. Not by us. It is a different group. I don't like them, they are sometimes violent."

Carefully, I pried open the door to the bus and motioned for Emilso to join us outside. Ignacio didn't seem to mind.

"Emilso, Ignacio says we'll be robbed again in ten miles."

Emilso checked his clipboard.

"No," he replied, unworried. Not on Saturdays."

"You have robberies scheduled?"

He held out his hands to signify that some things were out of his control.

"Ummm," I mumbled, trying to think of our options. "Can we go around them? Is there another road?"

Emilso shook his head in certainty but I couldn't tell if he was saying that there was no other road or that doing anything not on the schedule was out of the question.

I turned to Ignacio.

"Oh, no," he said. "This is the only road. But if you would like, I can make room for two people in my car. We can take you to Tikal by another way."

My doubt must have shown through because he quickly added, "You are safe with us, my friend. We are in your debt."

I suppose I'm gullible but I believed him. All the gunmen were being friendly and Xachua was in the lead. He was overjoyed that he had run into me again.

"What about everyone else?" I asked. "Are the... people" – (I almost said 'bandits') – "at the next checkpoint really violent?"

Ignacio shrugged.

"I don't like them," was all he said. "But they won't be here tomorrow." He turned to Emilso. "You could return to the park tomorrow."

Emilso deflated. That didn't fit with the program on his clipboard. He protested. The two of them argued. While they did I went back inside the bus and had a whispered conversation with Amy.

"Do you trust them?" she asked after I explained Ignacio's offer.

"Yes, I think so. But it doesn't matter. We can go spend the night in Flores and come back tomorrow."

"No! I want to see Tikal."

"Amy, they're terrorists."

"They're thieves."

"Okay, they're thieves."

"But you said you trust them."

"I said I think I trust them."

"But he owes you his life."

"He's a peasant with a gun."

"All the more reason to trust him. He's not afraid to get his hands dirty."

"What?"

"Mike, I want to see Tikal. If we go back to Flores the soldiers might not let us come back out here."

"And if you go into the woods with a bunch of guys with guns they might kill you."

She thought for a minute.

"You'll take care of me."

"I'm trying to take care of you by taking you back to Flores."

"You'll take care of me," she repeated. "Let's go with them. They might be very nice."

Getting off the bus again wasn't easy. Anne got hysterical that Amy was leaving. Then an older Dutch gentleman, misunderstanding the situation, gallantly offered to take Amy's place as a hostage. Finally we got outside where Emilso had folded like a lawn chair and agreed to Ignacio's suggestion that they turn the bus around. Amy and I leaving the group didn't faze him at all.

We threw our bags into the Bronco and climbed in after them. Ignacio and Xachua joined us while the other bandits piled into the jeep. Xachua drove us off the road into a field and bounced slowly through the high grass toward a treeline at the north edge. Behind us Emilso and his driver maneuvered the bus up the road to a wide spot where Ignacio had suggested they turn around. But then when they got to that point they kept going. Emilso had apparently decided to stick to his schedule. I looked at Ignacio. He shrugged.

"I warned them," was all he said.

We didn't drive far. We skirted the edge of the forest for ten minutes following tire tracks from earlier in the day, then cut through an adjoining stand of trees on a more discernible trail. From time to time Xachua chattered about something in his native dialect. In between his discourses Ignacio pointed out landmarks to tell us where we were in relation to the park.

After half an hour we joined a dirt road and turned to the west. The front right tire was going flat and we slowed down over the bigger bumps to avoid riding on the rims. Xachua guided us to a pair of frame houses at the base of a hill. The road curved away from the buildings into the forest but the upslope at the bend served as a driveway. We parked in the grass off the road. Our companion in the jeep did the same. Behind the houses were large gardens and beyond them a cultivated field of about two acres. There were a half-dozen women and children scattered around the field. Some of them started our way when we parked.

"This is my home!" Ignacio announced, climbing out of the Bronco. "Welcome."

Amy was quiet during the ride. Now there must have been doubt in her eyes because Ignacio quickly pointed to the southwest.

"The national park is right there," he said, pointing across the road. "The lodge is eight miles from here. It won't take more than an hour to take you there but if you don't mind I would rather wait until later in the day, toward dusk. It is safer for me. Right now you can have something to eat."

In the back of my mind I had the idea that we had just stumbled onto some revolutionary network, that Amy and I were about to be exposed to the private life of a modern Che Guevara. I imagined us sitting down and breaking bread with these social have-nots as they enlightened us about Marxist ideology and their goals for a more equal society. The land of the people would be returned to the people! The oligarchs of the capital would be overthrown and chased out of the country! This was a nexus of the URNG, I was convinced, and Amy and I would now see first-hand a view from the other side of the Central American class struggle. As diplomatically as I could, I asked Ignacio something along those lines, if that was what had driven him to rob the bus.

"No," he said. "We needed money."

The women and children from the fields came down to the house and gathered to stare at us. Except for one girl who appeared to be a teenager, the adult women could have been anywhere from twenty to forty-years-old years old. They wore colorful clothes and had the same round features of the Mayans near Antigua. The children were also dressed in deep reds and blues: I patted one boy on the head when he came to look at my shoes. Otherwise they all ignored me and clustered around Amy to feel her blond hair.

Nobody said anything about food but very quickly the women engaged in preparing something to eat. I offered to help and was immediately put in my place by Ignacio and the amused looks of his cohorts. Amy then took the hint and offered – the teenaged girl took her by the hand and led her into one of the houses, from which she emerged half an hour later coughing discreetly from the smoke and trying to wipe her hands clean of chicken feathers.

"What's for lunch?" I whispered.

She held up a feather.

We ate outside at a table between the two houses. There was a stone oven on the back side of one building. As we ate smoke from the oven rose and gave a campfire scent to the meal.

Conversation was slow. Normally a good talker, I was unsure what subjects were diplomatically acceptable given our situation. *So, does highway robbery pay well?* Amy stuck to science, asking all kinds of questions about the park and the ruins within. Xachua made her almost leap from her seat by describing

Mayan ruins *outside* the park that no one else knew about, but then dashed her enthusiasm by refusing to take her there. It was too far, his expression implied, and they were just a bunch of rocks anyway.

The boy who examined my shoes came back to inspect my watch. He was fascinated by the digital numbers and pointed at the seconds as they counted along. I let him put it on his wrist where it flopped loosely. I considered letting him keep it until I looked around and thought, what would he do with a watch out here anyway? Then I remembered something he might want: I'd gotten in the habit in Honduras of always carrying a pack of #2 pencils to give to kids we met in remote villages. It was cheap and simple but kids would fight over them whenever we passed them out, a pencil being something they could use. Whether in school, in church, or just drawing on the pages of an old book, kids liked to write. This boy, Xactu, was no different. When I pulled out the pencils all the children gathered around. I had twenty so everyone got their hands on two or three. I also gave Xactu a pad of paper. He had the gleam of Christmas in his eyes, gripping the pencils in one hand and paper in the other, eyebrows arched high as he watched Xachua to see if he would be allowed to keep them. Xachua nodded, whereby the children shrieked happily, sat down in the dirt and started drawing whatever came to mind.

By two in the afternoon we finished eating and exhausted the obvious sources of conversation. Xachua and the two other men drifted off without explanation. The women did the same. I began to get suspicious – of what I didn't know – and the feeling grew worse when Ignacio ducked into one of the buildings. All of a sudden Amy and I were alone.

"I want that guy Xachua to show me those ruins," she whispered to me.

"Where did the women go?"

"What?"

"The women? They all walked off into the woods. Where did they go?"

"Why are you worried about the women? Don't even go there, Mike. That girl is too young for you."

"What? What are you talking about? I want to know where everyone disappeared to."

Before my imagination could kick into overtime, though, Ignacio came back. He carried a tire iron and a shovel.

With the two of us working it took ten minutes to build a little ramp of rocks and dirt. Ignacio drove the front wheels of the Bronco onto the ramp and then propped a log under the frame of the vehicle on the right side. Satisfied it was stable, we dug away the ramp under the right tire and removed it to fix the flat.

"How is he going to repair the tire?" Amy asked when Ignacio went back inside the hut.

"I don't know. I'm just hired labor. Maybe he has a patch kit."

I sat down next to her and we looked around the homestead, not sure what to do. Ordinarily I would have suggested we go exploring but given our situation it seemed best to be quiet and unobtrusive.

"So, how 'bout them Bears?" I asked.

Amy ignored me.

"I want to go see those ruins," she repeated.

"Nope."

"Nope? What do you mean, nope?"

"I mean, let's just wait another hour or two and then grab the ride into the park."

"You don't have much of a sense of adventure."

I considered the events of the day since four o'clock in the morning and held my tongue.

"The others are probably on a tour by now," Amy added.

"I doubt it."

"Why?"

"Because you're talking about a bunch of tourists who aren't as gung-ho as you are about archeology. They've been up since the crack of dawn, survived a Third World airline, and been robbed by armed men. In fact, I'll bet they've been robbed twice. My guess is they're all in the bar getting hammered."

"What's this business about you saving Xachua's life?"

I told her the whole story about coming to Guatemala with Bob Harcourt and Jerry Miner, leaving out the bit about me cowering in fear while the shooting was going on. I didn't think it was relevant.

"Wow," she said when I'd finished. Then she thought about it some more and said, "Wow," again.

Ignacio repaired the tire. We put it back on the Bronco, reversing the ramp-building and log process. When that was done the three of us worked on the roof of a potato cellar that was dug into the earth behind Ignacio's house. Part of the roof had collapsed. We had to dig it out, replace the logs that supported the corrugated tin roof, and then shovel the dirt back into place so the whole thing was buried and everything inside stayed cool. By the end of the task it was five o'clock and I was covered in dirt and sweat. I wanted to ask where the other two guys had gone but realized after a while that they had houses of their own out of sight on the far side of the fields. No doubt they were there doing home projects of their own. Farming was hard work the world over. No wonder they robbed buses.

"We can go now," Ignacio announced when the cellar was complete. The sun hovered just over the hills behind the house, letting the trees at the edge of the forest throw shadows across the road.

"You won't get in trouble?" I asked.

He shook his head.

"The others have gone by now."

It occurred to me that he hadn't been concerned about the authorities in the park. Instead he had waited in order to avoid the other gang of highwaymen.

Everyone gathered to see us off. We went through a round of good-byes. As polite and proper as any lady in the city, Ignacio's wife wished us a safe journey and invited us back whenever we wished.

Ignacio drove us to the park. As we climbed into the Bronco, Xachua quietly gave me a small wooden bust carved from cedar. At first I thought that he was giving me something he had taken from an archeological site. Then I realized the carving was fresh, the smell of the wood rubbing off onto my hands. The face was of the bust was plain and relaxed, with indistinct features except for a high forehead and stringy hair that did passing justice in their resemblance to my own. Xachua had done it himself. It was for luck, he said. I shook his hand warmly.

The ride through the park took half an hour. It was beautiful terrain. The dirt road that ran past Ignacio's house led into the forest for two miles and ended at what looked like an abandoned logging site. From there we cut across a long meadow, forded two streams, and joined the paved road that came from the main highway. Ignacio carried us close enough to park headquarters that we could see lights winking on outside the tourist cabins. From there we got out and walked.

"Thank you for your hospitality," Amy told Ignacio as though we had stayed at a bed-and-breakfast. "You have a beautiful family."

"I hope you like our park," he replied. "We're very proud of it.."

"Oh, I'm sure I will."

"Will we see you on our way out?" I asked him.

He smiled.

"Oh, no. We only greet visitors on their way *into* the park."

Then he was gone.

That night we lay on the grass outside Amy's cabin, star-gazing. Muffled noise from the lodge reached us across the compound. I had been right: the others had in fact been robbed again and were still in the bar, drinking away the experience. All except for Anne who had already passed out. They had given us up for dead and made such a huge commotion over our return that after a while we made our excuses and escaped again out into the night. On the lawn behind the lodge it was so dark we could barely make out the buses parked in the driveway.

"How's your trip going, Mike?" Amy asked.

"To Tikal?"

"No, to Antigua."

"Good," I shrugged. "I came to learn Spanish. So far I've learned words I didn't expect, like plunger, rifle, and kidnapping, but overall I'd say I've improved. You?"

"Well, I wanted to do something different after graduating. Today has been different. We're not dead and I'm finally in Tikal, so I can't complain."

A buzzing rose from the nearby forest. Bats flew by to investigate, their shadows flitting drunkenly across the stars.

"How long will you be down here?" she asked. "In Panama, I mean. In Central America."

"Until the Air Force sends me somewhere else."

"You'll learn Spanish by the time you leave."

"I hope so."

"And you'll have adventures. Do things like today happen to you all the time?"

"Hardly," I laughed. "My nerves couldn't handle it if they did."

Something large – not a bat – glided by about fifty feet up. Right after it a shooting star dove for the horizon.

"You'll have to write to me from Alabama and tell me about the ruins there," I told her. "You've got too much in your head to keep to yourself."

"I'll do that," she agreed. "And you'll have to call me when you get back to the States and fill me in on your adventures down here. I hope you keep having them."

The large thing flew by again. It merged with the gloom of the treeline and disappeared but soon after the mournful call of a potoo told us what it was. It was the perfect sound for a dark night in the tropics: haunting and deep and likely to scare the hell out of you if you didn't know what it was. Potoos had disturbed my sleep nightly during a jungle survival course I did at Fort Sherman back in Panama. The low moan invariably found me in the darkness when I huddled on the ground, wet and scared and cowering from mosquitoes. Remembering that experience made me think of Panama, which reminded me of the C-27. I hadn't flown in weeks. If I was going to do as Amy wished and keep having adventures, it was time to get back to the cockpit.

"I'll do my best," I promised.

15. Monkey Stew

EVERYBODY WENT TO Jaime's when we stayed in Iquitos. He was a nice guy, he spoke English, and he knew everything that was going on in his corner of the jungle. And you could trust his food.

That was saying a lot because Iquitos varied decades if not centuries in development from street to street. It was a town full of contradictions. We couldn't drink the water and the food was often questionable, yet it was easy to find a bottle of Coca-Cola. There was no hot water in the hotels but the hamburger stand on Calle Arana had an espresso machine. And each morning as a fruit peddler's mare pulled his cart up the street past our hotel, a motorbike dare-devil screeched past him to drop off six copies of the Miami Herald. The papers were two days old but still.

By most standards Iquitos was the wild west. It called itself the gateway to the Amazon. In a few years it would become a mandatory stop on any Amazon basin eco-tour. In 1990, however, if you weren't from Iquitos and you were there, you were lost.

There were no roads to the town. The only way to get there was by boat or plane. Planes landed twice a day but only one came from outside Peru, a 707 shuttle from Manaus in Brazil. The port was sporadically busy: oceangoing vessels could make it upriver to Iquitos and during the rubber boom at the turn of the century had routinely done so. Nowadays, except for the occasional paddlewheel steamer headed downstream the town's business was local.

Some streets were paved, some were not. Traffic consisted of herds of motorbikes and three-wheeled *motocarros* that charged around in irregular stampedes, kicking up clouds of dust and exhaust. There were no suburbs. Where Iquitos stopped it just stopped and there was nothing but jungle for hundreds of miles.

Crime was common, especially petty theft, but violent crime was rare. Drugs traffickers were around but they were there to get away from it all themselves. The police and the government felt the same way: present in name, in practice both were a long way away.

The only violence in my years there was caused by Americans. The first instance happened when Dave, the SEAL team leader, had his watch stolen. He offered twenty dollars as reward for anyone who brought it back – and an extra ten if they beat the hell out of the thief. The SEALs spent a lot of time in Iquitos, supposedly looking for drugs but in reality forever being hamstrung by bureaucracy that kept them wasting their days by the pool. Dave was as frustrated as any of them which is why he overreacted on the watch. He wasn't serious about the beating but the street kids took him that way with the result that a Shipibo Indian named Ambrosio who was always hanging around the Plaza de Armas selling, of all things, watches was set upon one night by about twenty eight- to ten-year olds who punched and kicked him senseless. He had Dave's watch, though, and that was all the kids ended up taking from him. After that nobody ever stole from us.

The only other bloodshed I heard of came from a dust-up between two local drug merchants, one at the airport and the other at the docks. They had been partners at one time but after a misunderstanding began a mutual vendetta that drove them both out of business. The mix-up again was caused by us.

In early October just as the rainy season was getting into full swing Josh, Franklin, and I went down to Peru for two weeks to fly tanker runs around Sites 5 through 8. Site 5 was so remote it made Iquitos look like Manhattan. It sat near a village on a tributary of the Amazon and had a runway that was "sometimes there, sometimes not" as our survey said, depending on the flood state of the river. Site 6 didn't even have a river to recommend it. Sites 7 and 8 were on higher ground but just as isolated. All of them suffered from the disadvantage of needing fuel brought in to service their generators. The generators powered the radars and the radars were why the sites were there so someone needed to make sure they had enough gas. Josh hated the mission. He had come from flying tankers, KC-135s, and had no desire to go back. But it was flying.

We could download fuel the same way we uploaded it, through our single-point nozzle on the right side of the plane. If the guys on the ground had their rubber blivets ready and a hose pre-positioned, we could land, pump out three or four thousand pounds of gas, and take-off again in fifteen minutes. At six pounds per gallon the blivets filled up fast. The site could operate for another two weeks and we could be on our way before anyone on the ground, air, or radio realized we had landed. It was called hot-gassing, or hot-defueling, and was another reason the C-27 was so popular among ground forces.

Not that it always worked out. In September Story and I dropped two blivets into the grass in eastern Honduras. Task Force Bravo, based in the center of the country at Soto Cano Air Base, wanted us to create a Forward Area Refueling Point near Mocorón so their Blackhawks could buzz around in that part of the country and still have fuel to make it home. The spot they chose was a wide grassland that lay between the coastal jungle and the pine forests of the lowland cordillera, a flat dry area that could have been the Illinois prairie.

Landing amid the waving grasses we combat-downloaded the blivets, sliding them off the ramp while the plane was still rolling. We turned around by the trees, Bunny ran out with a hose, and like a malarial mosquito infecting a victim we pumped 4,000 pounds of JP-4 into each deflated balloon. Squatting in the brush like morose alien creatures, mock-ups for The Blob, their black rubbery skin swelled until each blivet was a huge lazy bladder of gas spread out across one corner of the prairie, a miniature service station just waiting for the H-60s to come along and relieve their suffering by siphoning off the pressure.

Three days later two helicopters landed with the wrong size hose. The pressure was too much for the connecting ring. It blew right off the nozzle, sending the hose dancing across the grass like a spastic cobra and spewing fuel in every direction. The rotors turned the gas into a cloud that enveloped the lead helicopter. The second helicopter beat feet immediately, launching himself into the air and making frantic radio calls to his wingman. Within seconds the cloud caught a spark from all the static electricity. It burst into an inferno around Lead, whose shocked pilot instinctively yanked collective and rocketed out of there. Nobody was hurt and neither aircraft was damaged – except for a few scorch marks – but several square miles of prime Honduran countryside disappeared in smoke. Days later it was still smoldering.

But if Josh was unhappy about hot-gassing he only pretended to be unhappy about Peru.

Josh bad-mouthed Iquitos in the same way he found fault with everything. It was hot, it was dirty, the people were poor, there were germs everywhere, he had better things he could be doing in Panama – but it was all a facade and an unconvincing one at that. He fooled no one in the squadron. Standing at the scheduling desk whining about another trip, a Br'er Rabbit pleading not to be thrown into the briar patch, he was so disingenuous that Maj Harmon would merely nod and ask, "Do you want to stay for three weeks or come back a week early?" and Josh would forget himself and instinctively respond, "I'll stay."

For one thing, Peru meant money. Though Sendero Luminoso had stumbled lately they still killed people with abandon and caused enough fear to make trips to the region risky. Add the fact that we were flying into drug-producing regions and then mix in the Tupac Amaru's car bombs in Lima and together that was enough for the Defense Department to label the country a hostile-fire region. That meant hostile-fire pay. It was only $150 per month but it was something.

But money scratched the surface. Saying that Josh flew to the Amazon Basin to make money would be like saying NASA went to the moon to pick up a rock.

It wasn't the flying, either. To Josh, flying was almost an inconvenience. He liked being a pilot but the responsibility of the plane weighed on him. He worried constantly something would go wrong. He was the kind of guy who would take the controls from his co-pilot at the slightest malfunction or hint of bad weather. Not that he flew better: he just wanted to be in control. He would make all the landings if the airfield "didn't look right." He would make all the take-offs. He insisted on doing his own pre-flight inspection and would re-compute landing data even after the copilot gave him the numbers. Usually the only time he let someone else fly was when he was about to throw a fit.

It was the adventure that drew Josh. In the jungle he was the picture of excitement, the stranger in the strange world, anxious to explore, to meet people, to do as the Romans did and learn new things. It was the people, the foreign-ness, the remote-ness of out-of-the-way places that attracted him as a flyer.

And Iquitos had all of the above. It was a place far away from our First World, not just in distance but in culture and outlook. In Iquitos even the chance of running into another American was remote. Which was good, because for Josh mingling with the locals only to find another gringo was like hiking into the wilderness and seeing a beer can on the trail. He wanted to feel like an explorer, the guy who finds a blank slate and leaves his own mark on it. Iquitos was such an opportunity. It was poor and chaotic. It was dusty, violent, and lawless. And it was a *loooong* way away.

All of which was perfect because Josh – his selfish, sarcastic, money-grubbing exterior aside – was starting to worry. A mid-life crisis was brewing. Nothing specific brought it on but suddenly the party animal in him had doubts that drinking and women were all there were. Dating was still fun and all women were still potential conquests but the meaning of it bedeviled Josh more every day. So now he swung in the opposite direction, being frustrated *because* he wanted to believe in something. He wanted to believe so badly that he occasionally latched on to the outlandish.

"You know," he said one day, his eyes lighting up in a way that arched his eyebrows and pushed his long, oval face even longer, "I just read about this Indian tribe in the Amazon."

"Cannibals?"

"No. Well, they might be but that doesn't matter. They've got this really mystical way of looking at the world."

"How's that?"

"They train their shamans in the coolest way I've ever heard. They take a baby from its mother and raise him in a cave until he's fifteen years old. In the dark the whole time. Dark, cold, wet. He never sees anything but dim shadows of rock and junk. Sleeps on bat guano. Stumbles around stalagmites. Stays warm around a fire but that's the only light he ever gets to see. They teach him history. They teach him language. They teach him about birds and animals and the seasons. They draw pictures and try to get him to imagine this stuff. They teach him about wars and poverty and hunger and disease and all the stories of their people and folklore and medicine and stars and the moon and everything else they can think of. Basically, they teach him about the world as it is, or anyway how we all normally see it. Then when he's been locked in there for years, when he's thoroughly cynical and depressed about reality, they tell him, 'Now we're going to show you heaven.' And they take him outside."

"Outside?"

"Yeah. Outside. Outside into the fresh air, into warm air. Out of the cave and into the jungle. The jungle! For the first time he sees colors. He sees light. He feels the sun. He stands on a hillside and looks out at the forest, the blue sky and green trees and red parrots and brown monkeys and soft, spongy ground. Warm, clean air, sweet fruit, beautiful calls of birds and insects. Flowing rivers, fresh springs, soil under his feet. And of course he's floored. Floored and overcome with emotion. Crying, wailing, on his knees in tears it's so beautiful. And they say, "This is our heaven. Lead your people through it.' And because he can now really see what's there – he's not jaded like the rest of us – he can appreciate it in ways that we never could. He can guide his people in ways that make sense."

Josh looked off into the distance, tempted toward tears himself.

"So what are you saying?" I asked.

"I'm saying...I'm saying...I'm not saying anything! But isn't that cool? The guy is the one person who's not blinded by all this stupidity that we push on ourselves every day, and all he had to do to get smart was spend fifteen years in a cave."

"That's all?"

"Well, what's the alternative? Once we've garbaged our brains with the modern world you would have to spend fifty years in a monastery to get to the same point. Fifty years at least..."

Fifty years on his knees was a harsh prospect. Josh convinced himself there had to be an easier way to uncloud his mind and see the world with the beauty and clarity that he thought it deserved. Somewhere out there was a clue that would guide him from his pointless revelry to inner peace. *Out there.* It had to be *out there* because he didn't feel it inside or with anything he knew. I nodded whenever he said things like that because it made him feel better. Searching in itself made him feel better. The sheer effort kept his mind off not knowing what he was searching for.

Iquitos was a great place to search. In part that was because no one there knew us.

Except, of course, for Jaime. Jaime knew everyone. He certainly knew us. In fact, he was the first in a seemingly endless parade of people I encountered in the jungle over the years who knew exactly what we were doing, where we were going, and who we were working with no matter how much we tried to keep it all secret.

His restaurant was down the street from the El Dorado, past Ari's Burger and all the way to the river. The street ended one block past Ari's. The ground there gave way rapidly, sloping down in a green expanse to the river's floodplain where huts stood on stilts above the swampy ground and people poled their way from one to the other in long *cayucas* or bamboo rafts.

The river itself – the flowing, navigable part of the water – was a full mile away across the bog. It was in sight even on rainy days, the master waterway of all South America, wide, deep, and steady in its flow. Gathering its strength from the largest watershed in the world, the Amazon carried more water than the Mississippi, the Nile, and the Yangtze combined. But that was at Belém, on the east side of the continent, where the river was wider than the English Thames is long and where it pushed fresh water 200 miles out into the Atlantic. Here in Iquitos, two thousand miles inland, the headwaters in the Andes were still a viable memory of the currents flowing past. Here the Amazon simply looked confident. It came in from somewhere between the trees to the south and made a lazy curve around the city before moving off to the east, disappearing on the horizon like a highway cutting across prairie.

Finding the river was the first step to finding Jaime, for his restaurant moved a lot. At night when streets were haphazardly lighted and the riverfront was – in Franklin's words – "dark as the inside of a Brazilian whore," finding it was a challenge. It was always in the same area, near the river's edge where the mosquitoes were thickest and the roads the worst, but Jaime and his cooks seemed to swap buildings as often as the river flooded. Originally they had been directly behind Ari's Burger and around the corner from the Marandú, the restaurant with the black boa over the door and a claim to fame that it served alligator tail from the gator of your choice. (There was a tank out back.) Jaime's had also been further down the *Malecón*, the waterfront street, next to the police station, until the station burned twice in two months and Jaime decided it would be safer to relocate. On our trip this month his restaurant was to the left off Napo Street, the one that ran into the river. A narrow path wound from the cobblestones to his small building, past tall piles of dirt and a stone wall topped with broken glass. The dirt gave the impression someone in the city was thinking of extending the *Malecón* in this direction along the top of the bluff. It also suggested they weren't sure how to do it without somehow extending the hill or eroding the buildings that lined its edge. The latter was the cheaper option and I could see another move in Jaime's future. For now, though, there was no road, just the path, and Jaime's restaurant, open only for dinner, sat in the dark beyond the wall with broken glass looking out where the river would be if there had been light to see it.

To avoid problems finding Jaime, we did research. The first stop on any trip to Iquitos was at Ari's burger. Ari's was an open-air cafeteria at the corner of the Plaza de Armas, next to the Weird Art Bar and across the street from a monument to the 1879 War of the Pacific.

Jaime's was where you got good food and the inside skinny on everything that was going on. Ari's was where you got cheap food and found out what there was to get the good skinny on in the first place. School kids gathered there on their way home from class; old men sat under the green awnings to swap stories, play a local version of backgammon, and watch the world go by. Teenage girls and boys flitted in and out to sneak glances at each other. Street urchins gathered by the dozen.

It was from the urchins, the *muchachos,* Latin Olivers with dirty faces and brushes to polish your shoes, that we learned the geography of the city and kept track of everybody's whereabouts. If you wanted to find somebody, you talked to a *muchacho.* If you wanted to hide from somebody, you talked to a *muchacho* (at least until someone else offered him more money to find you). If you wanted a prostitute, or drugs, or transportation, or anything else you talked to a *muchacho.* They lived on the streets, fought on the streets, ate on the streets, and occasionally died on the streets from violence, disease, malnourishment, or too much glue.

"*Oye, 'chacho,*" said Josh with a smile when the first kid hugged him even before we could pull chairs out onto the sidewalk. I learned they always hugged us on first sight, not because they were happy to see us but to see if we had guns. That was valuable information. "*Cómo estás?*"

"*Ben, ben,*" this one replied with a shy smile. They could steal, fight, swear, and use drugs but were still shy when talking to us. Two more stood beside me at my chair and a fourth sat on the ground at Josh's feet to polish his shoes.

"Hey, I feel surrounded," I laughed. "How're you guys doing? *Cómo están, 'chachos?*"

"They're good kids," said Josh, beginning a lecture. He'd been to Iquitos before and felt obligated to instruct. "Don't push 'em off. All they want is attention."

"I'm not going to push them off."

"*Quien está?*" one of them asked. "*Está day-ah?*"

"Am I what?" I replied.

"DEA," said Josh. "He wants to know if you're DEA. They say it as one word. *No,*" he said to the boy. "*No estamos DEA. Somos pilotos. Con la fuerza aérea.*"

"Why are you telling him that?" I was incredulous. "I thought we were supposed to keep a low profile."

Josh smirked. "It's not exactly a secret. Three guys with short hair fly a camo-colored plane into the jungle – gee, I wonder why. You can keep low in Bogotá. There's any number of reasons to be there. There aren't many for being in Iquitos."

He was right. The more I thought about it the dumber I felt, trying to play secret-spy in a town where we stood out like a squad car at a biker rally.

"Tonio," Josh called to one boy who had latched onto my leg with a big hug. He was maybe ten years old, skinny with an undersized build. He had quick eyes and a beautiful smile but a blotchy red mark that covered half his face.

Tonio jumped up and ran over to Josh, who hugged him and patted him on the back.

"*Qué pasa, guapo?*" he said. "*Cómo siguen cosas contigo?*"

Tonio smiled and ducked his head with a shrug, indicating that things were more-or-less the same as always. He was pleased with being called handsome.

"See the mark on his face?" Josh asked.

"It's hard not to."

"It's not a birthmark. It's an infection. Some bug here that gives you some disease. Supposedly he could get it cleared up in the States for about five thousand dollars."

"How do you know that?"

"I don't. I met a German girl here on my last trip and she told me that."

"What was a German girl doing here?"

"She was lost."

"She came a long way to get lost."

Josh looked up at the ceiling, trying to remember the details. "If I remember correctly, she was a biology student. She came to Peru to do research at some university near La Merced."

I pictured the country's map in my mind.

"La Merced? That's nowhere near here. That's in the mountains."

"That's the point. She got on the wrong plane and ended up in Iquitos. But it gets better. She figures while she's here she'll do a river tour, goes out on a boat and somehow drops her backpack with everything she owns into the river. Like that," he snapped his fingers. "Gone."

"Not good."

"No," Josh agreed. "She wasn't a happy tourist when I saw her. It took her weeks to get money sent and then a passport so she could go back home. She had plenty of time to see Iquitos, though. And apparently she learned something about tropical diseases. Or so she said."

Tonio didn't have a clue what we were talking about. He stood nonchalantly at Josh's side, occasionally thumping Josh's leg with his fist in time with something he was humming. The rash covered half his face and appeared to spread down his neck and over part of a shoulder. I wondered if it was growing or had reached its extent. Five thousand dollars. That didn't seem much to change a life. Tonio appeared not to notice the mark – he acted like any other kid.

"Does it grow?" I asked.

"Yeah, it's gotten worse."

"What happens eventually? I mean, does it kill him?"

Josh shrugged.

"I don't know. It can't be good, though. But it doesn't matter. Vince is hooking him up. Tonio doesn't know it but Vince has made arrangements to get him treatment in the States."

"Vince the mechanic?"

"Yeah."

"Why? What does he have to do with Tonio?"

"Nothing. But he likes him."

Tonio heard Vince's name and looked up excitedly.

"Vince está aquí?" he asked.

"No, guapo. No está."

"Cuándo viene?"

"Pronto. No sé exactamente, pero viene pronto."

"I thought Vince wasn't a nice guy," I said. "I mean, I've heard stories."

"He's got a past," Josh agreed. "If you cross him he'll kill you. But other than that he's okay."

"Other than that?"

"He's a good guy until it's time to be a bad guy. But he's helping Tonio. In six months, thanks to Vince this kid won't have people staring at him whenever he walks by."

We sat and watched the waitresses move around the cafe. The boys jostled and switched positions around our feet.

"*Sabes dónde está Jaime?*" Josh asked them.

Tonio nodded but didn't say anything.

"*Pues, dónde está?*"

Tonio gave Josh a crafty look that indicated no information came free. Then he pointed down to the river. With a wagging of his finger one direction and then the next he explained the best way to get to Jaime's new place.

Josh slipped some soles into Tonio's hand.

"Dígalo que estamos aquí. Y que vamos a visitarlo esta semana en su restaurante."

Tonio nodded and slipped the money – the equivalent of a dime – into his pocket. Smooth as he was, the event didn't go unnoticed by the rest of the boys. They crowded around and volunteered that they knew where Jaime was, too, and could deliver our message about coming to dinner as well or even faster than Tonio. Several even shoved our messenger to try to get him to share his fee. Tonio shoved right back and, when an opening appeared, slipped out of the crowd and took off down the street to deliver his message. Half a dozen boys ran after him.

We ordered orange sodas from the waitress. The boy at Josh's feet had been brushing merrily away on Josh's brown loafers and now decided to apply some polish. Black polish. Josh pulled his feet away just in time.

Franklin walked up. He looked sleepy as he always did.

"You take a nap?" Josh asked.

"No," said Franklin, hugging one boy after another. "I saw Angie."

"Already? We've only been here two hours."

"Well, she called me at the hotel. She knew we were here before we were finished checking in so I went to say hi."

Franklin spoke quietly. Nothing seemed to excite him. He was one of our best loadmasters and had experience in C-141s and C-130s before coming to Panama. He had a round face, dark brown skin, and an infectious smile that made him a favorite of the *muchachos.*

"Angie your girl here?" I asked.

Franklin frowned. "What're you talking about? I'm married. Don't be saying things like I have a girl here. She's Lennie's girl, mostly."

"He's married, too," I pointed out.

"Yeah, well, she's open-minded. If he's not around she'll be your girl, too, for as long as you're here."

"So what'd she have to say?" Josh asked. "They're usually up on what's going on around here. Anything good?"

Emanuel, the kid with the shoeshine kit, started to brush Franklin's shoes. Franklin patted him on the head and told him to go ahead. His loafers, too, were brown but Franklin didn't care.

"Well," he said, as though commenting on the weather, "two things. She says there's a bounty on us."

"What?!" I sputtered.

"How much?" asked Josh.

"She says fifty thousand dollars."

"That's not a lot."

"Who?" I said. "Who put a bounty on us? And what do you mean, us? Us three?"

"No, no," said Franklin. "The plane. You're worthless."

The waitress came by with our orange sodas. Franklin ordered some kind of frothy orange whip that was advertised on a big sign behind the counter.

"You know that's got egg in it," Josh cautioned.

"I know," said Franklin. "I drink them all the time. They're good."

"If you get sick I'm going to remind you you said that."

"Okay."

"Could we get back to the bounty thing?" I cut in. "You guys are pretty blasé about it. Who put it out?"

Franklin shrugged. "Angie says the Tupac Amaru."

"That's b-s." Josh wasted all of one second on the idea. "They've got to get better rumors than that."

"Why is it b-s? Downing a plane would be good PR for any rebel group."

"Not Tupac," Josh sniffed. "In the first place, they don't operate this far east – they're strictly urban, and mostly Lima at that. Never get far from a coffee shop. Second, Tupac's not bloodthirsty like Sendero. They've got more of a social conscience. If they had fifty thousand dollars they wouldn't waste it on us. They'd take a thousand and build a bomb, then use the rest to open a food pantry for the poor or something and preach about how it should be the government doing it and not them. And third, they don't have the money. 'Nuff said. What else did Angie have to say?"

"There's a party at Latin Lovers Saturday night."

"Now that's useful. What's the party for?"

"Some girlfriend of hers is getting married."

"Perfect. Lots of women looking to hook up. Did she say if Irena will be there?"

"I didn't ask."

"I bet she will." Josh rubbed his hands in delight. "Come on, Mike. Perk up. You might get a woman. Hey, I know that guy."

He nodded toward a rotund man walking through the plaza.

"From here?"

"Yeah, isn't he, ohhh....what the heck is his name? F-f-f-something. Fielo? Fernando?"

"Felipe?" Franklin offered.

"*Sí!* Yeah, that's it. Felipe something. He's the local node, the drug dude in the town."

"Oh, yeah," said Franklin. "He's got the villa the SEALs were renting."

"That's right. Nice place. I like the courtyard with the pool. Women get in there and just drop to the ground and spread their legs."

I tried to keep up. "The local drug lord is renting a house to the Navy?" I asked.

"Not a house, a villa. Huge. Dave has his whole squad in there and they have room to spare. I think they had a couple of live-in maids."

Franklin thought about it. "They were maids?"

"Why are the SEALs renting a house from a drug runner?"

"I don't think he runs drugs," Josh corrected. "He just coordinates logistics for the people who do."

"What's the difference?"

"There's a big difference. If I sell you a gun and you go kill someone, should I be charged with murder?"

"You should if you sold the gun to me knowing I was going to commit murder."

"Well, maybe he just sets up port calls and flights and stuff and doesn't know what they intend to do with, uh, with..."

"With their cocaine? Yeah, good point. There are a million legitimate uses for crack so how is he supposed to know if some pusher's going to use it illegally?"

"That's not what I meant. And anyway it's not crack until it gets to the States."

"Who cares? And you still haven't explained how the SEALs rent a place from the local drug kingpin."

Franklin interrupted in his quiet voice as Josh started to protest.

"I think it was the price. They needed a big place. He had one. That's all."

"It still seems odd."

"He may have legitimate businesses on the side," Josh insisted. "Rental properties, real estate. You have to think of the big picture, Mike."

"Noooo," I countered. "If that's your metaphor then your 'big picture' needs a new moral frame around it. I'm thinking of a big picture where we don't help the people we're trying to catch."

"Maybe there's some quid pro quo going on. Something we don't know about."

"Maybe. But I'm thinking of the small picture. Namely, me. I'm thinking about the bounty. I've never had someone willing to pay to have me killed before."

"Not you. Just the plane. But it kind of builds the ego, doesn't it? Want another soda?"

We ordered more Fantas.

"Oh, yeah," said Franklin, remembering something else although it was clear from the way he said 'Oh, yeah' that he'd been saving the best for last. "Angie also said there's another Chuck coming in tomorrow."

Josh put down his soda. "What?"

"Yup. Captain Whitcomb, Lieutenant Colmer, Bird…"

"How does she know that?"

Franklin didn't say. He knew the answer as well as Josh.

Josh was quiet. He was ready to get mad, I could see it coming.

"She knew the crew and everything?"

"Yup."

"That means one of them called down here."

Franklin didn't reply. He looked untroubled but the news bothered me. First, a bounty, fictitious though it might be, and now a local hooker knew our flight schedule.

Josh got up and tossed a handful of *soles* on the table.

"I'll be back," he said. "I'm going to call home."

Franklin nodded. "Thought you might want to do that."

It turned out it was Bird who had called down to Angie to let her knew he was coming. One of two ringleaders of the Puerto Rican loadmaster mafia, Bird was married and had a wife and kids with him in Panama but didn't mind sharing his affections with various women around the theater. Flutie and Evan, too, had already been to Iquitos several times and knew the girls there well, but it was Bird who took the extra step of phoning ahead to make sure their schedules were clear.

Major Byron, our deputy commander or DO, wasn't around to take Josh's call but Lt Col Rasmussen was. Needless to say, the excrement immediately hit the rotating air cooling appliance.

The next day's flight was cancelled. Rasmussen gave Bird an Article 15, the highest level of censure a commander can give without going to a court-martial. He also grounded Bird from flying and assigned him to desk duties pending a security investigation. When Angie found out she was mad as hell.

After the stop at Ari's Franklin and I took a walk around town. He gave me the tour as he knew it, showing me his favorite places to eat, where to find good souvenirs, what other hotels we occasionally stayed in, and which brands of bottled water I could trust. He identified two of the buildings that might have been the Iron House, one of which stood two doors from Ari's. The Iron House was, in fact, made of iron and had been designed by Gustav Eiffel, of Eiffel Tower fame. Somebody imported it piece by piece to Iquitos during the decadent days of the rubber boom in the late 19th century but unfortunately no one was sure which one it was anymore.

We went by the docks where the river boats came in and then to the street fair at Raymondi and San Martín where local Indians hawked trinkets and stone jewelry. On the road to the airport we found another fair that included small animals caught in the jungle. One man's collection caught my eye.

"Is that what I think it is?" I muttered to Franklin.

He stepped forward and took a closer look.

"Yeah, it is," he confirmed.

The Indian had half a dozen recently killed tarantulas on display. They were large, larger than my hand, hairy, and colored variously with red and black being predominant. Each was pinned to a piece of cardboard and mounted in a shallow wooden box with glass cover.

The Indian said something that I gathered meant would I like a closer look. I shook my head and stepped back.

Another vendor approached with a secretive cast to his eye.

"*Quiere Ud. comprar un jaguar*?" he asked in a hushed whisper, beckoning me to follow.

"Buy a Jaguar?" I said to Franklin even as I followed the man. "I would be leery of putting a Land Cruiser on these streets, much less a luxury car."

Franklin said, "I don't think that's what he meant."

It wasn't what the man meant. He took us around to the back of the fair where a refrigerator-size cage stood covered with a blanket. The man took hold of a corner of the blanket and said, "*Se cuesta sólo cincuenta dolares. Sólo cincuenta.*" Then he pulled the cover off.

Inside the cage was a baby jaguar, maybe two months old. It lay calmly on the floor of the cage with its long tail curled around its body. When the cover came off it looked up at us with confident eyes as though knowing instinctively that in this part of the world everyone else is prey.

The cat's chest rose and fell in the suffocating heat, its thick striped fur immaculately groomed. We could hear a low purr. It wasn't the purr of a house kitten, though, the shallow rattle of a domesticated feline. This was a full-bodied rumble, the resonant growl of an outboard motor or a powerful animal that left alone would rule a wilderness. I looked into the jaguar's eyes. He looked right back without blinking.

"How much did he say?" asked Franklin, bending down to look at the cat more closely.

"Fifty dollars," I replied.

"That's nothing," he said, starting to reach between the bars to pet the jaguar's back, then changing his mind. "We could take him home tonight."

The vendor hovered around expectantly, not understanding English but reading the body language of two people who were obviously falling under the jaguar's spell.

"I'd pay fifty dollars to get him and then let him go," I said. "No way would I take this guy with me anywhere."

"Why not?"

"Why not? The obvious reason is that it would be only a matter of weeks before he ate me. The other reason is I don't think it's right to encourage these guys to go catch animals to sell to tourists. You wonder where this baby's mother is."

I asked the vendor that very question. He shrugged and said the cat had been found alone, an orphan. The explanation was too pat.

"Capt Riker bought a monkey here over the summer," Franklin recalled, standing up straight. The jaguar cast him a glance then looked away. "They took it on the plane back to Panama and kept it in their house."

"Really?" I'd been to T.J.'s apartment, the one he shared with Steve up in El Dorado. I didn't remember any monkey.

"That's because after being there for two months, one day it jumped from the table to the couch and died in mid-air. They think it had a heart attack."

"Probably the stress of too much partying."

The vendor intervened again. "No, thank you," I told him. I wanted to give him a lecture on selling endangered species to tourists but realized it would be pointless. The man was trying to make a buck.

At the hotel I collapsed on my bed. It was only five o'clock but with the long flight, the heat, and now nothing pressing to do I suddenly felt like lying down for a while. The ceiling fan, its blades caked in dirt, turned slowly on its mount.

The El Dorado advertised itself as a four-star hotel. In New York four stars meant Leona Helmsley was going to meet you at the door. In Iquitos four stars meant the room had water.

For all that the El Dorado was perfect for our needs. There was a dresser, a mirror, a straight-backed wooden chair, an elaborate fountain pen (complete with feather) in an empty inkwell, an attached bathroom, and a double bed that mostly didn't sag in the middle. Beyond that it was spare. All the rooms were the same except for Josh's. On this trip he'd been given what we called the Doll Room. The Doll Room was a room exactly like all the others except that for some reason it was decorated with about three dozen rag dolls. Clowns, smiley-faced animals, wide-eyed children with features as distinctly Hispanic as rags can make them, they perched like eager pets on every flat surface in the room so that it was necessary to move them around just to have space to walk. Everyone hated that room. Your every move was watched by thirty-six pairs of eyes.

I dozed until a soft rustle from above woke me up . I opened my eyes, half-expecting to see rats running along the two beams that criss-crossed the ceiling above the fan. But the beams were empty. Their deep red surface showed parallel bends as they stretched across the room, a warp that was probably there the day they were installed, but no rats.

Then movement caught my eye. High on the wall to my right, just above the door frame, a cockroach the size of a Toyota Corolla stopped crawling and twitched its antennae to get its bearings. I don't know if it stopped because I opened my eyes or if it was just contemplating its next move, but it was high up, above the beams, and had a good vantage point for surveying the room.

I didn't move. I'd never seen a cockroach that big. Not really quite so big as a car, it was still large enough to wrestle small mammals into submission and make a homestead in the sewer of its choice.

I considered my options. Remove a boot to use as a weapon? Possible, but then it occurred to me I might need something more substantial. Perhaps the chair. If I leaped to my left, grabbed the chair, then swung high and got lucky… No. With my luck I would miss and end up having a super-roach with a grudge crawling around the room. I wished I hadn't left my pistol in the plane.

Suddenly a gecko came from nowhere and hit the roach broadside, grabbing it in its mouth so quickly even the roach had no time to turn.

Whoa!

The gecko was a streak of light. It moved so fast it just appeared on top of the roach. But if he was proud of his conquest he had no time to gloat – he had a problem. At least I thought he had a problem. The gecko was only eight inches long and the roach was easily half that. Looking at them together stuck on the wall was like seeing a carpenter's T-square some builder had left behind. There was no way the lizard could swallow its prey, not whole anyway, and it wasn't clear he could hang on to it long enough to chomp through given that the roach was still alive and kicking like mad. I had the animal kingdom operating right in my hotel room.

But if the gecko was worried he didn't show it. He ran across the wall in a curving line, the roach weighing him down until they reached the corner above the door. There both disappeared into a hole in the ceiling. Dinner would be served somewhere else.

Alone again I studied the walls. Then the window. Then, gingerly, the floor. I wondered if I was still asleep. Maybe I had dreamed seeing the roach. Maybe Marlon Perkins would walk in any moment to announce, "While Jim crawls into the wall to wrestle the super-roach, lets talk about geckos..."

But no, I was awake. And something told me it would be tough to sleep now. I lay down again...and loosened my boots just in case.

I wasn't the only one with insect issues. The next day we flew out to Site 6. 6 wasn't the most remote of the radar sites since it was only an hour away but since that was an hour across Amazon jungle its isolation was secure. It sat on a low table of a hill near the Colombian border, a steep gorge flanking two of its sides. It was an encampment cut into the trees with a dirt strip sticking down to the south. From the air the cleared area formed the shape of a lollipop.

The weather was clear when we arrived overhead. Because the camp had reported receiving gunfire we stayed high until late on the approach. Five miles out at five thousand feet we lined up on the strip and dropped the gear and flaps. Bringing the power levers to idle, Josh set the end of the strip in the bottom third of his windscreen and held it there. With the right winds, in this configuration we could drop out of the sky without anyone hearing our approach.

We wore body armor when we hopped off the plane. The troops who met us were in their t-shirts, dog tags shining in the sun.

"They only shoot at night," one sergeant explained. "So far, anyway. If we wore body armor all the time guys would be passing out."

The American camp began at the top edge of the airstrip. Two chest-high rows of concertina wire surrounded it. Inside the wire we entered a warren of sand-bagged passageways that led to the inner compound where everyone lived and ate. The sandbags were stacked eight-feet high and six deep on the outer walls. Inside they went to four deep but stood just as high.

Most of the Americans at Site 6 were Army. There were also four Air Force technicians and a civilian who maintained the radars. There were two radars. In the inner compound a Quonset hut and two metal boxcars occupied the center of the ¼-acre work area. Sixteen-foot-wide dishes perched on stands above the boxcars, reaching above tree-level and pointing at complementary stretches of the horizon. Everything was painted dark green.

The troops lived in tents. The canvas was draped over wood frames with aluminum pallets serving as floors. All construction sat inches off the ground. Wooden pallets served as sidewalks down the passageways and between the tents. The whole camp was built with wary respect for the environment in mind. It wasn't raining at the moment but like everywhere else in the jungle it did so at least once a day. Downpours, the sergeant advised, turned the camp into a river. There was no point in digging drainage channels because the water flowed naturally toward the gorge. It left the area of its own accord once the rains stopped. The only obstacles to the flow were the sandbag walls but they, too, had been designed with all entrances pointing downhill.

"You're one with your world," Josh complimented him.

"Hardly," the sergeant said. "We learn our lessons the hard way."

The Quonset hut held the dining area, a small science lab staffed one-deep by a lone civilian, and the recreation room where all had access to satellite TV, a video player, and a bookshelf of cheap paperbacks.

Ceiling fans and heavy screens on the windows kept the inside relatively cool. There was nothing anyone could do about the humidity, however. Notices tacked to a cork board had a moist feel and covers on the paperbacks had begun to curl.

A tinny, thwacking sound drew my attention to the window. There on the screen were a handful of moths, what looked like a june-bug the size of a golf ball, and the largest grasshopper I'd ever seen. The grasshopper was flapping its 5-inch wings and striking the metal frame of the window. All of them seemed determined to get inside.

"So who shoots at you?" Josh asked. "Locals?"

Three troops seated eating lunch in the dining area shook their heads.

"No," a sergeant first-class explained. "The locals are friendly. There's a village down in the gorge with about a hundred people in it. They're fine. We buy fish from them all the time. The trouble-makers are the FARC. The Putumayo's only a few miles away. They cross that and come over every now and then to take pot-shots inside the perimeter. Everybody thinks it's the Shining Path because we're in Peru but we're hell-and-gone from the Huallaga Valley. It's the FARC."

"Pot shots my black ass," another sergeant muttered. He was squat with a shaved head. "You weren't here in August during the attack. Bastards got right onto the airfield and tried to storm the compound."

"Here?" I asked. "Didn't the Peruvians stop them?" There was a Peruvian encampment of about fifty soldiers just the other side of the airstrip. They were there to defend the Americans.

The soldier sniffed. "You're joking. They fired a few shots and then came pouring inside our lines. We had a regular ol' firefight here for about six hours. That's why we built up the walls and dug the new foxholes. Stop them? It makes you wonder who's here to defend who."

"If it was so bad why did you volunteer for a second 90-day tour?" the SFC taunted. "To see if the FARC could kill you before the bugs did, or the jaguar, or the snakes?"

The second sergeant grumbled, admitting he didn't have much of a defense.

"I stayed for the money," he fessed up. "But another attack like that and my butt will be with these guys on the first plane out of here."

"That August attack was nothing," a soft voice behind us said. We turned to see the civilian standing at the sandwich counter slathering peanut butter onto a piece of bread. He was my height but stocky, with a loose shirt with sleeves rolled up to the elbows and baggy cotton pants. A mess of curly black hair blended into a beard of the same texture. He spoke as though each word was an observation on something he saw under the microscope.

"You should have been here in April when they attacked in force. There were only twenty-five Peruvian soldiers here then and half of them were killed." He bit into his sandwich and chewed thoughtfully, looking up at the ceiling and trying to remember if his figures were correct. "Yes, half of them. And the other half shot up rather badly. The commander even gave me a gun then, he was so convinced we were about to be overrun."

It was obvious the man was proud of the experience.

"Have you gentlemen met Dr. Sivey?" the SFC asked. "He's our resident biologist. He likes it here."

The way the sergeant said the last sentence summed up what he thought of Dr. Sivey.

"What's a biologist doing out here?" Josh asked the scientist.

Dr. Sivey was surprised at the question. "The same thing an astrophysicist would be doing in space," he replied, "or an archeologist in Egypt. Living a dream." He gestured with his sandwich around the room although its sweep was meant to include the jungle outside.

The third soldier at the table, a buck sergeant named Lewis, suddenly remembered something.

"Hey, doc, speaking of dreams – bad dreams – you want to see that bug now? The one I caught the other night?"

We all trooped outside. On the wood slats of the sidewalk outside the door were two white freezers, waist-high and voluminous enough to accommodate a fat man and friends. Their size dictated their location. Not only did they allow more room in the hut, they wouldn't fit through the door.

The freezers had power running to them via extension cords that snaked under the hut. Sgt Lewis hefted a cinderblock off the top of one of them and announced, "You're about to see the only ice within two hundred miles, gentlemen."

When he saw my look at the cinderblock, he explained, "For the monkeys."

He raised the lid on the freezer.

"Check this out, doc!"

At first I saw only frozen green beans and carrots. Then as the fog cleared away I made out what the sergeant was pointing at. A black baseball sat on a stack of pie shells. White lines of stitching traced its surface.

"Interesting," the doctor mused, and bent closer to see into the bin. After a moment of study he picked the baseball up and lifted it from the freezer.

"What is it?" asked Josh.

Now that it was in the light I saw what it wasn't. It wasn't a baseball. It was some kind of...bug. Or a beetle that had mated with an armored personnel carrier. The blackness of its shell flowed smoothly across a rounded body and blocky head as though it had been dipped in ink. The white lines were frost that formed in stripes across the shell, frost that melted in the heat of the open air.

"Holy entomology," I exclaimed. "That's an insect? Is it alive?"

"No, no," said the sergeant. "It's not alive – not anymore. I've had it in the deep freeze since yesterday morning. It's as dead as dead can be."

Dr. Sivey held the thing on the palm of his hand, hefting it to feel its weight and peering close to see the lines and details.

"It's beautiful," he said simply in his soft voice.

"Doc," the sergeant sighed. "You've been down here too long. My girlfriend's beautiful, a Harley-Davidson is beautiful. That's ugly. Scary. Downright nasty. I picked it up with a shovel and it tried to kill the shovel."

"Where did you find it?"

"Where do you always find stuff like that? In the latrine, of course. Right outside the shower. Walked in like it owned the place while I was reading a magazine. Scared the crap out of me."

"You were in the right place," Josh commented.

"Yeah, good th...very funny, smart guy. How would you feel if you were minding your own business doing your morning routine when all of a sudden Robo-bug here attacks your foot?"

"He attacked your foot?"

"He tried. I threw a boot at him and he went after the boot."

"Why didn't you just step on him?"

"Hello? Shower? Bare feet? Besides, stepping on that damned thing wouldn't kill it. Look at it! Reggie hit it with a shovel and you know what it did?

Hunkered down and looked pissed off, that's all. Then we threw it outside and you know what it did there? Got right up and headed for our tent. I think it would have cut its way in."

"To kill you," Josh added helpfully.

"To kill me! Damn right!"

"*Coleoptera invincipus*," Sivey murmured.

"Friend of yours, doctor?"

"Well, I recognize it. A rare species but not unheard of." He studied the insect closely, holding it up to his face and all but giving it a sniff. "I've never seen one this big before," he admitted in awe. "This is a remarkable specimen. Remarkable. Built for combat, for destruction, for plowing right into obstacles or enemies and tearing through them. That's how they stay around. Do you gentlemen know that one third of all living things is a beetle? Been here since the dinosaurs. A true survivor, this one."

"Alright, that's what I want to hear," Sgt Lewis said proudly. "Sergeant A.J. Lewis finds the big one. Maybe they'll name this dude after me. But I wouldn't be so attached to that survivor line, doc. This one here survived as long as the sun was out. Once he encountered a little arctic action he folded like a bad poker hand."

From where I was standing I had the vantage of the insect's profile, framed against the sun-worn face of Dr. Sivey. About two feet away was as close as I was willing to get but something caught my eye.

"Sergeant, you might still want to lock your doors at night," I suggested. "Doc, what are those things on the front of its face? Are they antennae?"

"Those? No, those are essentially horns, or teeth. They're mandibular extensions quite effective for attacking prey. Digging into their flesh and ripping them apart."

"In that case you might want to reconsider holding it because the left one just twitched."

Sivey moved faster than he looked capable, dropping the beetle onto the top of the nearest freezer.

The insect landed on its back. Two of its legs began to move. Then the mandible/prow/battering ram by its mouth budged as well. It twitched, fidgeted, and then squirmed. The whole body began to shake as it tried to rock its way back onto its feet.

"Son of a bitch!" Sgt Lewis cried. "It's unfreezing!"

"That would be thawing," Josh observed. He had never gotten close to the beetle to begin with and was now a comfortable distance away down the boardwalk. I joined him. I had seen movies like this and they all ended the same way.

"Been nice meeting you guys," I called. "We have to take off now."

"Oh my god, oh my god, oh my god," Sgt Lewis' concern was only half in jest as he watched the beetle try to right itself. "It's zero degrees in that freezer. That sucker should be rock solid!"

Dr. Sivey directed one of the sergeants to bring a coffee can from the kitchen.

"Jesus, that's a big bug," the first soldier commented. "Lewis, you better smash him now or he's gonna eat your black ass for sticking him in that freezer."

Sgt Lewis lifted a slat from a pallet and moved to squash the beetle but Dr. Sivey intervened. Just as well since I'm not sure the slat would have been enough. When the sergeant returned with a one-gallon aluminum can the two of them maneuvered the chilled bug inside and covered it with a pie tin and a sand bag. Moments later a *tick-tick-tick* sound came from the can. The noise turned into a *clack-clack-clack* as the unhappy fossil attacked the metal, plowing into the wall of the can with unrelenting will.

That night we headed to dinner late by our standards. It was eight o'clock, already dark and about the time activity on the Plaza de Armas slowed. The scorching Amazon day turned into a balmy tropical night. People stayed about but the crowds disappeared. Students walked to night classes, couples strolled in the plaza. A few *anticucho* grills opened up on the sidewalks, serving mystery meat the vendors claimed was beef. Traffic grew less frenetic – even the *motocarros* stopped pealing out from intersections.

"He knows we're coming?" I asked Josh as we felt our way down the path by the river.

"He knows."

"How? Yesterday Tonio said he couldn't find him."

"Tonio lies. Jaime was probably just closed or overseeing a shipment of guns somewhere."

"Then how can you be sure he's open tonight?"

"Tonio said so."

Jaime's was open. His restaurant was now in a one-story adobe house whose front room he used as the dining area. Two almond-shaped windows faced the river, letting a flicker of candle-light from inside fall into the courtyard as we walked up. The windows were devoid of glass but covered with reinforced screens. Jaime stood in the open doorway smoking a cigar.

"It's about time," he said upon seeing Josh. "I knew you'd be back. You're in love with our city."

"*Hola*, Jaime!" Josh replied. Jaime had him pegged.

Jaime was five-foot-eight with a round face and curly hair. His features were paler than most people in town. Not white but a light tan, the softened skin of an Iberian nobleman rather than the gritty brown of an Iquitos native.

An indistinct man at both first and second glance, there was something still relaxed and aloof about Jaime. Very relaxed. Weary. Languid motion came naturally to him. It wasn't his clothes – he wore baggy cotton pants over open sandals and an unbuttoned shirt. It wasn't the cigar, an El Credito. It was the movement, the stance, the heavy-lidded eyes. It was the way clothes hung on his indifferent frame and the way he blew lazy smoke into the night. Framed in the doorway he could have been a long-lost brother of Hedy Lamarr, casually accepting the evening's deep hand and keeping an open eye for possibilities. Anywhere else we would have used the words 'continental' or 'cosmopolitan' to describe him. In the jungle only a Spanish word would do: he was *suave.*

Tonight he was *suave* and tired. His eyes were content but there were bags under them.

He greeted me with wariness, for we were strangers. He knew Franklin already.

"How's Latrice?" he asked him.

"She's okay," Franklin said with his quiet smile.

"Just okay?" Jaime tapped ash from his cigar. "*Hombre,* she must be more than okay or you are not doing your job."

Franklin laughed. "Then she's good, very good!"

"*Eso es mejor.* That's better. And the *niños*? How are Brian and Clarissa?"

This was a man who had met Franklin once.

Franklin laughed again. "Okay," he replied.

Jaime threw up his hands.

He sat us at the first of four tables and brought out beer and fried yucca. The beer was *Cusqueña,* in tall brown bottles with the smallest amount of sludge floating near the bottom. The yucca was cut in thick strips like enormous french fries. It had a starchy, fibrous flavor that would have been rough going had it not been for what Josh called the "mystery green sauce," a bowl of which sat in the middle of every table. Jaime wouldn't tell us what it was but it was delicious.

Had I stopped to consider that the candles were lit because the electricity was out, that the screens were up to block malarial mosquitoes, that the bottles of beer had been re-used so many times their labels were gone, and that the mystery sauce no doubt came from unwashed vegetables and who knows what else, I might not have enjoyed the setting so much. Since I didn't stop to consider those things, in the tepid evening the ambiance of Jaime's place was perfect.

He spoke to someone in the kitchen before sitting down to talk.

"So, how goes the gasoline transport business?" His voice was soft, the tone casual and intimate. Anything we discuss, it said, is just between you and me.

"You call, we haul," Franklin answered.

"So business is good?"

Josh rolled his eyes. "You tell us. You're the one who knows everything down here. What's going on that we should know about?"

"Ha," Jaime scoffed. "What is always going on? Nothing. Nothing happens down here. Nothing but the same things that have happened forever. People work. The poor stay poor. Rich men come and go. Fools like me stay and try to run a business." He waved his cigar at the room, careful not to spill any ash.

"Is business good? You look tired."

He cocked his head in a gesture that could have meant anything.

"There is always something to do. People to meet. But I haven't starved." A long drag on the cigar.

I devoured the yucca. The green stuff was addictive.

"What's with the new place?" Josh asked. He found it hard to hide his distaste at the spareness of the room. "Your old restaurant was bigger."

"It was also made of wood," Jaime observed. His studied cool would have left Brando gasping.

"The *muchachos* told us about the fire," I offered. "Sorry to hear it. Everyone said it was nice."

Another long drag. "Thank you."

Conversation with Jaime was slow. Suave people aren't fast talkers. There was no hurry. There was nowhere to go. And it wasn't like Jaime had other things to attend to.

"How is the flying?" he asked.

"Good. The weather's been good the last few weeks. The rainy season is late."

"It will come."

I wondered what Iquitos looked like when it rained. How did those houses down in the bog cope?

"When it rains," I asked, "does the river level rise? Does it come up this hill?"

Jaime looked at me like I'd asked if day followed night. But he focused any thoughts about the question on the cigar's curling column of smoke.

"The river rises. The water comes up the hill. More important is the water that goes down. Sometimes our streets..." – he grimaced – "are like rivers themselves. You saw the piles of dirt at the end of Napo? That is the third time the city has put them there. They are trying to expand the road here, to have a,... oh, what is the word,...a boardwalk. But they take too long talking about it. Every time they put dirt there the rains come and wash it away. The same thing will happen with those piles now. You'll see."

"Why don't they move faster?" I asked. "Or put the dirt somewhere else."

Jaime smiled. "Why don't they move faster?" he repeated, enjoying the question. "Because then the rains could not wash away the dirt. Some things just are."

"A boardwalk?" Josh was skeptical. "Is Iquitos growing? Do they need more space?"

Jaime shrugged. It was a stylish shrug, one he started slow and then held as though massaging how much meaning to put into the gesture.

"Once upon a time Iquitos was *the* place to be," he explained. "Now it is *a* place to be. There are always more people. I don't know where they come from but they have to go somewhere."

"Speaking of people on the move," Josh said casually, "we saw Felipe yesterday. How's his business doing?"

"It depends. He has many businesses."

"The one that deals with pharmaceutical products?"

"Felipe is a businessman," Jaime allowed. "Not a good one. But he does many things and he knows many people. Unless you are shipping from the port, though, you won't run into any of his operations. He does all his business on the river. That is why he is such good friends with your associates in the Navy."

I didn't see the connection.

"You should." Jaime was patient. "They help each other. Having a house with American soldiers makes him look less dangerous. Not that he is dangerous, but you know what I mean. He is...shall we say...transparent. The Americans think they know all about him, they can trust him because after all there are American soldiers living in his house. *A la vez*, at the same time, it also makes him look more trustworthy to his business associates."

"How?" I was confused. "I would think someone who was so close to Americans would be more suspicious to a drug cartel."

Jaime flinched slightly when I said the d-word. He pointed his cigar at me.

"That is what *you* would think, yes! But *you* do not work in...*trade*. No one would be so foolish, so blatant to, ahhh, work both sides of the street so openly."

"But don't the SEALs..." I started to ask.

"The Navy is here so America gets to think it is doing something," Jaime explained. "Felipe is here so his associates think they are doing something."

I didn't follow the logic. Josh didn't, either. He looked at Jaime the way he looked at the old Chinese men in the Panama casinos – with amusement mixed with scorn. Franklin smiled to indicate he didn't care one way or the other. He was making thirty-five dollars a day in per diem.

"Uh, okay," I tried again, approaching from a different angle. "If Felipe works out of the port, who does the air side of the movement? Who works out of the airport?"

Jaime paused to get us more beers and coordinate for our dinner. A girl in her mid-teens came out from the kitchen to take our orders. Jaime recommended roast chicken which Franklin and I agreed to immediately. Josh insisted on having fish. She smiled and nodded and disappeared again. I worried that chicken was all they had and that now because of Josh the girl would be running down to the river in the dark with a fishing pole.

"A man by the name of da Silva coordinates business at the airport," Jaime said, lighting a new cigar and picking up where we had left off.

"So the two of them pretty much have a lock on trade here in Iquitos. They must be good friends."

Jaime was amused at the thought.

"No. *En realidad,* they don't like each other. Legal or not, the business pie here in Iquitos is small. Both men are hungry."

"Well, that will give you some good stories, I'm sure," Josh commented, bored by the discussion. "Maybe they'll fight it out. How is this guy da Silva?"

Jaime wagged his head. "I don't know him well."

That was a remarkable admission and he was embarrassed to make it. But he recovered.

"I know his daughter, however. She is here. Very pretty, very lively, *muy simpática.*"

"There you go, Mike," Josh suggested. "We can hook you up."

"Just what I need. A kingpin's daughter."

Again Jaime corrected me without sounding like he was doing it.

"Well," he said softly, "the situation is complex. There are many people involved in what you think is a single operation. It is not like one big plane full of..." – he searched for a word to substitute for the one he had been avoiding – "*cargo* flies away and makes a fortune for everyone. *De hecho,* I do not know of any such material coming through here. We are too far away. We are too open. Despite Mr. da Silva's efforts, all the airfields are in the *afueras,* far down the rivers. They are serviced by boats, which is why Felipe, as bad in business as he is, still can make money, how shall we say, *al margen,* 'on the edge' of the operation you are looking for. That is why it is so hard for you. You are looking for one thing but it is not one thing. It is many things and they are all around you."

"You say they are in the *afueras,*" Josh repeated. "Where?"

"In the *afueras.*"

"But where exactly?"

"Where are the airfields exactly?"

"Yes."

A tired smile grew on Jaime's face.

"Oh, *señor,*" he said through the smoke. "*Señor, señor.* Why would you want to know such things? What will you do? Stop by and visit?"

"I would just like to know."

Jaime watched smoke curl toward the ceiling. He didn't answer.

We flew to Site 8 the next couple of days, ferrying fuel. 8 was a dingy place even by radar site standards. It was only forty-five minutes away but even so was in the middle of nowhere, straight north of Iquitos near the Colombian border, halfway between the Napo and Putumayo rivers in a steamy landscape straight out of the Jurassic Age.

The airstrip was carved out of a bluff overlooking a no-name river feeding the Napo. For the life of me I couldn't figure out how anyone had chosen the location. Yes, it had a few hundred feet of altitude over the surrounding terrain. Yes, there was a village at the base of the bluff where the initial camp-builders could have started out. But there was nothing on the bluff itself – or hadn't been, anyway, until the Peruvians set up shop there sometime after their Ecuadorian war of the 1940s. Later someone showed up with either a truckload of chainsaws or one BLU-82 daisy-cutter and leveled the trees for a runway. Now there was a standard site setup: a handful of Americans to operate the radar, a handful of local soldiers to keep the Americans from getting killed by rebels, drug runners, or hungry villagers, and a dodgy, dirty strip for re-supply. All in the middle of a green sea of jungle, an endless canopy in all directions that hid activity on the ground perfectly until it ravaged its way into sight and blossomed like a sore.

Our first few trips to the camp were eventful only for the terminal ops. The weather was clear and the air was smooth, conditions that relaxed Josh enough that on our third run he let me make the approach. I wanted to do it even though my palms grew sweaty just thinking about it. The landing strip was long but it was narrow. The approach end dropped off the side of the hill while the ground at the far end rose up faster than we could climb. If we screwed up, our only go-around option was a hard climbing turn to the right. It was like shooting approaches to an aircraft carrier with the superstructure facing us on short final – you could come in high as often as you wanted but you could come in low only once.

Josh flew it twice and shacked the touchdown each time. He was good. It's said among pilots that one smooth landing is mostly luck, two is all luck, and three is a boldfaced lie. As well as he flew Josh could lie and get away with it. On my landing, I wouldn't say I shacked it but Josh only *started* to grab the controls then sat back, so it must have been okay.

The departure was just as fun. We backed up to the trees, ran the engines halfway up, then started rolling and went to max power. About three seconds after lift-off we ran out of ground as the hill dropped away beneath us. It plummeted to the river on an angle so steep you could have flipped a coin and never heard it land. At first that gave us vertigo, a stomach-dropping scare akin to falling off a building and hoping you wake up before you hit. But we grew to like it, to the point where the instant we cleared the bluff we would push over and dive out of sight, scaring the troops behind us who thought each time we were auguring in.

So the camp itself was straightforward. We flew there every day on a straight line from Iquitos. It wasn't until Friday when we made two runs on the same day that weather forced us to deviate west and come at the site from a new direction. Thirty miles out we overflew two riverside airstrips spaced a few oxbows apart. One was perfectly between the villages of Curaray and Yanchimanu, the other further downstream on the Napo. There were no roads to either, of course, as there were no roads anywhere in the region. And we couldn't see any reason for either strip. On our first run of the day we caught sight of a Beech King Air flying low and heading away from the area to the north. On our second run, about an hour before sunset, we watched a Cessna Caravan lift off from the Curaray strip and head the same direction.

Josh mentioned the strips to an Army major at Site 8.

The major shook his head.

"Oh, I don't think there are any strips out there," he said. "There's no reason for them. None of the villages can support an airport."

"It's not an airport," Josh explained. "They're just airstrips like you have here."

"I think what you saw was perhaps a logging area. The locals do that, you know. Cut down trees for farming. Slash-and-burn, they call it. It's a big problem here in the jungle."

Josh got the look on his face that I'd seen him get in innumerable restaurants. The one that says he's about to slap the waiter for being obtuse.

"Sir, we watched a plane take off from one of those 'logging areas.' How many of the local farmers have their own Beech King Air?"

The major wasn't listening.

"I appreciate your interest, guys," he said, clearly implying he didn't. "A lot of aircrew want to get involved in drug hunting. But we know from experience that the transshipments we're looking for happen out east. That's why our radar points that way."

"It only points one way?" I asked.

"Well, we can turn it but it's rather labor intensive. Takes most of an afternoon."

"Isn't that kind of limiting?"

"How so?"

"Well, the term 'Maginot Line' comes to mind..."

"We only need it to point one way," the major insisted.

"Why?"

"Why not?" he replied. "We're not here for traffic control. We turn it west, we miss half the horizon because of the hill. And we don't see anything. Why?" He pointed to the waning light spreading itself thin over the eastern sky. "Because the bad guys fly out there. It's flat. They come out of Bolivia, cut the corner of Brazil, use the fields south of Tabatinga to refuel, then head north along the

Colombia-Venezuela border to the Caribbean. Destination Florida. It's a straight shot."

"You see a lot of planes out there?" I asked, doubtful.

The major looked at me like I was a student he was helping along.

"Lots," he said, the inflection telling us we weren't cleared for the specific numbers.

"How many?"

"Lots." Then, his conscience perhaps feeling a tug, "Well, not as many as we used to, but that's because we're having an effect."

Josh wasn't shy with his skepticism.

"And the planes that aren't out west? The ones we didn't see? What don't they do?"

The major put his conscience away.

"Maybe," he suggested dryly, "they're botanists. Coming to fix the logging scars."

Later, flying west on our way back to Iquitos, it grew too dark for us to see anything more of the airfields. Josh insisted on flying over the area anyway, banking in a long curve so he could look down and purse his lips in thought.

"You know," he said, "I'd like to know what's in those trees."

We had dinner at Jaime's again on Saturday. Jaime was there and welcomed us but his manner this night was perfunctory. We arrived late and three of his tables were already full, taken by other customers, local people who didn't know us and perhaps weren't as accommodating to *norteamericanos* in their midst. Not that anyone said anything but we got our share of glances, particularly Franklin, the noteworthy thing being not that he was black but that by being black he was obviously American and therefore so were we. Jaime, knowing how to play to an audience, gave us the high sign to let us know it wasn't personal. He greeted us as sincerely as an alderman meets voters and then went back to schmoozing with the other tables. Josh had no opportunity to pull him aside.

It was over the weekend that Josh had his epiphany. We made a trip over to the SEALs' house.

Dave was there with four of his teammates from Rodman. They had returned the night before from a three-day excursion with the Peruvian army up the Amazon on a riverine patrol.

"How was that?" we asked.

"A waste of time," Dave admitted. He passed around beer and we sat by the pool in lawn chairs. "Theoretically we were 'patrolling' but nobody could tell us for what or for whom. We were just on an extended river cruise. The Peruvians are pretty harsh on traffickers in other areas of the coun try but out here not so much. They know drugs move through the region but they're all of the what-we-don't-see-won't-hurt-us attitude. They don't want to mess with it. We know the troops down here deliberately go where they *won't* find anything suspicious. They stick to those areas."

"So you cruised around on a little boat for three days and didn't see anything?"

"Didn't see anything, didn't do anything," a chief petty officer named Wharton said from the other side of the pool. He hid in the shade but let his feet dangle in the water.

"Well," Dave offered. "We could argue that we got some survival-type training with the locals."

"Not so," Wharton disagreed. "Getting bit up by mosquitoes doesn't constitute training. We looked at pretty jungle and that's it, sir. You know it as well as I do."

Dave didn't argue.

"Not my choice," he shrugged. "I'm convinced we're here for political reasons, not practical ones, even though my orders say different. Every time we come down here it's the same: hang out for a month, be nice to the locals, let the Peruvian army tell us they don't have any activity in this region, pretend like we're being effective when we're not, work on a tan."

He held out his beer to suggest what could he do?

"I have an idea," Josh offered. "Just how bored are you guys?"

The next day we had no tasking. Franklin woke up to find a tarantula the size of a coffee cup at the foot of his bed. He killed it with the fountain pen and stuck the carcass to his door in a William Tell-ish message to the hotel staff that they needed an exterminator. We spent the morning touring the city via *motocarro* taxis. In the afternoon we swung by the airport to check on the plane and fire up the satellite radio to call back home. The airfield was quiet, the ramp empty except for our plane and one Faucett twin turboprop unloading newspapers and boxes of fruit. The guard on the ramp slumped in his chair in the shade, the heat and silence too much for him.

That night we ate at the Marandú. Josh wanted to eat at Jaime's again but I pushed for the Marandú so we could sample the alligator. My luck being what it was, we showed up on the one evening where the tank was empty. No alligator, the owner informed us, wagging a gnarled brown finger in my face. He proffered the menu instead.

Franklin ordered the *pollo asado.*

"Chicken?" I asked. "You had that last night."

"I like chicken."

"But you're in the deepest, darkest jungle. You can have chicken anytime," I insisted.

"I like chicken."

"How about you, Josh?"

"I wonder what's in this *paella,*" he said, referring to a rice dish. Josh could never just order something.

He had to make it a big deal. Tonight was no different as he called the owner over and described in specific terms how he wanted to have various things on the menu altered to his liking. The owner waited for him to finish talking and then said, "*No.*" Josh got the *paella.*

"Y Ud., señor?"

I didn't know. I wanted something different and chicken and grilled beef wasn't going to cut it. A woman from the kitchen came by to serve a nearby table and set down a huge bowl of what looked like clam chowder. It smelled delicious.

"Excuse me?" I asked the owner. "What's that? *Qué es eso?*"

"Eso. Eso es aquí," he pointed to the menu. *"Potaje de la selva. Es una especialidad del restaurante."*

"Jungle stew," I mused. "What do you think, Josh? Is it safe?"

"It's stew," he replied, unhappy he'd been shot down. "What could be wrong with it?"

"Okay, *señor. Una potaje de la selva."*

"Mucho gusto. Que les aproveche. Bon appetit!"

The next day we took Dave along on a flight to Site 8. We circled the airstrips we had noticed earlier while he took notes. He noticed some structures along the river that we had missed. Back in Iquitos he discussed what he saw with his team.

That night I stopped by Josh's room to let him know I felt like crud. He sat in bed reading an old Barron's. All the dolls but one were piled up against the window, facing out, their arms outstretched as though they were watching a parade or trying to escape a fire. The lone exception was a single clown who Josh had hung by the neck from a crosspiece. Below him was the chair. It was knocked over.

"You're a sick man," I told him.

"I couldn't take it any more," he shrugged. "Someone had to do something."

"Speaking of being sick...I'm thinking I shouldn't have had the stew last night."

"Feel like crap?"

"Yeah."

"Doesn't surprise me. You never eat stew in a Third World country. Who knows what's in it?"

The effort to protest was too much. I would kill him later.

Being sick was frustrating though hardly a surprise. Everyone got sick at some point on these trips. Usually it was simple food poisoning that came and went in twelve hours. Sometimes it was something from the mosquitoes or maybe from a fruit vendor who coughed in your face. Mostly, though, it was stuff that guys got over quickly, the advantage of being young and strong and on lots of government-approved drugs. So far only Jem had caught a serious disease – malaria. Then, too, Tommy Goode was still in the middle of a mysterious rash he'd contracted after swimming in the Amazon. Since it afflicted only his penis he was petrified at first that it was the infamous candiru, a tiny fish that enters that part of the body and causes all kinds of problems with nasty teeth and hooks and claws. But the hospital at Howard assured him that no, it was just some strange skin infection. So usually any health problems were temporary. As world-wide deployable military members we were on so many inoculations and prophylactic medicines that I was surprised even a horrible jungle disease could find purchase in our systems. The doxycycline that made us sensitive to the sun and the primaquin that made us woozy after dinner were just the tip of our pharmaceutical iceberg. Because of all the drugs I already had in me, normally I hated the idea of taking pills. But at the moment I wished I had an entire medicine cabinet to dip into.

We had no more scheduled trips to Site 8 but at the end of the week the AOC radioed for us to take a load of gas to Site 7.

Site 7 was north of Iquitos, too, but more to the west, the third point on an extended isosceles triangle of the three locations. It was also on a hill but the strip was wider with no obstacles at either end. Its only quirk was a colony of butterflies that made its home in the nearby trees. Whenever we landed a cloud of them flew up and engulfed the strip. Every time we touched down – just as the wheels hit – thousands of fluttering blue wings cascaded over the plane as though we had landed on a ticker-tape parade. The same thing happened on take-off. The troops at the site tried to get the colony to move to no avail. They tried noisemakers, smoke, and even insecticides but the colony refused. The butterflies had been there long before the radar geeks and weren't about to uproot just for the occasional plane. We put up with it. The only downside was a few seconds of terror when we couldn't see out the front window. That and the mess of smashed bugs.

When we flew to Site 7, Dave and his team came along. They stayed inside the plane while we downloaded the gas. The troops at the site invited us to stay for lunch but we made our excuses and left as soon as we gave them their fuel.

"How far to the strips?" Dave asked when we were airborne again.

"Twenty minutes," Josh told him. "That is if my terminally-ill co-pilot is navigating right."

"I'm fine," I insisted. "I feel good today."

My stomach pains had gone from horrible that first night to intermittent over the following days. This morning it was as though they had never been. I was sure that whatever bug I'd ingested was gone.

We climbed to 10,000 feet and headed toward the village of Curaray, keeping ourselves offset from where Josh had spied the first of the suspicious fields. Once we had the area in sight we circled it to see if there was any activity. There was none. It was an empty strip by a quiet river.

We circled lower and set up for an approach. Josh didn't know if just flying by might provoke someone into shooting at us so he made the first pass at two hundred knots.

Nothing.

"It looks deserted," I commented.

We flew by again to get a better look. The landing area was dirt, mostly dry, with clumps of grass all over. The grass was short which suggested somebody attacked it regularly. The nearest water was fifty yards away through the trees.

"Well?" asked Dave, leaning up into the cockpit.

"Well," Josh replied. "I'm ready if you guys are."

The team was loaded for bear. Peru limited what weapons they could bring into the country but every man had a carbine with a grenade launcher attached. They wore body armor and helmets and each carried two sidearms. Franklin looked naked carrying just his rifle.

We set up to the northeast, not bothering to do anything tactical since the strip was unfamiliar and since it was empty as far as we could see.

"Give the team one minute," Josh advised Franklin.

He dropped us onto the dirt a quarter of the way down the strip and brought the plane to a halt abeam a clearing on the river side. Franklin had the ramp down and the SEALs moving by the time the gear stopped turning.

"You going to turn around?" I asked as the SEALs split up and went in two directions toward the clearing.

"No," Josh said quickly. His face was pressed to the glass watching the movement outside. "We have to taxi to the end anyway to take off so let's stay close in case they need us."

But Dave and his team didn't need us. Not for support and not for a hasty retreat. They disappeared into the woods going to the river and returned minutes later empty-handed. Then they searched the perimeter of the landing area, also with no results.

"It's a gas stop," Dave told us through Josh's open window.

"A what?"

"A gas stop, that's all. There's a fifty-gallon drum over there with some fuel in it. Not avgas but not diesel, either. It's light. Come take a look."

We hopped out. There was a pier by the river, a small shack, a fuel drum on a stand high enough to support gravity refueling via a hose to the runway, and a bunch of empty boxes. Scattered on the floor of the shack were old magazines, food tins, and shards of heavy wrapping paper.

"Pretty standard," Wharton said, kicking aside the paper and scattering a nest of mice.

"Standard how?" I asked.

"This is wrapping paper. Keeps the coke dry. Someone from Iquitos probably comes up here once or twice a week to load the tank. A plane comes in, takes what he needs, and continues north – or south, depending on whether he's coming or going. Avoids the hassle of landing in town. Too many people to pay off there."

Josh was disappointed.

"Sorry, guys," he said. "I thought it might be more than that. A lab, maybe."

Dave waved his hand.

"No big deal. I didn't expect to see labs out here, anyway. This is still something. It beats sitting by the pool."

"Yeah, it does," Wharton agreed. "What do you want to do, sir?"

Dave looked at me and Josh.

"We still going to the other one?" he asked.

"If you want to."

"Of course. How far is it?"

"Five minutes. Maybe fifteen miles."

Dave motioned to another team member, a short guy with a bushy moustache who didn't look

SEALish at all. Whereas Dave and Wharton were big, muscular men and fit the movie-SEAL stereotype, this guy – Andy – had more the look of someone who answered questions in the lumber section of a Home Depot.

"Can you rig something to torch this place in half an hour?"

Andy raised an eyebrow. "Is a pig pork?"

"Okay," said Dave. "Let's go."

"You're going to burn this?" Josh asked.

"Yeah. You mind?"

Josh hesitated, then laughed. "No!"

We took off to the east and found the next strip in a few minutes. We circled it twice then landed and found almost the same situation as at the first. 'Almost' because stacked by the fuel drum and wrapped in plastic was about three hundred pounds of packaged cocaine. The team was elated. With no one left to alert to our presence, they spilled the fuel tank and set everything alight. The shack and the coke burned with abandon. Then as we departed we saw a curl of black smoke rising from the first airstrip miles away. The two columns rose into the otherwise pristine air, temporary monuments to our zeal.

"Sorry I dragged you guys out here," Josh told the SEALs. "I thought there might be more. You probably figure this was a waste of time."

Dave shook his head. "Are you kidding? Not at all. That's the only coke I've seen in all my trips to

Peru. And this is more than we've done in months. By the way, you weren't planning on reporting any of this, were you?"

Josh hadn't thought things out that far.

"It's up to you."

"I'd rather we didn't. It'll be more fun to watch the locals wonder what happened."

"They'll figure it out soon enough," I pointed out. "It's hard to keep secrets here."

Josh considered that, too. "Let me think about it," he said.

Jaime had customers again the next night but he made time to stop at our table and chat. Or at least to stop by. He sat down with his El Credito and studied Josh through the curl of smoke.

"*Hola,* Jaime," Josh greeted him.

"Buenas noches," was the reply.

There was a long silence. I concentrated on eating fried yucca while Franklin just looked around with his usual inscrutability. Josh drank his beer.

Finally, Jaime added, "I spoke to Felipe today."

"Oh?" said Josh.

"Sí."

Another pause. It had begun to rain when we sat down and now was pouring outside, hard enough that the force of the water pushed a breeze through the screened windows.

"How's his daughter?" Josh asked.

"It is Mr. da Silva who has the daughter, not Felipe."

"Oh. Well then, how's Felipe?"

"He is not happy. It seems he had an accident with some of his..."

He stopped. He had almost admitted to knowing about something that before he had claimed ignorance of. He left his words hanging in the air and then backtracked. "He lost some property to a fire."

None of us said anything. Finally, feeling we had to comment, I said, "Bummer."

"Yes, it is a tragedy."

"Not a restaurant, was it?"

"No."

"Did he lose a lot of stuff?"

"Where did you fly yesterday?" Jaime replied bluntly.

Josh sat back and rolled his finger around the edge of his glass.

"Come on, Jaime. You know we don't discuss work with you."

"No, but where did you go?"

Josh laughed.

"'No, but discuss work with me anyway!' What's on your mind, Jaime?"

A screen collapsed. It sprayed water across the nearest table whose occupants leaped up in dismay. The girl serving beer rushed to replace the frame before mosquitoes invaded the restaurant. Jaime left us to placate his customers. When he came back he thought for a while how to get the conversation back on track.

"I just like to know things. I like to understand what happens around me."

"Felipe had a fire and lost some stuff," Josh summarized.

"Yes, he did."

"Here in town?"

Jaime eyed Josh above his cigar. Josh responded with a mien of total sincerity. I knew the look because he used it on me all the time.

"No, en las afueras."

"Ahh," Josh said. "*Las afueras.* So, it was connected to his business that you wouldn't tell us anything about."

Jaime puffed on his cigar. He studied every muscle on Josh's face, looking for a clue. There was none.

Josh motioned to the girl for another beer.

"Well," he said expansively. "I'm just a Jewish boy from Connecticut – and a gas-hauler at that – but it seems to me that puts Mr da Silva ahead then, doesn't it? How's his daughter, anyway? You still going to hook her up with Mike?"

Jaime stopped in mid-puff.

"You just carried gas yesterday?" he said thoughtfully.

"You call, we haul," Franklin repeated his favorite phrase.

"Business is good. What can I say?" Josh added. "We have the market to ourselves. No competition, unlike Mr da Silva..."

The screen fell in again, giving Jaime an excuse to get up from the table. For the rest of the evening he was lost in thought, giving his El Credito a great deal of attention.

"Ohhhhhhh, gaaaaaawwwwwd."

"Can't you look out the window? It'll take your mind off your stomach."

"Ohhhhhhh, gaaaawwwwwwd."

"Guess that's a no."

Oh course it was a hot day. Of course there were cumulus buildups dotting every corner of the sky from 5,000 feet on up. No matter where we flew, how high or how low, there was no escaping a rumbling, endless turbulence as though our plane was working itself upstream through rapids. The sun beating on the cockpit kept us hot as well. Even with the overhead screens closed and the air conditioning at max, 8,000 feet on a day like today wasn't high enough to beat the radiation that cooked us through the windows. Any other day I wouldn't have minded. Probably wouldn't have noticed. Bouncing around the clouds was fun, it made you feel like you were really flying and not just a chaperone for somebody's cargo. But today was different. There was no fun. Not in bouncing, not in broiling, not in breathing. My stomach was a cauldron of toxic waste and an unstable one at that. I got chills, an intermittent fever, and every thirty minutes a wave of nausea. It hurt to sit straight. The only thing I could do reliably was moan, channeling the sickness to an indifferent world.

"Oooooooooohhhhhhhhhhhh."

"Hey," said Josh. "Do you have to do that over the intercom? You sound like you're possessed."

"I am possessed. Possessed by that stew you let me eat."

"I didn't tell you to eat it. Franklin, did I tell him to eat that stuff?"

Franklin didn't look up from his magazine.

"I'm not getting involved," he replied. "I had my chicken and it was good, that's all I'm saying."

"My dinner wasn't bad," Josh offered in case we were interested. "The *paella* was bland but okay. There was some kind of nut in it, like pine nuts or something. Not as much rice. I should have sent it back. What was in your stew, anyway, Mike?"

"The jungle," I growled through my pain. "The fetid, steaming, nasty, heart of darkness jungle. I don't know. Meat, fish,...couldn't tell. It all looked like stew."

"Yeah, that's why you don't eat stew. You can never tell what it is. They can put anything in there."

"Probably some bad monkey," Franklin suggested, leisurely turning a page. "I've heard they do that down here."

The image was too much. I puked into a plastic bag I had next to my seat for just that reason.

Josh watched in revulsion.

"Dude, couldn't you go in back and do that?"

I didn't even look up. "Go to hell," I said.

We were flying to Caballococha, a small riverside town farther down the Amazon just this side of Leticia and the tri-border region with Colombia and Brazil. Someone at Caballococha had a boat engine that we needed to take to Site 5, which sat back to the west on the shore of the Apayacu River. In between we would hit Leticia for gas so we could download that to the radar site as well. It was a good day of short hops and strange airfields – one that I wouldn't enjoy at all. With my intestines knotted up as they were, the only day I would enjoy would be one spent in an intensive care unit swilling antibiotics and painkillers.

As usual, Josh did all the flying. At Caballococha, a quiet gravel strip located next to the more important port and boat docks, Franklin walked down to the water until he found the man we wanted. I had enough energy to climb down into the cabin and watch them carry the motor on board. Then we flew on to Leticia.

Leticia was a busier airfield. That meant there was another aircraft on the ramp when we arrived. There was no tower and no controller and everything except the runway was dirt. The sign above the arrival terminal said, 'LETICIA – GATEWAY TO THE AMAZON' which is what every town between here and the mountains claimed. Below that someone had hand-painted a more ambitious undertaking: 'World Center of Serenity, Peace, and Happiness.' The people who gathered on the road outside the terminal to watch us taxi in didn't seem any happier or more peaceful than anybody else but since I was in desperate need of intestinal serenity I took the sign at its word.

"Franklin, you haven't been to Site 5 before, have you?" Josh asked when we were airborne again.

"No."

"You know anything about it?"

"Nothing except that it's right by the water. Ozzie says they live with the locals, some native tribe. Or the village is right next to the site, something like that. He said when he landed here before he thought he was going to be eaten 'cause all these pygmy guys with bones in their noses and stuff came out to the plane."

"You're kidding."

"That's what he said."

"Hey, hear that, Mike? You may not have to suffer much longer. The pygmies at this next place might eat you."

"*Ooooooooohhhhhhhhhh.*"

The nausea came and went, peaking on the up side as much as on the down. I had a spell of health after we left Leticia and for a while felt so strong I wondered if I was delirious. My fever vanished and the rolling pain in my stomach went away, too, fading so quickly I wasn't sure I should believe my good fortune.

The feeling blossomed even more when we found the Apayacu. We dropped low and trolled upstream looking for the camp. When we did the turbulence really kicked our butt. It should have made me puke just as it had all morning but when Josh apologized I brushed his words away and offered to fly myself.

"You better?" he asked.

"I feel like a million bucks," I shrugged. "Don't know why but if you want me to fly through this, I'll take it. I'll show the damned jungle what we're made of."

Josh kept the controls and minutes later found the airstrip, a grass causeway that paralleled the bank and stuck out into the river current like the bottom of an anvil laid on its side. It looked dry on a flyover, the river's current not yet having swelled with the late winter rains. People from the now-visible radar camp ran out with an orange windsock to help us set up a pattern. Josh hemmed and hawed, re-computed his numbers, then announced an approach to the northwest. I felt the old excitement of an assault landing.

It was as he was setting up for the base turn that my fever returned, making my hands tremble holding the checklist. I began to sweat. My stomach expanded and convulsed as though a reactor inside wanted to overheat. The plastic bag was already full so even as I felt my throat tense, I knew I would have to wait until we touched down.

And that touchdown couldn't come soon enough. Josh flew with finesse, floating us down over the current-tossed branches of fallen trees to drop us soundly into the grass exactly on centerline. *Whummpp!* The nose came down, I grabbed the controls while he went for the steering, and we let the prop reversers drag us to a halt two-thirds of the way down the strip, abeam the blivet hoses.

Franklin opened the ramp. Josh shut down the engines and prepared the fuel panel for an offload.

"You coming out?" he asked.

I hunched in my seat, concentrating. The nausea was gone for a few seconds and I hoped that mental power alone would keep it away.

"Maybe," I said. "Let me see if I can keep this down."

"*Eeuunnhhh.* In that case I'm getting well clear."

A delegation from the camp came out to the plane. The detachment commander was an Army major but most of the technicians were Air Force, with a couple of contractors thrown in. Two troops got with Franklin to start downloading fuel. The others stood around looking at the plane. A chaplain arrived with three natives in tow.

"Excuse me, captain?" the chaplain asked. "Are you the aircraft commander?"

"Yes, I am," Josh answered. He regarded the tribesmen with alarm. They were short with shaggy hair and bare chests. Two wore cotton pants cut off above the ankle while the third wore a loin-cloth. No bone-piercings, contrary to Ozzie's warning, but some serious face paint. The one with the loin-cloth was the oldest and the senior man. He carried a stick with shells tied to the end and had bits of cloth braided into his hair. His face was disapproving. He paid no attention to Josh but stared at the C-27.

"This is our village elder, Pa-ichi. We share the camp with him and his tribe. They're a local branch of the Ashaninka Indians."

Josh listened as though someone was telling him his stock portfolio had been wiped out by a computer virus. Beautiful, exotic women appealed to him. Scrubby jungle dwellers did not.

"They like to examine boats or planes that come to the camp. It's, uh, I'm not sure how to say it," the chaplain groped for words, not as embarrassed as he wanted to appear. It was obvious he enjoyed his role as intermediary. "It comes from outside and touches their world, so they want to see it. If he approves, he'll bless your plane." Then, in an aside that made it clear the Indians didn't speak English, he added, "Don't worry, they'll approve. They always do."

Josh was impatient. "What do you want from me, padre?"

"Oh, just let them look."

"Fine, they can look."

The Indians set off on a stroll around the plane. I staggered back to the ramp as they did and found a seat at the side. The fever came in waves. My gut felt like it wanted to explode but nothing was making a committed move either way. Visions of the stew swam before my eyes. It had looked so good during dinner but now everything in the bowl moved on its own.

The chaplain lingered by the ramp. He was a thin man with an earnest face and graying hair.

"How are you men doing today?" he asked.

"Good," Josh said curtly. "You live with these guys, padre?"

"Oh, well, they live right there," he pointed. "Our camp is next to their village."

"How do you talk to them?"

He smiled. "Lots of sign language. We have a contractor who speaks their language but he's eating right now."

"So what's the deal with the plane? Big bird from the sky, that kind of thing?"

"Oh, no. They've seen planes. The thing is, this river is sacred to them. So is the land we're standing on. This bank floods every year and they used to plant on it – they can't now because we use it as an airstrip. It's funny, but I think they just want to know you're pure or something. You've touched on their land and they want to know you don't – oh, I hate to say this because it sounds condescending –that you don't have evil spirits." He shrugged, his sheepishness real this time.

Josh rolled his eyes. In a few months his midlife crisis would turn to the synagogue for answers but for now he had no patience for religion.

"Well, *I* don't have any evil spirits. Sergeant Andrews doesn't. Mike may. Mike, you have any demons in your stomach there?"

"Go to hell."

Franklin finished with the fuel and buttoned up the single-point panel. The Indians completed their circuit. They returned to the ramp where the old man spent some time staring at me from different angles. Then the three of them began an elaborate discourse in sign language with the chaplain. The padre was overwhelmed, his earnestness and nervous smiles unable to keep up. He turned to one of the airmen.

"Um, Airman Teague, could you go find Mr. Riaño, please?"

Teague ran off, as did one of the Indians.

"Problem, padre?"

"Well, I don't know. He's not happy with your plane."

"We're not either," Josh shrugged. "It's underpowered in the mountains and vibrates like an epileptic on crack. But it gets the job done and it's all we have. So, there you have it. Now," he clapped his hands, "it's been fun, guys, but we're out of here."

"Oh, no, you can't!" the chaplain surprised us by saying. "I mean, can you wait a few minutes?"

"For what?"

"Well, maybe Mr. Riaño can clear this up, but Pa-ichi doesn't want your plane to leave."

The chaplain stepped between us and the Indians as though that would keep our conversation private. Pa-ichi didn't seem to notice or care. He and his helper stood quietly, staring at the shadow of the tail.

Josh took a breath.

"Padre, we've got things to do. We can't just sit around because your medicine man thinks we have bad juju. Tell him we have to go. Act it out in interpretive dance if you have to."

"Uh, sir?" a sergeant nearby spoke up. "We had this happen once before with a boat. He may just have to bless you or something, do some kind of ceremony. Then the spirits get back in order and you can leave."

"Oh, please," Josh replied. "My spirits are in order."

"Mine aren't," I mumbled.

"Then you stay. Irena's going to be at Latin Limits in a few hours and I want to shower when we get back."

Franklin sat down. "It's Iquitos," he reminded Josh. "She won't care if you've showered."

The tail's shadow moved, or maybe it didn't. Pa-ichi watched it all the same.

Mr. Riaño trotted out to the plane. He was Peruvian, thin with a rectangular head that made him look like a totem pole. He moved in earnest, speaking to the chaplain to get the lowdown before moving respectfully to the elder Indian. Then he and Pa-ichi had a lengthy discussion that involved a lot of hand movements and clipped speech. When they were done, Riaño nodded confidently.

"He has to bless your plane," he announced. "That's all. He wants to cleanse you of the spirits you brought with you to the camp."

The chaplain clucked to say I-told-you-so.

"I have a date!" Josh barked.

"It'll be quick, sir."

Josh took another breath, held it while he thought of a dozen retorts, and then gave up.

"Alright, whatever," he waved his hand. "He's got ten minutes."

We waited. For a while Pa-ichi didn't move. Then the Indian who had gone back to the camp returned carrying a hen.

"Oooh," said Franklin. "We going to eat?"

But the hen appeared to be for show. The Indians walked around the aircraft again. There was no chanting as I would have expected. The old man merely waved his stick at a few places, voiced an observation or two, and paused at the nose to draw lines in the ground. The other two followed quietly, one stepping exactly where the old man did, the other carrying the hen as though at any minute he might toss it into the sky.

The three of them returned to their place under the tail, the chaplain and Riaño making room. I began to think his blessing might be working as my stomach seemed to have settled down.

Then with no warning the old man whipped out a short knife from his loin-cloth and cut the hen's head off. The Indian holding the bird thrust it up into the air and waved it around, blood and feathers spurting everywhere.

"Whoa, jeez!" Josh cried, ducking for cover. Even Mr. Riaño was surprised. The chaplain stepped back in alarm while the fuel troops ran to avoid being sprayed.

It was too much for me, especially with no notice. I fell to my knees on the ramp and puked over the side. It was a true power-spew, too, a fire hose pointed at the ground. Had I been well and observing myself from several feet away I would have been impressed. Since I wasn't, I watched instead as my last few meals mingled in the dirt with drops of chicken blood that fell like rain.

The blessing must have been a sight to see. Although I lay prone staring at the sand instead of capturing the look on the chaplain's face, I heard his reaction in the form of oh-my's and oh-dear's. I heard Josh, too, swearing up a storm. The local culture was taking a beating.

Finally things grew quiet. I wiped my mouth and looked up. Josh had blood on his boots and was ready to punch someone. The hen was spent. The chicken man held its limp and drained body at his side, waiting respectfully. Pa-ichi waited, too. He still focused on the ground but the scowl was gone, replaced by pursed lips and a calm, unfurrowed brow. He was satisfied. A grunt and jerk of his elbow ended the show.

Riaño turned to us and nodded.

"He says you can go now."

We stayed in Iquitos for two weeks. Every time I felt like dying the sickness in my stomach would disappear. Sometimes it would be gone for a day or two during which my appetite would come back and I would try to force something down. Then the nausea would return, making me puke but more often making my gut expand until it felt like I needed to download a bowling ball. It would stay that way for hours. The worst part was I couldn't download anything.

Nothing passed through my system. Constipation doesn't begin to describe what I had. It was more like the largest dam in the world holding back the largest river. Not only did I have a bug, it was a stubborn, greedy one at that. The guest that wouldn't leave.

When we returned to Panama I went immediately to the flight surgeon. That by itself is a sign of how worried I was. The medical profession is the natural enemy of the flying profession and no pilot goes to see a doctor unless he's convinced he's at Death's door. I felt like I had walked through Death's door, kicked off my shoes, and collapsed on his couch.

The flight surgeon gave me antibiotics and told me not to fly for a while. A week later I went back.

"How do you feel?"

"The same," I complained. "Bloated, nausea, fever. And I haven't had a bowel movement in a week."

"You haven't shit in a week?"

"Uh, yeah."

"No shit? I mean, really?"

"Really."

"That's not good."

"No shit."

He sat in his office and consulted a medical guide. Our doc, Jon Hinnaneman, was a nice guy. Young, single, short, and a party animal – Rod

Stewart without the long hair. He suffered from short-guy-complex but unlike Little Bud – who just got aggressive – Hinnaneman turned all his energy toward picking up women. It was a wonder he found any time to be a doctor because all he thought about was getting laid. Before I got sick we all thought he was the kind of doctor to have, a guy like the rest of us just trying to hook up. The kind of guy who would know his way around sexually-transmitted diseases they way I knew my way around a cockpit. Now I wasn't so sure.

"Hmm," he said, looking up from the book. "You've been taking all your pills?"

"Religiously."

He snapped the book shut.

"Then we need new pills! Drugs, Mike – they're awesome!"

He consulted other doctors in the clinic. They huddled, scratched their heads, and eventually prescribed a different antibiotic.

I took those for a week. The pain in my stomach went away briefly but returned. I was getting scared. I had stopped feeling hungry because I could never pass anything through my system. The bloated feeling in my gut got more and more intense. I drank tons of water and urinated fine but my colon seemed to have developed a life of its own. I had nightmares of a thirty-foot-long tapeworm that would one day crawl out of my rectum and choke me to death.

"Doc, this isn't funny anymore," I told Hinnaneman on my umpteenth visit. "I feel like I'm going to die one minute and explode the next. What the hell have I got?"

Hinnaneman examined me and shrugged.

"Something stubborn," he agreed. "You still can't take a dump?"

"No!"

"Okay, okay, okay. Give me a minute."

He sat down at his desk to consult the big book again. After some minutes he set it aside, dissatisfied, and stared into space, spinning a yo-yo. Then he leaped up and ran his fingers along a collection of leather-bound volumes on a shelf on the wall, the kind of encyclopedic collection every doctor has but you never see them use. He studied one title after another with a puzzled face that suggested he couldn't remember why he had bought the book in the first place, but finally settled for one at the end. A cloud of dust flew up when he pulled it off the shelf.

He sat down again and propped his feet up, flicking the yo-yo furiously as he read. It was twenty minutes before he spoke.

"Okay," he announced. "Got the answer right here."

He folded his hands in front of him and leaned across the desk, trying out a stern doctor expression. Hinnaneman the Party Animal was out. Hinnaneman the Family GP was in.

"Mike, you've got to work with me on this one," he said, as though somehow I had been letting him down. "We're going to go for the big guns."

He jumped up, ran from the room, and returned with a small bottle that contained three tiny blue pills. He held it across the desk but snatched it away when I reached for it, taking a second chance to observe the tablets through the orange plastic. With a frown, he gave in.

"Take these. One a day, starting now. They'll cure you. Nothing beats these babies."

"What are they?"

"Medical stuff, don't worry about it. One a day, no more. If you're not better by Monday we're talking surgery. Rip you open and pull that crap out by hand. At the very least we'll need stool samples to send up to Wilford Hall because science is going to be interested in whatever the hell's in your gut."

"Stool samples?"

"Yup. Poop in a jar. Can get messy if your aim is off."

"But that's only if these don't work?" I said hopefully. "Right? I mean, these should take care of it?"

"Oh, yeah," Hinnaneman nodded, leaning down to look at the little blue pills and displaying a confidence he normally shared only when a woman unhooked her bra. "Oh, yeah."

"They're small."

"Trust me."

I took a pill right then. The next day I took another. On Sunday, lying around the Tamanaco apartment with no energy to go out, I took the third. Nothing happened. Nothing felt different. It was as though I had swallowed a cubic foot of air. I didn't even have Rolo to complain to – he had flown to Honduras with Flutie and wouldn't be back until mid-week.

Nauseous, listless, desperate to sleep, I wondered if it was menstrual cramps that were bringing me down. Maybe the C-27's constant vibrations had shaken my DNA apart and turned me into a woman. Or maybe I was pregnant with some alien baby. What could have been in that stew that had taken over my body? My vision blurred. Flayed alligators and monkeys swam before my eyes.

Sunday dragged on. I couldn't go out on the balcony because it was crumbling. When the power went out I didn't have the energy to go downstairs to fix it. I sat on the couch in our drab, unfriendly flat and stared out the window, watching the ocean and overcome with self-pity. The thought of surgery weighed on my mind. And stool samples?

After a while the power came back on. I turned on the TV. One channel had a documentary about a cholera epidemic in India. Another showed a movie about a virus escaping from a government laboratory and wiping out a town. I turned the set off.

Then at nine-thirty that night there was a rumble.

I was lying on the couch when it happened. The windows were open and at first I thought the wind had shaken the building.

Rumble, rumble.

No, that was definitely me. I put a hand on my stomach. Something was moving.

Rumble, rumble, RUMBLE!

I fell off the couch and hurried in a half-crouch down the hall to the toilet. *Give the team one minute!* I wanted to yell. Something was happening and it was happening quickly. Suddenly I had to use the bathroom like I'd never had to before.

I barely made it. No sooner did I sit down than there was an explosion of biblical proportions. Epic proportions. Had Homer been relating the event he would have said, "There was a bowel movement such as ten men today could not do." The porcelain beneath me groaned from the pressure. The explosion went on and on until I worried the neighbors would hear. Whatever came out didn't want to stop. It was as though I was giving birth after all...to an anaconda. In two minutes I was sure I had lost five pounds and an inch off my waistline.

But that wasn't the half of it. There was also the smell. Never, never, ever, not once in my life, not once in my worst dreams, had I smelled anything more foul than the putrid air I myself created that evening. Paint peeled off the walls. Mildew in the corners dried away to nothing. The ever-present ants that burrowed their way through concrete in the walls and marched in endless rows along the base boards stopped in their tracks, fell over, curled up and died. It was amazing that our magazines didn't spontaneously combust. I could scarcely breathe.

The explosion stopped. I flushed the toilet several times without looking. Oh, god, I thought. Oh, god. Oh, god. Oh, god. *That was horrible!* Please tell me it's over.

Rumble, rumble.

Oh, no. Not again...

BOOM!

Another explosion, another five pounds gone. Even remembering that I was talking three weeks of food to get rid of I still couldn't believe the volume of waste I expelled that night. More importantly I couldn't believe that any human could smell as bad as I smelled at that moment. I was embarrassed to be me. I couldn't move. I couldn't stop. I was a passenger in my own body, hostage to the damage that some berserk bacterium was inflicting.

Half an hour later I staggered back to the front room. The whole apartment, 2000 square feet of it, reeked of death. It was just as well Rolo was gone. He would never know how lucky he'd been. A fumigator couldn't have done a better job. I was sure the people downstairs had keeled over in their chairs and were now lying like dead roaches on their living room carpet. Struggling for breath, I swung the balcony doors wide to let the ocean breeze wash through. The curtains blew horizontal in the wind, pointing the direction for the odor to go.

I lay on the floor in my shorts, using magazines for a pillow and looking through the bars of the balcony railing to where the lights of boats bobbed in Panama Bay. I was too tired to move. My body was spent.

As the lights wavered on the bay my mind drifted, too, unable to remember how I had ended up in a penthouse apartment in Central America gasping for breath because my intestines had just expelled a creature that could have inspired Lon Chaney. Visions of the Marandú floated before my eyes. The stew was there, and the alligators with their jaded smiles. The boa was there over the door, the sign of traditional medicine, and although it was stuffed the head turned so the snake could eye me for himself.

Then the Marandú shifted and I saw down the street, to a man offering up a jaguar, and hordes of children waving for me to follow them through the dust. There was a gecko on a ceiling, a spinning fan, and a lurching tarantula. Josh walked by with a woman on each arm, happy in his element. Out of the night Dave and his companions ran up and set the jungle alight, and as the flames rose a determined beetle battered his way through the brush.

There were natives and butterflies and an unhappy hen while I lay prone in the dirt spitting blood.

Last, before I fell asleep I saw Jaime. In my mind's eye he lounged in a chair blowing curls of smoke, relaxing in the night, *suave,* supporting the weight of the air as lightly as a dancer holds his partner. The darkness was broken only by candlelight which played on his features as he studied his El Credito. Together we looked past the balcony to where dark waters flowed to meet the jungle and sky. *Some things just are,* he said, while before us the Amazon rolled on.

ABOUT THE AUTHOR

Michael Bleriot is a military and civilian pilot. He has flown on six continents and counts himself fortunate that most of his aircraft he returned in more or less the same condition he borrowed them. To date the number of his landings equals the number of takeoffs.

Made in the USA
Lexington, KY
15 January 2013